GCSE ENGLISH

LONGMAN REFERENCE GUIDES

Series editors: Geoff Black and Stuart Wall

TITLES AVAILABLE
CDT
English
French
Mathematics
Science
World History

FORTHCOMING
Biology
Chemistry
Geography
Physics

ENGLISH

LONGMAN
REFERENCE
GUIDES

Mary Pascoe
Paul Pascoe

Longman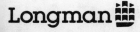

Longman Group UK Limited,
Longman House, Burnt Mill, Harlow,
Essex CM20 2JE, England
and Associated Companies throughout the world.

First published 1989

British Library Cataloguing in Publication Data

Pascoe, Paul
  English. – (Longman GCSE reference guides).
  1. England. Secondary schools. Curriculum subjects:
  English language. G.C.S.E. examinations
  I. Title
  420'.76

  ISBN 0–582–05072–3

Designed and produced by The Pen and Ink Book Company Ltd, Huntingdon,
Cambridgeshire

Illustrated by Chris Etheridge

Set in 9/10pt Century Old Style

Printed and bound in Great Britain

ACKNOWLEDGEMENTS

We are grateful to the following for permission to reproduce copyright material: André Deutsch Ltd for the story 'I Used to Live Here Once' by Jean Rhys from *Sleep it off, Lady*; Faber & Faber Ltd for the poem 'Preludes I' by T.S. Eliot from *Collected Poems 1909–1962* by T.S Eliot; Authors' Agents for an extract from *Brighton Rock* by Graham Greene, pubd Wm Heinemann Ltd, and the story 'I Spy' by Graham Greene from *Collected Stories*, pubd The Bodley Head Ltd.

Throughout your GCSE course you will be coming across terms, ideas and definitions that are unfamiliar to you. The Longman Reference Guides provide a quick, easy-to-use source of information, fact and opinion. Each main term is listed alphabetically and, where appropriate, cross-referenced to related terms.

- Where a term or phrase appears in **different type** you can look up a separate entry under that heading elsewhere in the book.
- Where a term or phrase appears in **different type** and is set between two arrowhead symbols ◄ ►, it is particularly recommended that you turn to the entry for that heading.

CONTENTS

PART 1 | ALPHABETICAL LISTINGS OF KEY WORDS

ABBREVIATION

An abbreviation is a shortened form of a word or phrase, used instead of the full form for convenience or to save space.

Some words are so commonly used that we almost forget they are abbreviations. For example, the word 'exam' is now so frequently employed in place of 'examination' that people no longer write the full stop after it to show that it is an abbreviation. 'Member of Parliament' sounds very long and formal; we are all used to MP. Some new words have come into being in this way. ASDA is the abbreviated form of ASsociated DAiries, NATO stands for North Atlantic Treaty Organisation.

Abbreviations do not always seem to relate to the words they represent. This is because some of the words we use in English are borrowed from other languages. A case in point is e.g., which is borrowed from Latin, with the abbreviation being the shortened form of *exempla gratia* – 'for the sake of example'. Similarly, i.e. is short for *id est* – 'that is'. Most dictionaries provide a list of this kind of abbreviation, usually at the back of the book. For your purposes, looking these up is more likely to be a case of curiosity rather than of real need. So when can you use abbreviations in writing?

If you are writing for yourself – for example, when you are making notes – then abbreviations save time and space. When you are writing for other people, it is better to avoid them.

◀ Dictionary ▶

ACCENT

A common misunderstanding is that only certain kinds of speaker have an accent. Everyone speaks with an 'accent', as the term applies to the sounds we make when we pronounce words.

Most people have a way of pronouncing words which identifies them as coming from a particular place. This is called a *regional* accent. Some people (a very small percentage of the population) speak in a way which is *not* linked to a particular part of the country. This is called 'Received Pronunciation' (RP), or sometimes 'BBC English'. However, if you listen to the radio or watch television, you will hear presenters and announcers who have regional accents.

Sometimes this 'received pronunciation' is referred to as if it is 'posh', or in some way superior to other kinds of accent. You should not allow this view to affect you and make you try to imitate it, *unless* your accent actually makes it difficult for others to understand you. When you take part in class discussions or other oral work, you will *not* be marked down if you have a regional accent. What is important is that you should speak clearly and appropriately.

▶ SHOWING ACCENTS IN WRITING

In your own writing, you may feel you would like to convey the distinctive sounds of someone's accent. This is quite an ambitious thing to attempt, and you may find it difficult using conventional **spelling**. The flavour of someone's speech can be shown through 'new' spellings, such as 'luv' to indicate a northern vowel, or 'bruvver' to indicate a Cockney accent, but it is a device to be used sparingly. More than a few lines like this becomes difficult both to sustain and to follow, as you can see from the following extract.

> 'You'd ha' thought he'd ha' done it yesterday an' given us time to get another man.' An' he sighs. 'I don't know,' he says. 'If it in't a cornet player wi' a split lip, it's a drummer wi' nobbut one arm.' He looks at Thomas. 'Wes'll have to do wi'out drummer, Thomas, that's all.'
>
> Stan Barstow, *The Drum*

◀ Dialect, Oral communication ▶

ACCEPTABILITY

Language is a social phenomenon, inextricably linked to the society which uses it. What is 'acceptable' in English, therefore, is simply what most people who speak English *regard* as acceptable. Indeed, one of the ways in which the language changes is that words and structures which were once considered 'unacceptable' gradually became acceptable. This is not decline – just change! For example, for many years it was considered *ungrammatical* (a word sometimes used to mean 'unacceptable' in this context) to split an infinitive. Can you spot the split infinitive in the following sentence? 'She wanted to completely finish her work before going out.' Such a usage nowadays, whilst not recommended, is generally acceptable.

Judgements about acceptability are almost always linked to **audience** – who is the language for? – and **purpose** – why is it being used? What is acceptable in a formal context seems merely pompous or ridiculous in an informal one. Vocabulary and sentence structure which are acceptable in a classroom may not be acceptable among friends. What is acceptable in speech is not necessarily acceptable in writing.

◀ Appropriateness, Audience, Bad language, Correctness, Register ▶

ACCURACY

Just what is meant by 'accuracy' when it refers to English? At the simplest level, it is checking that you have copied or written down words correctly.

ACTING

You should be able to spell words given to you in your stimulus material, or in your passages for understanding.

Accurate spelling, together with accurate **punctuation** (the use of capital letters, commas, etc.) is sometimes referred to as *mechanical accuracy*.

 READING

You should try to attain accuracy in reading, of both stimulus material *and* questions. Read all your material carefully. Questions, in particular, are worded in such a way as to be helpful to you! A hasty glance will *not* ensure that you do what you are asked to do.

 WRITING

When you start writing, check that you are accurately recording what is actually in the passage, not what you *think* is there. Look back to make sure.

Check that you really are answering the *question set*, all parts of it, and that you are answering from the viewpoint requested ('advantages', 'disadvantages', 'both sides' and so on).

Accurate selection or identification of *individual words* is sometimes required. Don't in this case offer a chunk of writing with the key word or words hidden somewhere inside. This is sometimes called 'slab quotation', and is not a substitute for accurate selection.

Finally, accuracy in *choosing the right word or expression* is important in your own writing. Choosing the precise word, rather than a rough approximation will always gain you credit.

◀ Ambiguity, Correctness ▶

ACTING

GCSE English is not a test of your dramatic abilities, and if the idea of acting fills you with dismay you need not worry. However, acting in various forms could be helpful to you, and you might like to consider these suggestions.

 ACTING AND ORAL WORK

Acting could help you in your **oral communication** assessment. You could choose to prepare an excerpt from a published play to act out in a group situation. *Preparation* is the key word here. Acting is a skill which needs practice; don't try to read the words off the page for your assessment without several rehearsals. Discuss with your fellow performers how you think the piece should go. Be prepared to modify your approach and to accept criticism. You could also devise your *own* script to act out. You may be given a situation and asked to imagine you are one of the people involved. After some discussion with the other people who have been given roles, you will then act out the situation. This is sometimes called 'role-play'.

▶ **ACTING AND COURSEWORK**

Strange as it may at first seem, acting can be useful to you with your coursework as well. If you choose to write a **play script** then it is essential that you (and some willing friends?) act it out. This is the only proper way to assess its quality. Are some of the lines difficult to speak? Do they sound unnatural or stilted? Is the pace of the dialogue too quick or too slow? Would it interest an audience (or reader)? Does it need editing? Only by acting out the script will you be able to answer these vital questions.

In a different way, acting can also help your reading and understanding. Whether they are fact or fiction, difficult pieces of writing can sometimes become clearer to you if you *read them out loud*, imagining that someone else is listening and that you are trying to make the sense clear to them. It is not always possible, of course, to read aloud – in exam rooms or libraries, for instance – but there is the technique of 'silent acting', or reading the words out loud in your head.

◀ Editing, Play Script ▶

ADJECTIVES

All the italicised words in these two sentences are adjectives:
- The *lingering* scent of *old* leather and *rich* food filled the *book-lined* room.
- *Sharp* sleet and *driving* rain beat mercilessly against the *shuttered* windows.

Adjectives help to provide vividness and interest to your writing. Compare the simple sentence 'The cat sat on the mat.' with 'The sleek, pampered Siamese cat lounged on the silken, deep-piled carpet.'

Adjectives do have to be well chosen, though. 'Big', 'little', 'old' and so on are not going to enhance your writing very much. In the example above, all the adjectives stress the comfortable, even luxurious life the cat seems to have.

Choosing a number of adjectives from *the same area of meaning* can help to focus or concentrate your writing. For example, when describing a scene in the rain, you might use 'moist', 'damp', 'sodden', 'watery', 'soaked' . . . (A thesaurus can be useful here.) Or you might concentrate on adjectives *appealing to a particular sense*, such as touch or smell.

Adjectives can help to *sum up* a significant aspect of character, such as neatness, especially if key words are repeated. For example: 'Her polished black shoes matched her neat well-tailored suit. Her carefully groomed hair was tidily pinned up in an elegant chignon and her well-groomed hands with immaculate pale pink fingernails were folded neatly on her lap.'

You should be careful not to over-use the adjectives; long lists of adjectives before a **noun** do not usually work – two will be plenty. Though, as with all general rules, you can occasionally break this one for special effect.

. . . the out-of-bed-sleepy-head-Polly-put-the-kettle-on townhall bell . . .
Now in her iceberg-white, holily laundered crinoline nightgown, under

virtuous polar sheets, in her spruced and scoured, dust-defying bedroom in trig and trim Bay View . . .
The slowblack, slow, black, crowblack, fishingboat-bobbing sea.

Dylan Thomas, *Under Milk Wood*

 USING ADJECTIVES

Adjectives are not obligatory! An adjective in front of *every* noun can be very tedious. The novelist, Graham Greene, wrote in his autobiography *A Sort of Life* about his problems in making his writing dramatic and exciting. He found something of a solution to his problem in *avoiding* too many adjectives. He wrote, 'An adjective slows down the pace.' If you are sparing in your use of adjectives the ones you do use will be more effective. Here is an extract from Greene's novel *Brighton Rock*.

> A mounted policeman came up the road: the lovely cared-for chestnut beast stepping delicately on the hot macadam, like an expensive toy a millionaire buys for his children; you admired the finish, the leather as deeply glowing as an old mahogany table top, the bright silver badge; it never occurred to you that the toy was for use. It never occurred to Hale, watching the policeman pass; he couldn't appeal to him.

Ernest Hemingway, the American writer, uses very few adjectives in this passage from *In Our Time*.

> The two boats started off in the dark. Nick heard the oar-locks of the other boat quite a way ahead of them in the mist. The Indians rowed with quick, choppy strokes. Nick lay back with his father's arm around him. It was cold on the water. The Indian who was rowing them was working very hard, but the other boat moved further ahead of them in the mist all the time.

Adjectives should also really 'say' something, and not state the obvious or the expected. If you describe old people as having 'wrinkled' faces and 'gnarled' hands, you may not be showing any real care or thought in your choice of words. Such adjectives are in too-common use to be effective, and so they 'say' little.

It is not always necessary to put the description before the noun. Phrases using adjectives can be placed after the noun they describe, as in 'The sleek, pampered Siamese with the lustrous yellow eyes . . . '

Remember that many words which you might at first think of only as nouns can be used as adjectives. Also look out for new or unusual combinations of words, *hyphenated* to make new adjectives, as in these examples from *Cider with Rosie* by Laurie Lee.

- A Sevres clock . . . pink-crushed with angels, . . . some airy figures from Dresden . . . like pieces of bubble-blown sunlight.
- Sickle-bent bodies
- The cat's-breath, death-green elder . . .
- A pepper-smelling cupboard

These are sometimes referred to as *compounds*.

Your writing will improve as you widen the range of adjectives you know and can use. However, in the excitement of discovering 'new' words, make sure you know how to use them properly and appropriately. Adjectives need to be in keeping with your subject matter and with the style you have chosen. Inappropriate adjectives can produce intentional or – as in this example – unintentional comic effects: 'He was struck on the head and is receiving some very serious attention.'

Your understanding of other people's writing will improve if you look carefully at the kind of adjectives chosen. Try to work out the *reasons* for their choice. Look at the way in which the italicised adjectives in this sentence suggest the writer's disapproval: 'The rapidity of change and the speed with which new situations are created follow the *impetuous* and *heedless* pace of man rather than the deliberate pace of nature.' (Rachel Carson, *Silent Spring*)

◀ Appropriateness, Register ▶

ADULTS

◀ Mature students ▶

ADVERB

Adverbs can extend or qualify the meaning of a **verb**. In these three sentences the italicised words are all adverbs.

- She drew their meeting *abruptly* to a close.
- He was *unfortunately* obliged to attend a meeting.
- She talked *rapidly, occasionally* stuttering over difficult words.

As you can see, adverbs frequently (but not always) end in -ly.

Where do you put an adverb? You can put it *in front of the verb*: 'She carefully untied the parcel.' You can put it at the end of sentence: 'She untied the parcel carefully.' If you really want to stress *how* or *why* something was done, you can put the adverb at the *beginning*: 'Carefully, she untied the parcel.'

Additional stress or emphasis can be created by *repeating* the same adverb: 'Slowly, slowly, he edged towards the frightened animal.'

In English we do not normally use strings of adverbs, though, as with most rules, this can be broken at times.

Is your adverb really necessary? A poorly chosen verb, supported by an adverb, will *not* be as effective as a verb which includes the meaning of the adverb. For example, 'to walk slowly' is not as effective as 'to saunter', 'to dawdle', and so forth. 'To talk rapidly' is not as effective as 'to babble', 'to gabble', and the like.

ADVERTISING/ADVERTISEMENT

Advertising has become such an important subject in modern society that it is possible only to provide an outline in this short entry. During your GCSE course you will be concerned with advertising in some form, so it is worth considering in some depth. You will almost certainly do some work on advertising in class, and most libraries have a selection of books dealing with aspects of the subject. If you use a course book in English, it may well have a section dealing with advertising.

A number of features can frequently be spotted in advertising.

 ## PURPOSE

A clearly stated or implicit **purpose**. The purpose of the Government's campaign about AIDS is clearly stated and *explicit*. On the other hand, the free gifts and jackpot prizes offered by some organisations have the *implicit* purpose of influencing you to buy their product.

 ## AUDIENCE

Having a sense of **audience** means, more often than not in advertising, identifying the *customer*. Advertisers do a great deal of market research into the likely customers for their products. As a result, advertisements are often highly selective in their appeal. A recent series of advertisements by a major bank took the form of little stories featuring different sorts of people, each of whom had reason to be grateful to the bank. One advertisement concerned a young woman working as a publisher's assistant who wanted the money to visit her friends in Australia. Another featured a young couple further on in their careers, who wanted a mortgage so they could move to a bigger house. Yet another figured a couple in late middle age who were attracted by the advantages of putting their savings in the bank. Each advertisement had a direct appeal to a *particular kind of person*, with market research having identified that kind of person as important in the analysis of bank customers.

 ## DIRECT ADDRESS

Direct address makes *you* feel personally involved. One of the most famous advertisements ever was published during the First World War. It portrayed Lord Kitchener pointing directly at the onlooker and proclaiming 'Your Country Needs *You*!' If the poster had read 'The Country Needs Soldiers', it would not have been nearly so effective. The fact that you may have seen numerous variations on that famous poster, is a tribute to the simplicity and power of direct address. Whenever you see the little word 'you' in an advertisement, you should take note.

 ## EMOTIONAL APPEAL

Most advertisements appeal to our emotions in some way. The reason is a simple one: the heart is a much more powerful persuader than the head. Why are housewives supposed to long for a *dream* kitchen when, in fact, what they are being sold is a workshop? Why are the pieces of machinery we call cars given names such as 'Cavalier', 'Sierra', 'Escort' and so on, which tell us nothing whatsoever about their mechanical soundness? The answer is because the advertisers want to present their wares in such a way that we *feel* we need them. Playing on our emotions in this way need not, however, involve deceit, and it should not be assumed that all advertisements are, in some way, lies. Nevertheless, emotional appeal can be a bit like a deceit, in the sense that subtle suggestions may be slipped in without our noticing them. But most people actually enjoy this kind of 'nice' deceit! So if you are to gain some understanding of how advertisements work, you must try to identify what basic emotions the advertisers are trying to tap. Sometimes you may have to study an advert very closely, because the advertiser's methods may not be immediately obvious.

'Reading' advertisements is very similar to reading a text. You need to look for the clues to their implicit meaning. Studying an advertisement is a special kind of close reading. A few of the more common forms of appeal you will come across are to:

Our acquisitive sense

The desire to own things is a very powerful instinct. 'All this could be yours,' we are told in all sorts of different ways. More often than not, *pictures* have an important part to play. People with whom we readily identify are shown already enjoying the pleasures of ownership of a product. Sometimes beautifully produced photographs display the goods in a desirable light.

Our need to belong

Some advertisers play upon the notion that their product is the key to belonging to a special set of people. Usually this is done by *association*. For example, instant coffee may be associated with sophisticated white middle-class people having a sophisticated after-dinner conversation. A fizzy drink may be associated with bubbly young people having a good time. Sometimes this is referred to as *lifestyle advertising*.

Our sense of self-esteem

We all like to think that we are sophisticated or clever or cool or sexy or feminine, or that we possess any number of desirable qualities. Many advertisements project us into situations where these qualities are in evidence. We are all very ready to recognise ourselves, provided, of course, that the image is flattering. Many advertisements for the Army present 'The Professionals' being cool in a crisis. The point is, of course, that the potential recruits should say to themselves, 'That's ME!'

Our desire to feel superior

This sort of appeal follows on from our sense of self-esteem. Sometimes advertisements suggest that they are offering the key to the success that you deserve. *Prestige* is a common quality which is stressed, often by use of pictures in conjunction with the text (or *copy* as it is known). Expensive-looking cars are pictured in even more expensive-looking settings, while aristocratic-looking people savour suitably aristocratic sherry. Frequent use is made in the advertisement of words such as 'executive', 'exclusive', 'luxury', 'select', 'superior', 'sophisticated', and so on.

Our desire to be up to date

Nobody likes to feel they are behind the times. Advertisements have always made full use of words and phrases such as 'new'. . . 'latest' . . . 'just arrived'. And more recently, being up to date has become equated with technology. As a result, a whole host of new phrases has entered advertising all suggesting that the product is the latest innovation. The latest model is 'advanced', 'high-tech', 'state of the art', 'computer designed', 'computer controlled' and its 'on board computer' is probably 'programmed' to 'digitally display' its 'multi-functional operation'. Whether any of these terms makes sense is of less importance than the *impression* they make. Very often, the technological image is reinforced by the use of impressive-sounding code numbers. You may find yourself washing your socks in a 'Series 6 HT 7000X'. Manufacturers have been known to achieve success with poorly-selling lines simply by giving them a more appealing name.

Humour

Many advertisements are witty and appeal to our sense of fun. Advertisers of convenience foods, confectionery and drink products are especially fond of suggesting their products are enjoyable and make people happy. Whether these advertisements 'work' or not, the advertiser's aim is to fix the name of the product firmly in our minds; this is particularly important when the products are all very similar. Few people will fail to name the lager that reaches . . .!

Fear

Although it is not judged acceptable in the UK for advertisers to exploit our fears in an excessive way, a number of advertisements do so in a quiet way. Often advertisers offer relief to an obvious, but unstated fear. For example, many insurance schemes offer *security in old age* as an alternative to the *implied* poverty which will not be shown in an advertisement. Various products stress their high level of *safety*. Security and alarm systems must, of course, rely for their very existence on people feeling at risk from burglary. In addition to the real fears people have about their safety or well-being, there is the fear of feeling inferior or left out. Products are described as being *essential* to every home. Or we are informed that no business person can *be without* the latest gadget that is used in all the top firms. The fear that we are missing something that others already have is often exploited by advertisers in combination with our desire to keep up to date, and our sense of self-esteem and need to belong.

Sex

The use of sexual associations in advertisements is very well known and often unsubtle. Be on the look-out, however, for the *hidden* or *low-key* sexual association. You may be invited to have a 'romance' with the most unlikely products, or to caress the smooth lines of the latest motor car.

Self-assertion

Sometimes advertisers invite us to put aside our natural reluctance and 'let our hair down'. The advertisement can sound all the more appealing if the suggestion sounds just a bit naughty, as in: 'GO ON, OPEN UP THE LYLE'S GOLDEN SYRUP'.

 ## USE OF PICTURES

Pictures have already been mentioned in connection with emotional appeal. You will be aware that almost all advertisements these days are made up of two major components – the *picture* and the *text* (or *copy*). Very often, the picture dominates. When examining advertisements, it is most important to consider the picture and the text *together*.

The first thing to remember is that pictures in advertisements are there to create an impression. Sometimes they may illustrate the product in use, but more often they are there to give us *feelings* about what is being advertised. For example, if a car is depicted standing on a deserted beach, it is unlikely that you are expected to admire the vehicle's resistance to salt water. You would be expected, however, to *associate* the car with such things as romance, freshness and the 'freedom' of wide open spaces. This car, the advertisement might suggest, will not be stuck in suffocating traffic jams.

The combinations of text and image are endless, but a number of fairly common factors are worth considering:

Many advertisements show people

Pictures of people are used for many reasons, three of the most important being:
- to suggest something about what is being advertised
- to suggest something about the intended customer
- to suggest something about the audience of the advertisement

If the person depicted looks glamorous, there is a chance that some of the glamour will rub off on the product. We tend to identify the people in the picture with the kind of people who will buy the product, especially if they are attractive and represent the way *we* would like to be. A picture can make several suggestions at once.

Many advertisements suggest optimism

The basic suggestion is often that if you buy the product or service, you will somehow be better off. As a result, some types of advertisement tend to depict 'happy people, with happy faces, with happy problems'. Even so, to see what is going on you need to examine the images in some detail.

Advertisements use stereotypes

Generally the people portrayed are recognisable **stereotypes**: the smart executive type; the family man or woman; the super-fit sporting type; the well-off businessman or businesswoman; the successful 'career girl'; the homely retired couple; the cheery working-class male beer drinker and, of course, the impossibly elegant, sophisticated, beautiful person who exists only in advertisements.

Look carefully at the people, their dress and their surroundings. The images are usually constructed carefully to reinforce the message of the advertisement as a whole. Always remember that what we think about the *people* influences what we think about the *product*.

Pictures appeal to our basic senses

Advertisers wanting to suggest richness and luxury often use warm colours and fill the pictures with mellow leather and glowing antique furniture. Even if the product is a modern mass-produced hi-fi, constructed of steel and plastic, placing it among articles in traditional materials can give an association of quality and craftmanship. On the other hand, the same hi-fi seen in a brilliant white setting might appear smart and technologically advanced.

Look for the colour codes; are they perhaps strong and 'manly', soft and 'feminine' or brash and 'youthful'?

Other 'devices' used include 'romantic' soft focus and idyllic natural settings. Shampoo is basically a detergent, but flowing tresses of hair caught in sparkling sunlight create an altogether more attractive image, especially if the shampoo is called 'Rosemary and Orange'!

 WORD ASSOCIATION AND CONNOTATION

This area is dealt with more fully under **connotation**, and is a particularly important aspect of advertising. Advertisers have to be constantly thinking of the right words for the product. Food must have connotations of freshness and wholesomeness; toiletries, such as toothpaste and deodorants, should appear clean, fresh and safe; cars have to be powerful, responsive, modern and so on. The precise words will vary, but they must call up positive, pleasing and perhaps exciting images. Similarly, the names of products have to be chosen carefully so they give a good impression. A certain hairspray, which was known in the UK by the romantic-sounding brand-name 'Mist', was a disastrous failure in Germany because the German word *Mist* means something which is distinctly unpleasant!

Word-play

This is frequently used to identify a product in our minds. Advertising slogans often stick in our minds because of a catchy use of **word-play**. Everyone knows that *Beanz Meanz Heinz* and that people who *Drinka Pinta Milka Day* have *Gotta Lotta Bottle*.

Image building

Advertisements try to create a clear *image* of the product. A successful image is built up by a careful and consistent use of the kinds of technique which have been outlined in these notes. The image may associate a *company* with a particular section of the market. For example, if you think of some of the main High Street clothing shops, such as Burton, Laura Ashley, Next, C & A, Marks & Spencer, you will probably have a clear image of their style and the kind of customer they seem to serve. The *products* themselves can also be given images. You may associate certain goods with elegance and sophistication, others you may think of as excitingly modern, while others you may consider as simple down-to-earth good value. Sometimes advertisers set out to *change* their product's image. When Daley Thomson was employed to advertise Lucozade it ceased to be associated with ill-health and convalescence and came to be linked with fitness and activity. At the same time, the drink's rather dull image was replaced by a bright and cheerful one which was put across through a series of advertisements.

▶ USES OF ADVERTISING

Not all advertisements are concerned with selling products. Government departments, charities and organisations of all sorts advertise. You may even have done some advertising yourself. The basic principles are the same as for selling products, however. A good advertisement must create a sense of need; the audience must recognise that it needs to do what the advertisement wants, whether it is to buy a new dress, to give money to charity, or to stop smoking.

ALLITERATION

◀ Figures of speech ▶

AMBIGUITY

Ambiguity results when there is potential for a word or words to be interpreted in more than one way, as in these two sentences:
- She has put the cat down.
- His hair needs cutting badly.

The **context** is often enough to tell us the meaning which is intended. In the first sentence it is more likely that the cat is being lowered to the ground than taken to the vet to be destroyed, and in the second it is unlikely that someone would need a bad haircut. The effect of ambiguity can be amusing – whether intentionally or unintentionally.

Writers sometimes wish to use ambiguity deliberately, to make their readers laugh, or to make what they have to say more memorable. This usage sometimes involves **puns**.

Ambiguity can sometimes cause us confusion, as the meaning is obscured:
- She told her mother that one of her dresses was missing.
- According to the regulations you have to pass in English, a foreign language and maths or a science.

Ambiguity can also arise from the way that sentences are put together; in particular, in the use of pronouns which relate to an inappropriate noun.
- 'Mr Patel asked whether the local bakery could provide some of the cakes and where bran could be obtained for the bran-tub. Mrs Flower suggested that Messrs Brown and White would probably provide cakes and that nowadays *they* were usually filled with sawdust.'

Obviously the 'they' in italics is bran-tub, but in English sentence structure a pronoun (such as 'he', 'she' or 'they') refers back to the nearest **noun**, in this case 'cakes'.

Reflexive pronouns require some care in their use, just in case you produce something like this!

- 'The rifle-range owners like to shoot themselves.'

◀ Puns ▶

AMPLIFICATION

Amplification is the provision of extra information in order to make the meaning clearer or more vivid.

When speaking or writing, we sometimes forget that, however vivid our thoughts may be, unless we express them fully, they may not seem very interesting to other people. Good communication, of course, depends on choosing your words carefully, but very often it is also important to express yourself fully. Remember always to put yourself in the reader's or the listener's position and ask yourself the question, 'What would I have understood by these words?' Then you can decide whether you need to amplify.

Amplification is most obviously necessary when there is insufficient information to make the meaning clear. Examiners often find, when they are assessing responses to passages for understanding, that students succeed in making a number of *half-points*. They fail to do justice to themselves, simply because they have not provided enough explanation or illustration. If, for instance, you are describing **character**, it will probably not be enough to say that a person is 'intelligent' or 'brave' or 'sensitive'. You will almost certainly need to explain *what exactly you mean* by your comments and *why* you have come to your conclusions. You must also make clear to the examiner that you have thoroughly understood all the *evidence*, so it may be necessary to refer in some detail to the text in support of your points.

 PRESENTING AN ARGUMENT

It is also necessary to provide sufficient amplification when you present an **argument**. Your logic may be perfectly clear to you, but unless you fill in all the stages of the argument, you may not make much sense to anyone else. Suppose, for example, you were writing an assignment in which you were defending the Monarchy against the accusation that it is an out-of-date institution. You might wish to say that the Royal Family are more popular than ever because they perform all kinds of good works and that they are like superstars that brighten people's lives. Although these may be good points, they need some amplification and explanation. What *evidence* is there that the Royal Family *are* more popular? What kinds of 'good works' do you mean? What do you mean by 'superstars' and *how* do they brighten people's lives? The amount of extra detail you should supply will depend on your overall plan and on what points you want to emphasise, but always remember that the reader should *not* be relied upon to fill in what you have not clearly stated. Bear in mind, too, that good *examples* in support of your ideas are of more use to the general reader than vague statements. It would, for instance, be better to support your statement about the Royal Family's good works by referring to Princess Anne's work as President of the Save the Children Fund, than to pass on immediately to your next point.

▶ IMAGINATIVE WRITING

Amplification is also vital in imaginative writing. Although very skilful writers can create vivid pictures with the minimum of words, most people's writing would be very dull without enough detail. For example, the subject 'The Explosion', is likely to conjure up vivid and possibly horrifying images. But if a student wrote like this, we would not be able to picture the scene very easily:

> Suddenly there was a flash and a huge roar. It was a bomb! Glass was scattered everywhere and dead bodies lay in the road. There was a lot of screaming and shouting. Fortunately I was not hurt so I tried to help the injured.

Put like that, the description is too vague and general. The reader wants *more detail* in order to feel involved: where and when did the explosion take place? What was going on at the time? What was the narrator doing and thinking about? Apart from glass and dead bodies, what other sights confronted the narrator? How did individuals react? And so on.

Of course, amplification alone will not necessarily make the writing interesting; the story could simply be long and boring rather than short and boring. Even so, extra detail is likely to make a better impression than a few sketchy points. You will often need to amplify in order to create the right sense of proportion and structure in a piece of writing. Remember that certain sorts of writing and speech depend on a sense of timing. A 'shaggy dog story' is a long and elaborate joke that needs to be told at great length if it is to get a laugh. It cannot be told briefly. Similarly, if you are to create suspense, you must find ways of *delaying* the shock so that it can have its maximum effect. In the film *Alien*, the terrible creature which destroys almost everyone on board the spacecraft is hardly glimpsed throughout the entire film. Instead, a great deal of time is taken up with nothing happening. There are long scenes set in dark, empty, decaying cargo holds, with lengthy shots of twisting pipes, cables and heating ducts. As we peer into the darkness, these scenes build up our fear and expectation of sudden horror, and the longer it is delayed, the more the tension increases.

Likewise, you should remember that you will sometimes need to amplify your description for a larger effect which would be lost if you were too brief. In the following example, the student has tried to capture in words the effect of a surprise party.

> I became dispirited as I walked up the path to my empty home, knowing that I would have to spend the entire evening alone, when the previous day I was wondering who would be the first to ask me out.
>
> I turned the key to open the door and slowly walked in. I went into the

kitchen, put the kettle on and then walked into the back room. It seemed dark. I was sure that I had opened the curtains that morning, so I turned the light on and to my amazement, there were my friends and family, all shouting, 'Surprise!'

The basic ingredients are there; the dispirited walk home, the thoughts about what might have been, the empty house and the puzzlement over the closed curtains. However, the effect is too rushed. The surprise could have been held back by amplification. The writer could have dwelt more on the depressing emptiness of the house and more details, like the out-of-place curtains, could have been included. The extra information would not only have helped to create more of a sense of surprise, it would also have made the character's state of mind more vivid.

Remember – it is also possible to say *too much*! Try to keep a sense of proportion and to avoid giving information without any clear sense of its purpose.

ANTI-CLIMAX

An anti-climax occurs when you get an unexpected change from the important or the serious to the trivial or ridiculous.

This can happen within a single sentence. It can also occur at the end of a paragraph, or even a complete story. For instance, you build up the suspense of thinking there is some mysterious force in the house when you get home, only to find it is the cat!

Anti-climax frequently produces a mocking or comic effect, sometimes referred to as bathos. So take care not to use anti- climax accidentally. Don't build up expectations in your reader or listener which you can't satisfy, as in this passage:

The driver looked horrendous. His arms were all twisted and his elbow was sticking out of the skin. I was sick to my stomach. He had blood all over his face and there was glass down one side of his face . . .

After several hours of waiting we discovered that the man's injuries were a lot worse than we had at first thought. His legs were broken and he had lost a foot that had got trapped under one of the pedals of his car, one of his lungs had collapsed and he was suffering from shock.

Sometimes *lists* can have an anti-climax effect. A series of items followed by 'etc.' or 'and so on' can sound feeble, and so create an anti-climax.

ANTITHESIS

This is the technical term for various types of *contrast*. Antithesis can be used in pairs of words, as in 'Freeman and slave, lord and serf, oppressor and oppressed'. It can also be used in longer sentences. These advertising headlines use antithesis to make their point:

■ 'Higher quality, lower prices' (*Wilson and Glick kitchens*)
■ 'Low risk drivers should not pay high risk premiums' (*Royal Insurance*)
■ 'Far from engineering the driver out, we engineer him in.' (*Lancia cars*)

In your own writing, you will find that antithesis is a useful device to express neatly, and forcefully, the relationship of contrast or opposition. It can help you sum up a situation or an argument. For this reason, it is quite often used in speech-making. Look at this example from Martin Luther King's Washington speech:

> I have a dream that one day even the state of Mississippi, a desert state sweltering with the heat of injustice and oppression, will be transformed into an oasis of freedom and justice.

Antithesis can help to mark the turning-point in an argument or a story.

APOSTROPHES

Apostrophes have two main uses in English.

 ### APOSTROPHE OF POSSESSION

The apostrophe can indicate that the item following it belongs to the word or words preceding it – the *apostrophe of possession.*

Some people have a lot of difficulty with apostrophes of possession, but the main rules are quite simple in practice.

- *If the word is singular, add an 's.* For example, 'The dog's bone' means there is only one dog.
- *If the word already ends in an -s because it is plural, put the apostrophe after the -s.* For example, 'The ladies' cloak-room'.
- *If the word ends in -s but is in fact singular, it is customary to add 's.* For example, 'Charles's house'.

 ### APOSTROPHE OF OMISSION

The apostrophe can show that one or more letters of a word have been missed out – the *apostrophe of omission.* For example, *didn't* stands for *did not; it's* stands for *it is.*

You do not normally use the apostrophe of omission in formal writing, but you may need to use it when writing **dialogue** or a **play script**.

Finally, when you are in doubt about using an apostrophe, *don't.* Many people get so worried about apostrophes that they add them to almost every word ending in -s. 'Best tomatoe's and King Edward potatoe's' can be seen in many greengrocers' windows!

APPROPRIATENESS

You will find this term used throughout this guide. It is a key concept, the essence of which is summed up by the phrase 'Proper words in proper places'. Just as we adapt our *behaviour* according to where we are and the company we are in, so we should adjust our *language* to the **context**.

In judging what is appropriate, you should pay due attention to the relative formality of the writing. A chatty style is appropriate for a letter to a friend and certain kinds of personal writing, but it is usually inappropriate for an extended narrative. The words 'mum' and 'dad' are appropriate in an informal context, but 'mother' and 'father' are more appropriate in many narrative contexts.

Always bear in mind that *speech* and *writing* are essentially different. In speech you convey a lot of the meaning by stress and gesture. In writing, however, you must be much more careful about how you put your words together, because they alone have to carry your meaning. As a general rule, *try to avoid writing in the way that you speak.*

ARGUMENT

Argument is basically the organisation of information into a clear order which leads naturally to a conclusion. Argument can follow the strict rules of logic, or it can be used more loosely in order to persuade.

The **National Criteria** require you to 'understand, order and present facts, ideas and opinions'. Although there are many ways of satisfying these requirements, you will probably have to involve yourself in some form of argumentative work. At first, this work may not appear particularly difficult, because we all have ideas and opinions, and we probably express many of them every day. However, simply having strong opinions is quite another matter from being able to put them across in a connected and effective order. Certainly, examiners usually find that students have most difficulty when attempting organised discussion, whether in written or spoken form.

Arguments can take many forms, and their purposes are enormously varied.

UNBIASED ARGUMENT

The strictest forms of argument are those employed by such people as philosophers and scientists. They may not always succeed, but their aim is to search after truth in as unbiased a way as possible. You might be surprised that this argument by the philosopher Gilbert Ryle is about *pleasure*:

> Some sensations, like some tickles, are pleasant; others, like some other tickles, are unpleasant. One scalding sensation may be distressing, when the equally acute scalding sensation given by a gulp of hot tea may be pleasant. On rare occasions we are even ready to say that something hurts, and yet we like it, or at least do not mind it. If pleasure were correctly classified as a sensation, we should expect it to be possible correspondingly to describe some of these sensations too, as pleasant, some as neutral and others as unpleasant, and yet this palpably will not do. The two last would be contradictions, the first either a redundancy or worse. If I have been enjoying a game, there need not have been something else in progress, additional to the game, which I also disliked or enjoyed, namely some special sensation or feeling engendered in me by the game.

Even if you do not fully understand Gilbert Ryle's argument here, you may sense how he attempts to deal only with what is essential to his subject. Each statement is carefully constructed and is as precise as possible. When a point may not be absolutely true, he covers himself by offering the alternative possibility: '. . . and yet we like it, or at least do not mind it.' You may also notice how he avoids obvious personal involvement. Few people have the intelligence and skill to argue so closely. Certainly you will not be required to do so at GCSE. It is, however, worth bearing in mind that we must sometimes try to see things as clearly as possible and not be influenced by personal opinion or bias.

 PERSUASIVE ARGUMENT

In this next example, by contrast, the writer is anxious to put across a deeply felt point of view:

> The public, on the other hand, are extraordinarily vulnerable to the effect of television. The young are hypnotized by the box at which they stare, sometimes for hours. For adults, the television box is what André Malraux called a 'dream factory'. Every night millions of people enter this world of dreams which are concocted by a very few people. Therefore there is a great responsibility on those responsible for creating the myths and images of television, that they should be myths and images which are elevating and not degrading to our society. In addition to that, the television box has been called the hidden persuader. It is something which is capable of influencing our subconscious and even our conscious mind. Although in the television code there is provision against subliminal advertising, nevertheless the fact remains that such is the impact of television that whether we like it or not we are all subconsciously or unconsciously influenced by it . . .

> Maurice Edelman, quoted in Mary Whitehouse, *Cleaning up T.V.*

We can see here how Mr Edelman's methods are very different from those of the unbiased argument of Gilbert Ryle. For unbiased argument, Ryle has to keep his vocabulary *neutral*, because his main concern is to analyse and work towards a conclusion. Edelman, on the other hand, wishes to influence the reader with his own opinion. You will notice how he uses keywords to *reinforce* his argument: 'extraordinarily', 'vulnerable', 'hypnotized', 'dreams', 'concocted', 'responsibility', 'elevating', 'degrading' . . . The colloquial-sounding word, 'box', is used to suggest the idea of mindless enslavement to something which is basically trivial.

For GCSE you are more likely to meet an argument that, like Mr Edelman's, is designed to persuade you in some way. Putting forward a point of view, however, need not involve using passionate language. This next example is written in a very cool style, but is expressing an unusual and individual outlook.

Bicycles are not only thermodynamically efficient, they are also cheap. With his much lower salary, the Chinese acquires his durable bicycle in a fraction of the working hours an American devotes to the purchase of his obsolescent car. The cost of public utilities needed to facilitate bicycle traffic versus the price of an infrastructure tailored to high speeds is proportionately even less than the price differential of the vehicles used in the two different systems. In the bicycle system, engineered roads are necessary only at certain points of dense traffic, and people who live far from the surfaced path are not thereby automatically isolated as they would be if they depended on cars or trains. The bicycle has extended man's radius without shunting him onto roads he cannot walk. Where he cannot ride his bike he can usually push it.

The bicycle also uses little space. Eighteen bikes can be parked in the place of one car, thirty of them can move along in the space devoured by a single automobile. It takes two lanes of a given size to move 40,000 people across a bridge in one hour by using modern trains, four to move them on buses, twelve to move them in their cars, and only one lane for them to pedal across on bicycles. Of all these vehicles, only the cycle really allows people to go from door to door without walking. The cyclist can reach new destinations of his choice without his tool creating new locations from which he is barred.

Ivan Illich, Energy and Equity

This writer, like Gilbert Ryle, was trained as a philosopher, and this passage is similar to the first in that it attempts to argue in a clear, seemingly scientific way. There is quite a lot of *technical language*, such as 'public utilities', 'infrastructure', 'proportionately' and so on. His method is also *analytic*, with some use of statistics: 'It takes two lanes of a given size to move 40,000 people across a bridge in one hour . . .'

However, if you look closely, you can see that he is organising his ideas and using language to *win us over to his point of view*. Throughout the first paragraph, the advantages of the bicycle are contrasted with the disadvantages of the motor vehicle. This antithesis is repeated: the bicycle is cheap, while the car is expensive; the bicycle is durable, while the car is obsolescent; the bicycle can go almost anywhere, while the car needs special roads . . . In the second paragraph, the statistically large amount of space occupied by motorised transport is contrasted with the remarkably little space needed by bicycles.

There are two important points to be learned from this extract. The first is that, although Ivan Illich compares the bicycle with the motor car, he keeps *stressing his main point*, which is that the bicycle is superior. He does not actually enter into a discussion of their advantages and disadvantages. Very often, students simply present a list of arguments for and against an issue, without providing any clear central point of view. Although there are times when you must deal with objections to your case, your arguments may lose force if you swamp the reader with lists of conflicting opinions. What is more, you may run the risk of contradicting yourself.

The second point is that the argument is presented in such a way that it *appears* that the author is demonstrating a truth. He does not introduce *himself* into the argument at all. It is as though we do not have to take Ivan Illich's word; no sensible person could fail to agree with the facts!

▶ PRESENTING OPINIONS

Too often, students confuse their personal opinions with the issue at stake. Even if you have strong feelings about an issue, simply by announcing that they happen to be *your* feelings, you do not give authority to your argument. It is of little interest to the world at large that Jane detests fox-hunting, that Leroy wants nuclear disarmament or that Ivan Illich may not personally approve of motor cars. It is the arguments themselves that count.

Sometimes arguments can be presented in a more relaxed, less formal manner. When the subject is suitably light-hearted, it is possible to present your point of view in an almost conversational tone. Here, for instance, is Bill Cosby writing about the generation gap in his book *Fatherhood*.

Nothing separates the generations more than music. By the time the child is eight or nine, he has developed a passion for his own music that is even stronger than his passions for procrastination and weird clothes. A father cannot even convince his kids that Bach was a pretty good composer by telling them that he made the cover of *Time* a few years ago. The kids would simply reply that he isn't much into rock mags.

'OK,' says the father grimly, standing at his stereo. 'I want you guys to forget that Madonna stuff for a few minutes and hear some Duke Ellington.'

'Duke Ellington,' says his son. 'Is he a relative of Prince?'

Yes, the kids will listen to neither the old masters nor the great popular music that Mom and Dad loved in their own youth . . . When I was a boy, Patti Page made a record called 'How Much Is That Doggie in the Window?' It swept the country, but you wouldn't sell ten copies today because it couldn't be filmed for a video. A cocker spaniel scratching itself in a pet-store window lacks the drama a video needs, unless the dog were also coming into heat and 50 dancing vets were singing 'Go, you bitch!' Today's parents grew up with the silly notion that music was meant to be heard. We have learned, of course, that music has to be *seen*, that the 1812 Overture is nothing without the sight of 20 regiments of Russian infantry . . .

I doubt that *any* father has ever liked the same music his children did. At the dawn of time, some caveman must have been sitting on a rock, contentedly whistling the song of a bird, until he was suddenly jarred by music coming from his son, grunting the sound of a sick monkey. And aeons later, Mozart's father must have walked into the parlour one day when Mozart was playing Bach on the harpsichord.

'Turn that crap down!' the father must have said.

And Mozart must have replied – in German, of course – 'But, Dad, this stuff is fresh.'

Bill Cosby is, of course, taking a witty view of an aspect of life, but he is also making a point and developing it. Like the other writers, he has his eye firmly on his subject.

Examples of argumentative writing, especially of a persuasive kind, are to be found regularly in newspapers and magazines. Look, in particular, at the comment and opinion columns.

◀ Assertion, Generalisation, Persuasive writing, Sequencing, Spider diagrams ▶

ASSERTION

Assertion is making a forceful statement, often without any supporting evidence. Sometimes people mistake assertion for **argument**. They make statements without examining the evidence or considering alternative views. For example, in the 1970s it was a popularly held and commonly asserted view that Britain was being overrun by immigrants, but official figures showed consistently that, in raw numbers at least, more people were leaving the country than entering it. The facts show that this was a false assertion.

Assertion, unsupported by sound evidence, is often a sign of prejudice and intolerance. Throughout history, people have suffered because of lies which other people have asserted as truths with total confidence. If you have read Bernard Shaw's *St Joan* or Arthur Miller's *The Crucible*, you will know that there were those who sent innocent people to their deaths on the basis of mere assertion.

 ## CATEGORICAL ASSERTIONS

Try not to make *categorical* statements; that is, statements which sound as though they are absolutely true under all circumstances and allow for no alternative viewpoints. You can usually avoid this trap by examining the evidence and asking yourself, 'Is this really true?' For example, suppose you were writing an assignment which involved discussion of the kinds of television programme people like to watch. You might be tempted to begin with the assertion, 'Everybody watches soap operas.' A little thought and common sense ought to suggest to you that this statement could not be literally true, and you might be prompted to consider that many people like quite different things. In fact, about a third of the population watch the most popular soaps at any given time. This is, of course, an enormous audience, so you would be justified in making a statement such as, 'Soap operas are phenomenally popular.' If you made the second statement rather than the first, it is less likely that you would be led into the assumption that the whole of the population would like to see more and more soap.

Equally, you should avoid treating your personal likes and dislikes as though they were absolute truths. If you were to claim, for example, that Shakespeare is boring and nobody likes him, you would be saying more about yourself than about the qualities of Shakespeare's plays.

 ## CONSCIOUS ASSERTIONS

Assertions can be used positively when you use them *consciously*. You could, in fact, begin an essay with the statement, 'Everybody watches soap operas,' if you were intending deliberately to exaggerate. You might wish to be humorous, ironic or provocative, in which case outrageous assertions may be perfectly appropriate.

◀ Generalisation ▶

ASSIGNMENTS

The term assignment is often used to refer to a piece of **coursework**. It has no special significance, except that it suggests a complete activity involving considerable preparation and **planning** rather than the traditional overnight item of homework.

When put together, your assignments should represent a variety of writing skills, usually containing some **open** and some **closed writing**, and at least one piece which reflects the reading of a work of literature. However, the kind and number of assignments you will have varies from syllabus to syllabus.

Your teacher or tutor will give you an outline of what kinds of assignment you will need to produce, and it is useful to keep your own check on how many of the required assignments you have completed. But do not let your natural concern for your progress get out of hand. A poor assignment does *not* mean disaster. Not all the assignments set will be of equal importance, especially in the early stages of the course. Some will undoubtedly be practice pieces, intended to get you used to the demands of GCSE. Remember, too, that it is a *selection of your best work* which will be used for final assessment. If you do not have the regular support of a teacher or tutor, you may be advised to take an examination which requires fewer assignments.

◄ Coursework, Gathering information and ideas, Planning assignments ►

ASSOCIATION

◄ Connotation ►

AUDIENCE

Audience is a key concept, and is referred to many times in this guide. The term is used to indicate the person or persons at whom any communication is directed. In ordinary conversation or in **oral** work, the audience is usually in front of you. If you know your audience well, you will speak with confidence because you will instinctively choose the right words and, if necessary, adapt to their reactions.

You need to develop a similar sense of your audience in written communication. However, when you are writing, the audience is usually invisible. Naturally, you may first think of your teacher or the examiner as the audience, but this is not necessarily the case. They will, of course, read your work, but your writing might have to be in the style of an article for a popular newspaper, in which case your audience might, for instance, be a typical *Mirror* reader.

Always ask yourself the question, 'Who's this for?' Then put yourself in the readers' shoes and think about how *they* will respond to your words. Will they understand? Have you struck the right note? Is the information the kind they would expect to read? If you intend to write leaflets and pamphlets, remember that they are always intended for very specific audiences, as are many forms of advertising.

Often, the nature of the audience will not be altogether clear. For example, you may be given a story to write on a particular subject, but with no information at all about the audience. In such a case, you have a choice: you can either make up your own audience, or you can assume that the audience is a reasonably intelligent, interested adult, such as your teacher or examiner!

When the opportunity arises, you should always try out your writing on a real audience. Children would be the best judges of the success of a children's story, for example. Remember, GCSE encourages you to treat writing as a real activity for real people.

◀ Advertising ▶

AUDIO RECORDING

A simple tape recorder can be very useful both for oral and written work. Audio recording provides a good way of being your own 'audience', and of trying to assess how well you are doing. You need privacy, since 'talking to yourself' is difficult at first, but when you have got over the initial awkwardness it may well help you. Try recording an essay, or some other kind of writing. Play it back, listening carefully to what you are saying. Is it coherent? Is the information in the clearest order? Does it have pace and variety? Are some of the sentences difficult to read? Is that because they are not put together very well? Are you trying to put too much into one sentence?

If oral work makes you nervous, audio recording can also help. You can practice reading out loud, or giving a short talk. Do you *honestly* interest yourself? Is your voice monotonous? Do you vary your pace and tone? Can you hear the words clearly? Remember, though, you are not assessing your accent, but rather how you are using language to communicate clearly and accurately.

◀ Accent, Dialect ▶

AURAL TESTS

An aural test is a specific assessment of your listening skills involving some written responses. Obviously it is important to listen carefully in your oral assessments as well, but some groups make aural work a separate item.

> The test will be based on a pre-recorded cassette supplied by the Group and a transcript will be issued after the first hearing. Candidates will be asked to respond in writing to a recording of original spoken material, with attention to the manner, language and interaction of the speakers, as well as to its content . . . The questions will require candidates to respond in a variety of ways, both to what is said and the way in which it is said.
>
> Midland Examining Group. Syllabus A

As you can see, you are not entirely dependent on what you hear, since you are given a transcript (a written, word-for-word version of what is said), but you must also note the emphasis on how the words are *spoken*; information on speed, pitch, tone of voice and accent, is only available to the *listener*.

To help you further, you are allowed to hear the tape *more than once*. The first time introduces you to the material, perhaps allowing you to become used to the voices, and to get a general impression. The second time you hear the tape is usually *after* you have been given the questions. You can therefore listen for specific points. You will also be allowed to make notes as you listen to the tape.

AUTHENTICATION

At the end of the course you will be required to sign a declaration that your coursework is all your unaided work. If it is discovered that a candidate has, in fact, used unfair means, *the penalties can be severe*. For example, the candidate could be disqualified from *all* subjects.

 ## SOURCES

You may, of course, use sources, but if you use someone else's words you must acknowledge the fact.

There are several ways to indicate the use of sources.

- If you have quoted directly from a text, you should indicate that you have done so – first, by the use of quotation marks, and second by an acknowledgement of the source at the end of the extract. There are many examples of this practice in this guide. Quotation marks need not be used for *long* extracts.
- If the quotation is very brief, it can be included in the body of your text and the source placed in brackets immediately afterwards.
- You may also introduce a quotation directly, using such statements as: 'As Norman Tebbit once said . . .' This last technique should be employed sparingly, and be used only for fairly short quotations by reasonably well-known figures; casual reference to the immortal words of Sándor Petfi will succeed only in making the reader feel small!
- If you have used a number of sources, it is advisable to add a bibliography.

 ## DISCUSSING IDEAS

Remember, you must on no account copy other students' work, even if you change the words slightly. It is perfectly in order, however, to discuss your ideas when you are planning an assignment, and you are free to act on helpful suggestions. *No one except you* must take an active part in the actual writing, though. Sometimes parents are anxious to help, and take pains to make improvements to their children's writing. More often than not, the presence of a helping hand is easily detected, and the teacher or tutor is required to report even *suspicion* of unfair practice. The Northern Examining Association regulations state clearly that 'Any candidate who uses, or is suspected of using or attempting to use any unfair means is to be reported immediately . . .' The other examining groups have similar provisions.

AUTOBIOGRAPHY

◄ Biography and autobiography ►

BAD LANGUAGE

'Bad language' is the term usually used to describe swear words and other crude expressions unacceptable in polite usage. Many people use swear words from time to time, for instance, when they are very angry or surprised, as in this piece of dialogue from Barry Hines's *The Blinder*, where the main character, Lennie Hawk, is being told off.

> 'I suppose it was t'old tale, it couldn't happen to thee, the great Lennie Hawk. You silly bugger!'
> 'All right! All right! I know!'
> 'Tha' does now! I though tha'd have had more bloody sense.'

Bad language can also be a characteristic regular feature of the way certain kinds of people express themselves. In his novel *Catcher in the Rye*, J. D. Salinger creates a central character whose habitual language can be seen in these two passages:

> Aah, go back to sleep. I'm not gonna join one anyway. The kind of luck I have, I'd probably join one with all the wrong kind of monks in it. All stupid bastards. Or just bastards . . .

> If you really want to hear about it, the first thing you'll probably want to know is where I was born, and what my lousy childhood was like, and how my parents were occupied and all before they had me, and all that David Copperfield kind of crap . . .

So what should you do when you create in a story or a piece of dialogue a situation where you think a character would use bad language? There is no simple answer to this question, but these three points will help you:

- Swear words are *not* an easy way of making your writing more vivid. Lavish use of them won't make your character or plot automatically more 'real'.
- Think about the people who are going to read your work. Will your use of bad language cause offence? People's attitudes to bad language (and what they consider to be 'bad language') can vary enormously. A good rule of thumb is, *when in doubt, don't!*
- If you *do* decide that swearing is appropriate, use it *sparingly*.

BATHOS

BEGINNINGS

Where do you start? Almost everyone finds it difficult to know where to begin a piece of writing. The start has to be good: first impressions last, and you have to interest your reader from the very beginning. If you start well, then the rest of the piece of writing is more likely to be successful. So it is worth taking time to think about how to begin. In **coursework** you will have the opportunity for second or third thoughts; take advantage of this. In an examination room there will be more pressure on your time, but do not be panicked into beginning to write before you have thought carefully about the best way to do it.

 IMAGINATIVE WRITING

Some of the ways in which you might begin imaginative writing or stories are listed below.

Shock

Give your reader a shock or a surprise, as here – 'Eunice Parchman killed the Coverdale family because she could not read or write.' (Ruth Rendell, *A Judgement in Stone.*) This seems a shockingly unusual motive for murder.

Arousing curiosity

Make your readers curious. In this passage we are kept in suspense waiting to find out what 'it' is.

> It probably did not last more than a second, but the impression it made upon Maigret was quite extraordinary. It was like one of those dreams which, we are told, pass in a flash but seem to go on for ever. Years later, Maigret could still have pointed to the exact spot where it happened, the paving stone on which he had been standing, the stone wall on which his shadow had been projected.
>
> Simenon, *Maigret and the Toy Village*

Outlining character

Present your readers with details about a *character* at the very outset. When you read the following extract, you will be instinctively wondering how the information which is included is going to be significant in the rest of the story.

> Jimmy Garvin lived with his mother in a little house in what we call the Square, though there wasn't much of square about it. He was roughly my own age, but he behaved as if he were five years older. He was a real mother's darling, with pale hair and eyes, a round, soft, innocent face that seemed to become rounder and softer and more innocent from the time he

began to wear spectacles, and one of those astonishingly clear complexions that keep their owners looking years younger than their real age. He talked slowly and carefully in a precise, old-fashioned way and hardly mixed at all with the other kids.

Frank O'Connor, *The Paragon*

Is this boy going to be a loner all through the story? Is his mother's attitude going to play a significant part? Does the repetition of words such as 'innocent' suggest the boy is naive and may be exploited in some way? How does this fit in with the idea that he is very grown-up for his age? The use of character detail at the start may be a useful way of capturing the interest and attention of the reader.

Using dialogue

Snippets of conversation are always intriguing, and dialogue can also help to establish character and place, as in this passage:

'I think I knew his father,' said my uncle. 'Was he in India during the war?'
I said, 'I've really no idea. I don't know Mark all that well, I only mentioned him because I . . .'
'That'll be him,' said my uncle, with furrowed brow. 'He was in Calcutta in '43. Man with a limp. Played the trombone. Waiter! Could we have a menu?'

Penelope Lively, *Servants Talk About People: Gentlefolks Discuss Things*

From these few lines we learn about the uncle's past, his rather abrupt way of speaking, his nephew's somewhat hesitant manner, and the fact that they are talking in a restaurant.

Direct approach

Try letting your reader straight into the gist of the story or plot, as in the opening of this story, *Seventeen Oranges* by Bill Naughton:

I used to be so fond of oranges that I could suck one after the other the whole day long – until that time when the policeman gave me a scare at the dock gates when he caught me with seventeen hidden away in my various pockets, and he locked me up, and ever since then I've never looked at an orange – because I had my fill of them.

Despite giving you some of the plot, this beginning may help arouse your interest to find out the details behind the events which are outlined.

A variation on this idea is to start by explaining to your reader how you come to be telling the story, or what your relationship is to the events. That is the technique used by John Wyndham in this example:

The question I find most difficult to answer; the one which always crops up sooner or later when the subject is mentioned is, approximately; 'But how on earth did you come to get yourself mixed up in a crazy affair like this, anyway?'
I don't resent it – partly, I suppose, because it does carry the implication that I can normally be regarded as a reasonably sane citizen – but I do find it scarcely possible to give a reasonably sane answer.

John Wyndham, *Web*

Creating atmosphere

You can start your writing by establishing a *mood* or *atmosphere*, if this is going to be important. For example, the beginning of Ursula Le Guin's novel *The Farthest Shore* makes clear that it is set in a fantasy landscape.

> In the Court of the Fountain the sun of March shone through young leaves of ash and elm, and water leapt and fell through shadows and clear light. About that roofless court stood four high walls of stone. Behind those were rooms and courts, passages, corridors, towers, and at last the heavy outmost walls of the Great House of Roke, which would stand any assault of war, or earthquake, or the sea itself, being built not only of stone, but of incontestable magic. For Roke is the Isle of the Wise, where the art of magic is taught; and the Great House is the cental place of wizardry; and the central place of the House is that small court far within the walls, where the fountain plays and the trees stand in rain or sun or starlight.

As you read this beginning, what at first seems ordinary – March sun, ash and elm trees, a fountain – takes on a new dimension with the references to magic and wizadry. There is also a hint in the style of the passage, in its formal tone and deliberate repetition, of a special place and atmosphere.

Another kind of atmosphere is created at the beginning of this novel:

> Snow covered the airfield.
>
> It had come from the north, in the mist, driven by the night wind, smelling of the sea. There it would stay all winter, threadbare on the grey earth, an icy, sharp dust; not thawing and freezing, but static like a year without seasons. The changing mist, like the smoke of war, would hang over it, swallow up now a hangar, now the radar hut, now the machines; release them piece by piece, drained of colour, black carrion on a white desert.
>
> It was a scene with no depth, no recession and no shadows. The land was one with the sky; figures and buildings locked in the cold like bodies in an icefloe.
>
> John Le Carré, *The Looking Glass War*

The scene is bleak, cold and depressing.

Action

You don't have to begin at the beginning – you can plunge straight into the action of your story. As your narrative unfolds, you can provide more information once your reader is caught up in events.

▶ ARGUMENT

Not all your writing is going to be imaginative. What about the beginning for *argument* or *discursive* writing? Obviously, you will still need to capture your reader's attention and interest, but you will need to do it in a different way.

You may be writing in response to a question asking for your views for and against a particular issue, or some other invitation to talk around a topic. *Never* start by repeating the question, writing something like 'People have many different views on the causes of violence in modern society' or 'There are several points to be made for and against going abroad for your holidays'. This kind of beginning only irritates the reader, who is waiting for you to *say* something.

Start with the *first point* you want to make. You may think this a bit abrupt. Nevertheless, a good point, clearly made, will be much more effective than an introductory paragraph, which is likely to have little impact. Some people feel they have to 'write themselves into' an answer, winding themselves up, as it were. If you have thought carefully *before* putting pen to paper, this should not be necessary.

You do *not* need to begin by explaining what you are going to say in the rest of the work. If your ideas are clearly expressed and logically constructed, it will be clear what line of approach or argument you are taking.

You could start with a *short* anecdote or story which illustrates either the whole issue, or the first point you want to make. Perhaps you could start with a *question*. This is often 'thought-provoking' and can be useful in highlighting an idea or topic. Or what about a very challenging, deliberately provocative beginning? A shock beginning may provoke your reader and draw attention to your argument.

A final note in this section. This entry on Beginnings is quite extensive in order to give you a variety of ideas and examples. But remember, you have to write a *complete* piece of work! Make sure you strike a balance, especially in examination conditions, between the beginning and the rest of the work. Don't get so carried away with the opening section that the rest is rushed and under-developed.

◀ Argument, Persuasive writing, Point of view ▶

BIBLIOGRAPHY

This term describes an alphabetical list of books, magazine articles and other texts giving their author and title and details of publication. Sometimes you may find a bibliography headed simply 'Further Reading' or 'References'. Normally a bibliography will be found at the end of a book or section of a book.

When you research a topic for your coursework or project, you will need to refer to a number of different sources of information. A good way of identifying possible sources is to look at the bibliography of the first book you find. This will give you ideas about where else you might look. If libraries have to order books specially for you, they will welcome all the information which a bibliography gives about the date of publication and publisher, as well as the author and title.

Keep a careful note of what you have read when you do your **research**. When your piece of writing is completed, you will then be able to put in a list of books consulted at the end of the finished work. It will look something like this:

Begley, G. *Keep Mum! Advertising Goes to War*
Elliott, B.B. *A History of English Advertising*

Field, E. *Advertising: The Forgotten Years*
Turner, E.S. *The Shocking History of Advertising*

As an alternative to a bibliography at the end of your work, you can use *footnotes*. You put an asterisk * at the end of a quotation or reference, and, at the bottom of the page, you give details of its source.

BIOGRAPHY AND AUTOBIOGRAPHY

What is the difference? Biography is the story of *someone else's life*. Autobiography is written *about yourself*. Most of the following comments apply in various ways to both.

If you think you would like to try writing a biography or autobiography, visit your school or local library and skim through some published examples just to find out some of the different ways in which the task can be handled, and to see some of the kinds of style used.

 PRODUCING A BIOGRAPHY

There is not cut and dried way of going about writing biography. However, here are some of the points to keep in mind, and some of the stages involved in producing the finished item.

Choice of subject

Who are you going to write about? Rather than a film star, sports personality or long-dead historical figure, it might help to choose someone you know *personally*. Consider relatives, neighbours or local figures, all of whom may have had interesting experiences. Older people often have fascinating stories to tell about their youth, perhaps of school days or of working in jobs or conditions quite different from those you know today. Your writing will be much more lively and original if you can base it on a living person you can talk to.

Information sources

What sort of information do you need? *Primary sources* (letters, school reports, diaries, and so on) are preferable to *secondary sources* (other authors' printed biographies of your subject). Depending on your choice of subject, you may have to consult secondary sources, but remember that your GCSE coursework has to be *original*, *not* composed of extracts or re-wordings of other people's writing.

Researching the subject

How do you go about obtaining the material you need? If at all possible, *talk* to your chosen subject. *Prepare a list of questions* before the interview. Taping the interview can save you a lot of hassle in trying to make lots of notes while you are talking. But you may have to be patient – a tape recorder can put

* An example of a footnote.

people off and make them unwilling to talk. Give your subject time to relax by asking some very straightforward questions first. Encourage your subject to talk; don't interrupt just because they are not telling you exactly what *you* thought you wanted to know! What *they* volunteer may turn out to be much more interesting. Ask their friends and colleagues questions about them as well. See if you can get hold of cuttings from local newspapers, photographs, programmes – anything your subject is willing to let you look at and take note of. Do handle this material very carefully, because it may have important sentimental value, and it is likely to be irreplaceable. If there are already published biographies of your subject, make notes from them, but don't copy out chunks of writing.

Deciding on scale

How much of a person's life can you cover? A full-scale biography can run into many thousands of words. Obviously that will be beyond your scope. Try concentrating on a *particular period* or episode, rather than trying to cram in a list of dates and events.

 PRODUCING AN AUTOBIOGRAPHY

A number of stages will be involved. You may not feel that enough has happened in your life for you to select from it, but it is still important to *pick key periods*. For example, you might start with your earliest memory; a time when you were seriously ill or had to go into hospital (to have your tonsils out?); your first day at school; the birth of a brother or sister. Aim to make the reader feel as you did at the time, sharing your **point of view** and it will be interesting, even if the event itself may not be all that unusual or original.

Here are two examples from writers who chose to start their autobiographies at moments well into their childhood.

> One thing about living on a hill, there was always lots of sky to see and when you weren't busy you could study it. Sometimes the clouds would race along like lean white lions; like heraldic lions on the shields of knights I used to think.
>
> Sometimes they were grey and flat and slow. Old elephants pushing each other.
>
> I used to watch that sky a lot when I was a kid.
>
> Leslie Thomas, *This Time Next Week*

> We were about halfway down the gully when my sister screamed and called out, 'I've found him!'
>
> But she hadn't; it was just a rusty old can gleaming wet in the dew among the leaves. It wasn't George by any stretch of the imagination; I'd know George anywhere and he wouldn't be down in the gully, of that I was pretty sure. He'd be up top, in the Great Meadow where the grass was fresh and tender, and there were hosts of dandelions which he liked.
>
> Dirk Bogarde, *A Postillion Struck by Lightning*

AUDIENCE

Who is going to read what you write? Don't just think of a teacher or examiner. You should always have a particular **audience** in mind. Remember that biographies and autobiographies are real pieces of writing which exist in the real world. Why not try writing something for a younger age-group, for example, or for a specialised audience?

WRITING FORMS

What form is this piece of writing going to take? Not all biographies or autobiographies come in book form. The field of journalism offers many possibilities for biography. Local newspapers carry articles about local people who have distinguished themselves in some way; some magazines invite readers to tell of their experiences, or feature a 'reader of the month'; colour supplements of newspapers have features such as 'A day in the life of . . .' Autobiography lends itself to a diary format. You could also devise a **play script** or radio script, dramatising some scenes from your own life or the life of your subject.

How do you decide what to include? Don't get too obsessed with facts and dates. Biographies contain **opinion** and interpretation as well. You may want to explain why a certain event was so important, or how a particular episode reveals something typical about your subject. However, you do need to keep a balance, and to give your readers enough information for them to be able to make up their own minds. *Biography is not the same as personal writing*, and your feelings shouldn't be intrusive.

A few special points about autobiography. It is very difficult to stand back and look at yourself **objectively**. Concentrating on your own thoughts and feelings is therefore quite appropriate, but *do* take care not to start too many sentences with 'I', and *don't* keep saying 'I felt . . .' or 'I thought . . .' There are ways of sharing how you felt without simply stating it. Autobiography can lend itself to a more poetic treatment. You could even interweave sections of poetry and prose. Be adventurous and experiment! Autobiography can also be *self-limiting*. It is difficult to include events at which you were not present.

In passages for understanding, you may encounter autobiography. Remember that you are not simply looking for facts; you are looking for the personality *behind* the facts. What you have in front of you is the truth as that person saw it, and another person might have provided a different response or version of events.

Something to watch out for – not everything written in the first person ('I') is autobiographical. The 'I' in the story may *not* be the author. Sometimes a writer adopts another personality and then writes from that point of view.

BRACKETS

Brackets – also known as 'parentheses' – are used to cut off additional information from the rest of a sentence. They can contain afterthoughts, extra examples, or comments on the main sentence. For example: 'Now you know all about brackets (I hope!).' 'This was the first (and only) time we ever went to stay.'

Grammatically, the words in brackets are an *addition* to the sentence, which should still make sense without them. For example: 'He was extremely cautious (as it is observed by a learned historian) of punishing men who had found no other accusers but themselves.'

In writing which makes reference to other people's work you can indicate the source of the material simply by putting their name, and perhaps the title or date, inside brackets. For example: '. . . variation in the degree of uncertainty which the speaker may attach to what he is saying (Turner and Pickvance, 1969).'

Brackets do need to be used sparingly or they can make your writing seem rather jerky or disorganised. Very frequently you can substitute commas, or even dashes, for brackets. For example: 'How well I remember that evening – now many years past – when we first met.'

Finally, remember that brackets always come in *pairs*; don't forget to close them.

BROADSHEET

Broadsheet is the formal term which is sometimes used to describe large-format newspapers. It can also be used to distinguish 'serious' newspapers from the small-format *tabloid* newspapers. For example, the *Independent* is a broadsheet, while the *Sun* is a tabloid.

Some examining groups use the term broadsheet for the stimulus material that is handed out prior to the examination.

BROCHURE

A brochure is different from a leaflet in that it usually contains a number of pages. Brochures can contain an interesting blend of information and persuasion, and you may like to try your hand at producing one for your coursework. You may find it a good opportunity to use language in new ways, without having to write complete sentences on lined paper in 'essay' form.

Get hold of some samples of brochures to see the kind of language and techniques which are used. Travel agents are one obvious source of brochures, but many different kinds of organisation produce them. They are frequently aimed at very specific audiences. For instance, the major banks produce glossy brochures about their financial services for school leavers; hi-fi manufacturers lure prospective purchasers with technical data; and car dealers will offer you fully illustrated brochures of their range of cars.

Professionally produced brochures make use of a range of colours, a variety of types of print, glossy photographs and pictures. You will not have all these resources at your disposal, but you should try to make the finished product look as real as possible. At least use the same shape and size of paper, and leave spaces for illustrations. Do not worry if you are not very good at art; you will *not* be assessed on your artistic skill. What *is* important is that you show understanding of the *significance* of using pictures, different colours and types of layout, and so on.

The writer of a brochure has to think very carefully how to present information in an interesting and exciting way. Choice of words and their **connotations** are very important. So, if you decide to write a brochure, you will need to think carefully about:

- *what* you are going to say
- *how* you are going to say it
- how you are going to *set it out* on the pages.

◀ Advertising/advertisement, Persuasive writing ▶

CAPITAL LETTERS

Strictly speaking, capital letters are not part of **punctuation**, but a *convention* we use in writing; you can't talk in capital letters. Their correct use does, however, make it easier for a reader to understand your work. The following is written in complete sentences, but without capital letters. You can see for yourself how difficult it is to read.

'his eye was cold and hostile. others, it seemed to say, might like archie moffam, but not he. daniel brewster was bristling for combat. what he had overheard had shocked him to the core of his being. the hotel cosmopolis was his own, private personal property, and the dearest thing to him in the world after his daughter lucille.

P.G. Wodehouse, *The Indiscretions of Archie*

Capital letters are used in these cases:
- *proper names* – Mary, Ranjit, Australia, Sri Lanka
- *titles* – the *Daily Telegraph*
- *important words in titles of books, plays, films and so on* – *Gone with the Wind*
- *the first word of a sentence, or the first word of reported speech* – 'She answered, "No, thanks," in a very quiet voice.'
- *adjectives derived from place-names* – American, German, Japanese, Pakistani

CASE STUDY

This is the name sometimes given to a task in which you are given a number of different sources of information and then asked to produce a specified piece of work.

A case study tests your skill in three different areas: selection, understanding and writing.

A number of points are worth noting.
- Read the *information* (or *data*) carefully. What are the sources of this data? Is it all *fact*, or is some opinion? Is it written from a *biased viewpoint*? Do you need to read between the lines?
- Look again at the *task set*. Is a particular **audience** mentioned? Will this affect your choice of material?

- Select from the data the parts you actually *need* to answer the question. You will have to use your judgement about what to leave out, for not everything which you are given will be relevant or useful.
- Now *choose the format*, unless the question already specifies this.

You are now ready to write up the case study, using your notes. It is important to remember that you are *re-using* the information or data, but doing so in your own choice of words, not stringing together chunks of the original material.

CHARACTER

The idea of character is likely to crop up in several areas of your GCSE work. Passages to test your understanding will often focus on character and on the interaction between characters and events.

 ASSESSING CHARACTER

Sometimes the writer may openly *comment on* or *sum up* the person involved. In that case, you can see the character revealed quite simply by the writer. More usually, you will have to draw conclusions from the way a character *acts*. If, for example, a person frequently interrupts others when they are trying to put forward their views, spends more time talking than anyone else, and takes the last biscuit without asking if anyone else would like it, then you might deduce that that person was opinionated, domineering and selfish.

You need also to be able to distinguish between an *isolated incident* or passing emotion and a *permanent character trait*. We are all impatient at some time or other, but only some of us have impatience as a permanent aspect of our character.

Sometimes, the assessment of character requires the more sophisticated skill of reading 'between the lines'. It may be a question more of what someone *doesn't* say than what they *do* say.

Apects of character

You should try to widen your vocabulary in order to be able to sum up character accurately. Someone who rushes into things without really thinking through the consequences, for instance, could be neatly labelled 'rash', 'impetuous' or 'heedless'.

If you are asked to *label aspects of character* make sure that is what you do. If you write that the woman 'gets up to offer her seat to the old man', you are describing an *action*; if you say that the woman is 'courteous' or 'thoughtful', you are describing *character*.

A number of aspects of character are worth considering in your own writing. You may want to *be* a character. This is sometimes called *adopting a persona*, as you take on the personality and outlook of another person and write from their **point of view**. Sometimes when you work on passages for understanding you may have to 'be' one of the characters in the passage. You could also choose this approach in a piece of coursework.

CREATING CHARACTER

How do you go about creating a character? Some of the points mentioned above in the section on revealing character are also relevant here, but there are other considerations as well.

- Would the person have a distinctive way of speaking? Would this help you to pinpoint the character?
- Is the character of a person central to the plot? If so, you may think it worthwhile to start by establishing this character in some detail.
- Remember that outward physical appearance may – or may not – be a guide to character. Mention only that which is significant. It is not obligatory to list height, colour of eyes, hair. Be selective! Choose to emphasise features important in building up the particular character you have in mind.
- Don't feel that every character needs to be created in the same depth; some people in a piece of writing are obviously going to be more important than others.

Sometimes, carefully detailed characters are *not* necessary. If your emphasis is on fast action, you don't want to slow it up with lengthy descriptions of character. Think of your own reactions to character descriptions; do you read them carefully or do you skip over them, wanting to get on with the story? Make sure that the aspects of character you write about are the kind *you* would find interesting to read.

Names

What about giving your character a name? This may, at first, seem a trivial consideration, but think of the different ways you would react if you thought you were going to meet people called Peregrine and Francine, or Fred and Marlene? Names have *associations* of social status and period. For example, it is not common nowadays in the UK to be called Augustus or Agatha. In your reading, the names which writers give to their characters may also be a clue to the kind of writing it is or to its tone. Charles Dickens, for example, names one of his characters Mr M'Choakumchild (he is a schoolteacher), whilst a very stern factory owner is called Mr Gradgrind.

In **oral** work you may be asked to imagine yourself as some other character in a given situation; this is sometimes called 'role-play'. You will have to make decisions about how your character might react, and how he or she would express feelings and reactions.

◀ Stereotype ▶

CHARTS

A chart is a useful way of conveying information in a clear and concentrated form. One of the most common forms of chart which you are likely to come across for GCSE, is a *pie chart*, as pictured overleaf.

The *shares* of the total going to particular components are shown as slices of a 'pie'. In this example, we can quickly see that most of the government's revenue comes from taxes on income, and another significant proportion comes from taxes on expenditure (such as VAT). Taxes on capital clearly

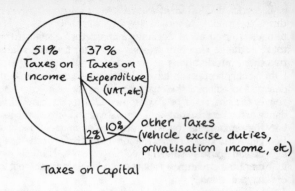

Sources of Government Revenue in 1989

make up only a small part of government revenue. So the pie chart provides a quick and clear picture of the breakdown of a total into its various component parts.

The main difference between a chart of this kind and a table is that charts usually contain *interpretation* or suggest some kind of *ordering of information*. You may encounter charts in stimulus material for coursework or case studies. It is also a convenient way of displaying information in informative writing or brochures. Remember, though, that charts do usually need to be accompanied by *written comment*.

◀ Flow charts, Tables ▶

CHECKING

Checking over our own work may not be very enjoyable, but it is very necessary. All professional writers have to **proofread** their work. Try to read your work objectively, as though it belongs to someone else. You may have to read it twice – once for the sense, and once for the mechanical **accuracy**. In examinations you should always leave some time for checking over your work. Many errors arise from simple haste and are only slips of the pen, which become immediately obvious on second reading. In coursework, you have ample opportunity to check your own writing, and to re-draft what is unsatisfactory.

In examinations, as well as checking your own writing, you should make sure that you obey any instructions given on the exam paper (the **rubric**). Check and re-check as you work through the paper. And be sure that you have seen *all* the question paper – it is amazing how often, in the anxiety of examinations, candidates fail to see a section, or even to turn over a page!

CHRONOLOGICAL ORDER

This involves placing events in the order in which they happened – in a sequence of *time*.

In certain kinds of *factual writing* – for example, itineraries or instructions – this is the most appropriate way of ordering events. It is often infuriating not to have information in chronological order. For example, it is not helpful to be told: 'Beat the eggs for five minutes until frothy, having first separated out two egg whites'.

In **narrative** writing, chronological order may also be quite appropriate. In descriptions of events, chronology can be significant, in that time-spans or sequences can be a key feature of what happens. However, there is always a danger that chronology can take over; check that your writing does *not* become simply a list of actions and happenings linked with 'and then' . . . Look at some of your own expressive writing which deals with chronological events. Do you keep using 'and', 'then', 'so' a lot? If so, try not to! Apart from its being poor style, you are probably becoming over-concerned with a series of events.

In many kinds of writing, both factual and imaginative, chronological order may seem the obvious choice – is it the best though? *Start at the beginning and work through to the end* is advice often given, but it may not produce the most interesting writing. Starting in the middle of events, or even almost at the end, can be very effective. You can the fill in the earlier events at appropriate stages in the narrative. Or, having captured your readers' attention and directed their interest to the key event, you can go back and start at the beginning.

◀ Beginnings, Flash-back, Sequencing ▶

CLICHÉ

A cliché is a word, expression or idea which was once original and interesting but which has now been used *so often* that it has lost all its freshness and impact. At times we all resort to clichés – they are ready-made expressions which save us time and thought. When you read the following, ask yourself how many times you have used them – be honest!

> I don't mean to be rude, but . . . do your best . . . like a bat out of hell . . . not the ghost of a chance . . . jumped out of my skin . . . without a second thought . . . at this moment in time . . . in this day and age . . . a dream of a shot . . . one last lingering glance . . .

In your own writing you will generally want to *avoid* clichés; you don't want your work to be labelled as stereotyped and boring!

There may, however, be some occasions when it might be appropriate to use clichés. For example, you may wish to portray a situation in which it would be natural for a person to talk in clichés, perhaps a man talking to his workmates about a football match. It might also be appropriate if you wanted to suggest a **character** who was limited in outlook and expression. The clichés would then help to define the person using them. Using a cliché can also provoke your reader into reassessing just how much in language is taken as being true, when this may be far from the case. For example, exactly what attitudes are implied by 'business is business' and what does the estate agent's description 'deceptively spacious' actually mean?

If you come across what you think are clichés in literature or other passages for understanding, you must always ask yourself *why* they are there. It may be for one of the purposes mentioned above, or it may be a poor piece of expression. In discursive or argumentative writing, clichés can be a cover-up for shallow thought, or ideas with little substance to them. It is not by accident that many politicians talk in clichés!

Proverbs are one special category of cliché. They usually contain some general truth or folk wisdom, often summed up in some kind of illustration or metaphor. 'Too many cooks spoil the broth' is a proverbial expression of the way in which too many people performing a task together will get in each other's way and so be inefficient. Many proverbs are so well known that it is possible simply to write or say the first few words, such as 'A stitch in time . . .'

CLOSED WRITING

In closed writing the subject matter, form, **audience** and **purpose** are *laid down for you*. In fact, for writing to be 'closed', it is not necessary that all these four requirements should actually be stated, at least not explicitly. Closed writing will often involve such activities as the writing of reports or instructions and other 'factual' exercises. However, in certain types of closed writing, techniques normally associated with imaginative writing are used to the full. For example, contemporary advertisements are frequently written in a narrative form, complete with characters and storyline. Although they read like fiction, they are written to very tightly defined criteria.

The **National Criteria** require that opportunities should be provided for you to write in 'closed' situations. When attempting closed writing, make sure that you have satisfied the stated requirements for the task.

CLOSE READING

Close reading is an important skill which you can only develop with practice. Most of the time when we read, we are only concerned with gathering the basic sense. If the text is a novel, we are anxious to find out *what happens next*. If it is a newspaper, we are concerned with *basic facts*. This kind of reading is concerned with understanding **explicit meaning**, but in some writing *implicit meaning* is just as important. Implicit meaning is much more difficult to see, and it will not normally be uncovered by a quick read through. Reading a text can be a little like getting to know a person. At first, you notice only the most obvious features, such as appearance and voice. With greater familiarity, you become aware of the subtler features of the person's character which were hidden from you at first. You may even discover your first impressions were wrong. Some kinds of writing, particularly literature, require a similar kind of getting-to-know-you process.

Exactly how you go about close reading will, of course, depend on the nature of the text, but you will need to employ some or all of the strategies described here.

LITERARY PASSAGES

- Read through to ensure that you have grasped the *basic sense*. Use a dictionary if necessary. If there are any parts that you still do not understand, make a note of them – their meaning may become clear later.

- Read through again, this time more slowly, and try to form a picture of the overall structure and design. Ask yourself, 'What is this writing really about?'

- Try to get the *feel* or *mood* of the passage. It is very important from the start that you judge the atmosphere and tone of the writing. Is the passage optimistic or sad? Is it serious or perhaps tongue-in-cheek? How do *you* react to it?

- Jot down or make a mental note of *specific words* to describe your response to the passage. Many students completely misjudge passages from the outset, and it is not uncommon for humorous material to be treated as though it were deadly earnest.

- Try to gain some impression of the *development* of the passage. Compare the ending with the beginning and see how the one grows out of the other. Consider alternative possibilities. What *choices* did the author make?

- Look for particular clues or hints about the 'hidden' meanings. Note any features that strike you as interesting or even odd. You might find, for instance, an unusual choice of word. In a story by Stan Barstow, the principal character steps out of the hospital after visiting his wife, who has just had a terrible accident, to find '*horror in the sunlight*'. After a quick, superficial reading you would readily associate the word 'horror' with the husband's state of mind. After closer reading, however, you would need to ask yourself why the author chose to use 'horror' in connection with sunlight, which we normally find anything but horrible.

- Basing your thoughts on the clues you have uncovered, build up a picture of the *story behind the story*. The passage may focus on relationships that seem to extend well beyond the immediate circumstances described. This strategy may be particularly important if you are asked to do a write-on, where you have to extend the story in some way.

NON-LITERARY PASSAGES

- As with literary passages, read through first for *surface sense*. Decide the purpose of the passage. Is it intended to inform, instruct or persuade?

- Read it through carefully to see how it is constructed. What are the stages in its development? They may be marked out for you in paragraphs. What are the *key points* in each paragraph?

- Try to spot the difference between *main points* and less important ones. In particular, try to make sure you can see what are points and what are examples.

- When considering **persuasive** writing, it is useful to adopt the *opposite* *viewpoint* to the author's. Do not take anything for granted. What are the *objections* to the author's claims?

- Look out for words that are used in clever ways. In **advertisements**, think about **connotation** and word association. In advertisements, you can be almost certain that not all is exactly as it seems at first!

- Consider carefully the intended **audience**; there may be features of the text designed to appeal to a particular group of people. Often the appeal will be through certain emotions. If so, write them down.

- Decide in your own mind *your attitude* to the subject matter; you may be asked to develop your thoughts later.

▶ PERSONAL RESPONSE

In all close reading, it is most important that you relate the *details* of the text to an understanding of the *whole*. To do this you will need to keep the text constantly under review. Check your developing ideas against the text. This may mean switching back and forth between sections of the text. A pencil is a useful aid, and a highlighting pen can also help you find your way around a text, but ask your teacher's permission first!

More often than not, of course, your response will be geared to answering specific questions that you have been set. Remember that GCSE questions are becoming increasingly *open-ended*, and tend to take the form of invitations to write about our personal response to the passage. Form your own clear view of the passage, so that you can approach the questions with full understanding.

CLUES

Reading texts can sometimes be likened to a game of detection. In one sense, all stories are detective stories. If you are an active reader, you will constantly be trying to outwit the author and to guess what will happen before you are told, while the author will be trying to mislead you and spring surprises. It is a very profitable activity, especially in discussion with a friend, to take a passage a little at a time and try to *predict* what will happen next. If you treat this exercise seriously, you will become aware of the importance of small details; they are the crucial clues.

The clues may not only be connected with the plot; they can also concern character and setting. Dialogue is frequently rich ground for clue-hunting. In Stan Barstow's story 'One Wednesday Afternoon', Jack's mother comes to the factory where he works to tell him his wife has been involved in an accident.

'It's Sylvia, Jack,' she blurted. 'She's had an accident.'

If you paused there, you probably would not notice anything remarkable, except perhaps the fact that she blurts. Is she distraught, or can't she wait to pass on the news?

A few moments later, the picture becomes clearer:

She ran clumsily alongside him as he started for the gate. 'All that hair,

Jack . . . She wouldn't have it cut short an' sensible. An' I bet she never ever wore it fastened like other women.'

Even in that tiny extract you can see a picture of a woman who resents her daughter-in-law and who is almost revelling in her misfortune. Notice the words '*like other women*'. Do they suggest that Sylvia was simply careless or that she was rebellious? Do they offer any clues about the mother's attitude to her son's marriage? Go back to the words '*She ran clumsily alongside him*'. How do you picture the situation? What do you imagine Jack is thinking? Is he taking any notice of his mother? Would you guess that, a few moments later, he turns on her and shouts: 'Shurrup! Shurrup!'

As well as making you more competent in answering questions about texts, finding the clues will increase your enjoyment of reading.

◀ Close reading, Implicit meaning ▶

COLLOQUIAL

'Colloquial' describes that kind of English which is acceptable in speech but not in formal writing (for which **Standard English** is needed). A colloquialism is not always easy to define. There is a very narrow line between the colloquial and **slang**. One person may regard a word like 'bloke' as slang, whereas someone else will think it is a colloquialism. Another cause of difficulty is the fact that our language changes, and what is considered slang at one time may later be considered a colloquialism (and eventually even become Standard English). Do you, for example, disagree with your parents about what *they* consider to be colloquial?

In your own *writing*, colloquial English will be appropriate (and therefore acceptable) only when you write dialogue. Sometimes people try to get round the difficulty of wanting to use what they realise is colloquial language by placing the words inside inverted commas; writing: *I felt really 'browned off'*, instead of *I felt very bored and disheartened*. Normally it will be preferable to look for formal equivalents of colloquialisms.

◀ Slang, Standard English ▶

COLON

◀ Punctuation ▶

COMMA

◀ Punctuation ▶

COMMENT

When discussing texts in your writing, you need to distinguish between making statements which merely *recount* the subject matter and making comments *about* the subject matter. Generally, you will gain higher marks for sound comment than for factual statement. Comment involves some sort of thought and judgement. Take a simple example from *The Secret Diary of Adrian Mole Aged 13¾* by Sue Townsend:

Being in a gang is not as exciting as I thought it would be. All we do is hang around shopping precincts and windy recreation grounds. Sometimes I long to be in my bedroom, reading, with the dog at my side.

If asked what this extract tells us about Adrian, you might say that he dislikes being in the gang. That would be quite true in one sense but you would only be re-stating what Adrian has already told us. If you were to say Adrian disliked the discomfort he experienced, you would be making a very simple *comment*.

A more thoughtful comment would be on the lines that the passage shows that Adrian likes to see himself as superior, preferring to enjoy civilised adult pleasures, rather than childishly hanging about the streets. More valuable still would be the comment that Adrian tries to convince himself that he is not disappointed at not being one of the gang, by assuming a supposed superiority. Notice how comment is based on the text, but *does not retell the story*.

◀ Close reading, Clues, Implicit meaning ▶

COMMENTARY

Starting on page 161 there is a section devoted to examples of *real work* produced by GCSE students. Each one has a commentary which tries to show you the positive qualities of that particular piece of writing and also features of the writing which can be improved with care and practice.

You are not required to write commentaries on your own writing for GCSE. However, your work can only improve if you *train yourself* to comment objectively on pieces of work and to think positively about what skills you can build on, and which weaknesses need attention.

COMMUNICATION

The **National Criteria** suggest that work in English should include a wide range of communication skills. Communication involves speech, writing, gesture, picture, sign and any other way of making our meaning clear to others. For GCSE English you are mainly concerned with speech and writing, but remember that in everyday life there are all sorts of signals that have meaning for us. How much do you learn about a person by the way they dress, for instance? Television programmes, newspaper features, magazine articles and advertisements often communicate in ways which extend *beyond* speech and writing. When you are dealing with anything other than plain writing, you should try to make yourself aware of all the factors that make up the act of communication.

COMPOSITION

Composition is a vague form not much in use now. It was used to refer to continuous writing, other than a letter. GCSE requires you to have a much clearer idea of precisely what kind of writing you are producing and for whom.

COMPOUNDS

◀ Adjectives ▶

COMPREHENSION

You will sometimes come across this term in some older course-books, where it describes a task designed to test understanding, but it is a term not much in favour now. For GCSE, **understanding** is the term more usually linked to the idea of responding to a set task in a way that shows you have grasped what is going on.

CONJUNCTION

◀ Joining Words ▶

CONNOTATION

Many words do not simply refer to an object or thing in a *neutral* way, but have all kinds of associations and emotions attached to them as well. These can be described as connotations. The idea of connotation shows why you need to be careful when you use a dictionary. Because they do not grasp a word's connotations, other people learning English sometimes say things which amuse us. Out of **context**, 'savage' and 'wild' may mean very similar things, but their connotations differ – 'wild flowers' is acceptable, but 'savage flowers' sounds ridiculous.

Connotation is a fundamental idea in the use and study of language. We use connotations both consciously and unconsciously in all our daily talking and writing, to convey attitudes and opinions and try to influence the attitudes and opinions of others. Why, for example, are the people who do the vital job of emptying our dustbins now sometimes referred to as 'waste-disposal operatives' or 'refuse-disposal operatives', rather than the older term of 'bin men'? Why would an army officer be reluctant to admit to ordering soldiers to 'retreat' but be willing to say they had made a 'tactical withdrawal'? Why are so many 'cakes' now referred to as *'gateaux'*?

When we talk of choosing our words carefully, one of the things we have in mind is the appropriateness of their connotations. If we want to suggest approval of someone who is unwilling to change their mind, we might use 'determined', 'resolute', 'firm' or 'strong-minded'. If their refusal to change their mind irritates us, then we might use 'stubborn', 'pig-headed' or 'obstinate'. Which is worse, an 'error' or a 'fault'? Which is younger, a 'baby' or an 'infant'?

The connotations of words are particularly important in forms of **persuasive writing**. When we read newspaper articles or skim over advertisements, we are being influenced by the associations of the words we are reading, either consciously or unconsciously. For example, some recent legislation has gone through Parliament making sweeping changes to this country's education system. The use of the term 'Education Reform Bill' implies that the existing system was unsatisfactory and that the changes which have been made are all for the better. But, depending on your own political views, you may see the changes as changes for the worse. If a newspaper describes a group of people as 'campaigners', they are giving them more status and approval than if they call them 'protesters' or 'demonstrators'. A 'crowd' is thought of as more orderly than a 'mob'. Sometimes even numbers and letters can have connotations: 'X' or 'GT' plus some number on a car has associations of speed and power – and probably expense.

The connotations of a word can change with the times. 'Gay' still exists in our language as a word indicating a light-hearted mood or something brightly coloured, but many people would now hesitate to use it in those senses because of the connotations of homosexuality which it has acquired.

◄ Advertising/advertisement, Persuasive writing ►

CONTEXT

The context of a word or idea is made up of the surrounding words and ideas. In the context of a discussion about travel, someone saying 'I got a ticket' will mean something different from a person saying the same thing in the context of parking a car.

Context can help you to understand the meaning of a word you aren't sure of. By looking at the surrounding words, you can often make an intelligent guess. The idea of context is also important when you are using a **dictionary**. A dictionary tries to give all the meanings of a word. When you look up a word, you have to read all the definitions until you come to the one which fits the context best.

Context – what sort of writing, for whom, whether written or spoken, the topic and the purpose – will also influence your own choice of language when you write. Words which may suit one context may not be appropriate in another.

◄ Clues, Correctness, Dictionary ►

CONTRAST

◄ Antithesis, Sequencing ►

CONTROLLED CONDITIONS

Some pieces of coursework may be required to be done in controlled conditions, which usually means under close supervision by the teacher. Often pieces needing controlled conditions will be done under **examination** conditions.

CONVERSATION

◄ Dialogue ►

CORRECTIONS

◄ Checking, Fair copy ►

CORRECTNESS

The term 'correctness' in the context of English can mean many different things. This entry deals with correctness in the sense of **mechanical accuracy**. At the end is a list of other entries within this book which you might also want to read.

Naturally, you will want your writing to be as correct as possible – no punctuation errors, no misused words and no spelling mistakes. There may be a reference on your examination paper to the importance of 'writing in clear English', which is another way of reminding you about correctness.

Just how important is correctness in your writing? In GCSE assessment is *positive*, not negative. You will be marked for what you *can* do. Although marks are not taken off for spelling and other mistakes, poorly spelled, unhelpfully punctuated work will obviously *not communicate as well* as language that is used correctly, and will therefore gain fewer marks.

Sometimes students concentrate so much on trying to be correct that the *content* of their work suffers. Anxiety over correctness should not stop you from trying to write in as interesting a way as possible. It is difficult to get the balance right between being clear and being interesting, but examiners will generally look more favourably on attempts at adventurous expression than on correct but dull expression.

Remember that in coursework you can check and re-draft your work, and that **dictionaries** are also available in examination rooms.

◀ Acceptability, Accuracy, Appropriateness, Standard English ▶

CREATIVE WRITING

Creative writing is a term much less frequently used nowadays than it was a few years ago. It was originally used to refer to writing which was intended as a release from the rather mechanical exercises and formal compositions which were once common. Today, it is most likely to be used in a general way to refer to **open writing**. Many would say, however, that all forms of writing are in some ways creative, just as all forms of writing demand particular skills and disciplines.

CRITICISM

This word sometimes causes confusion. In the context of English, 'criticism' means the process of judging or evaluating; it is *not necessarily* fault-finding and negative. So, if you are asked to *criticise* a writer's argument, you should be able to find both strengths and weaknesses. Your criticism need not be 'critical' in the destructive sense.

CROSSING OUT

Naturally you will want to present your work as neatly as you can, but you should not be afraid of crossing out, especially in examinations. Few people can write straight on to a page without making mistakes or changing their minds. Sometimes crossings-out are an indication of a thoughtful candidate who takes care over language. There is no need to obliterate all errors with correction fluid – your **Examination Group** may even ban it, in fact!

If you make a false start or change your mind about something, remember to *cross out clearly what you don't want the examiner to read.*

DASH

A dash (–) has a variety of uses in English. The ways in which it is used can be complicated, but this entry outlines the two main ways in which you are likely to want to use it.

In very informal writing, such as letters to close friends, the dash can operate as a substitute for a full stop. For example, 'Went to a smashing party last Saturday – lots of people were there – I didn't get home until 2.30 – Dad went mad!' Do you use it in this way? Take care that in your GCSE work you only use it in a 'chatty' context where appropriate, and don't let it become a habit.

In certain circumstances, a dash can be used as a substitute for **brackets**, to separate some additional item from the main part of a sentence. For example, 'David retired to a quiet corner – he often did this when they had visitors – and started to read.' This use is quite common in some forms of journalism but, when the dash is over-used, it can make writing seem rather disorganised or 'breathless'.

DATA

Data is the formal term given to a collection of facts or evidence on a given topic. In your GCSE work you may have to collect data in preparation for writing on a given topic. If you want to write about the work of the NSPCC, for example, you will need to collect together information in the form of facts and figures, in order to support your arguments convincingly.

Some **Examination Groups** *offer* you data in the written examination, as part of a **case study**, or as **stimulus** for some other piece of writing. Data can be in the form of numbers and charts but, as with words, you need to be able to interpret and evaluate the material you are given. Simply reproducing data without interpretation or comment will not be highly regarded by examiners.

DEADLINES

The term deadline is used for any date or time by which a piece of work needs to be finished, or to have reached a given stage. In order to structure and pace your GCSE English course, your teacher will give you deadlines. Don't think of them as an irritation or something to be ignored if you can get away with it. Coursework is designed to give you the best possible chance to produce the best work you can, and the best work is not produced all in a rush at the very last moment. Make a careful note of the dates you are given. An effective way of ensuring that you meet these deadlines is to count backwards from this date to when you think you need to start – and then add a few days! Work almost always takes longer than you think.

Your **Examination Group** will also issue deadlines and *final dates* by which it will expect you, and your teachers to have completed various tasks. These dates really are exactly as their name suggests, *final dates*. Completion of the coursework component is a vital part of the syllabus. After you hand in your completed coursework *you* can sigh with relief; your teachers still have a lot of work to do, marking and moderating it.

DETAIL

It is almost impossible to over-stress the importance of detail in every aspect of English. Small details very often make writing believable, and when you read a text you will find real understanding comes from attention to detail. Remember that *good writers do not waste words*, and it is often the seemingly uninteresting details which provide the keys to understanding and enjoyment. *All* writing gains from attention to detail, but it is particularly important in narrative and descriptive writing. Look at the pieces of writing quoted in this guide and you will see that it is often the tiny details that make them convincing.

In your own writing, try to avoid being too general and vague. There is no need to describe everything, but keep your inward eye on your subject and try to concentrate on those details which seem to have a meaning or sum things up. There are no rules to follow, but you should study as many examples as you can. A sensitivity to detail is crucial in speaking, writing and reading.

◀ Close reading, Commentary, Implicit meaning, Short story ▶

DIALECT

Dialect is a variety of English, such as *Cockney* or *Scouse*, linked to a particular part of the country. In general use, dialect is often confused with **accent**. For example, you may hear people making comments such as 'I don't like the Birmingham *dialect*', when what they mean is they don't like some of the sounds associated with the Birmingham *accent*. Dialect is concerned with vocabulary and grammar as well as pronunciation.

Sometimes you may come across the idea that dialects are rougher and inferior forms of the **Standard English** from which they are derived. This is not the case. Historically, Standard English (despite its name) is *one dialect* of English, which has, over the centuries, achieved general usage and prestige.

How does all this affect you? As in many aspects of English, the 'rules' concerning writing and talking are slightly different. For GCSE you will generally be expected to write in Standard English. After all, your work may be read by people unfamiliar with your dialect, but every English speaker and user is familiar with Standard English. The main exception here is in **dialogue**, where you may want to 'flavour' a character's speech with some dialect forms. It can be very effective, but use it sparingly. Long speeches in dialect are difficult to follow, especially if they involve inventing 'new' spellings to represent the sounds. You may lose your readers' interest.

In your **oral work**, *some* dialect is acceptable, especially if you're talking to people you know well.

DIALOGUE

Dialogue comes in two forms – as *supposed extracts of speech in a story*, and as the *words actually spoken in a play*. This section deals with the first of these. For dialogue in plays see **play script**.

Dialogue is not the same as *talk*. If you tried to write down exactly the way people speak, it would be full of *ums* and *ers*, it would break off and then start again, repeat words and phrases, and seem very slow or rambling. For this reason, attempts to reproduce spontaneous dialogue are only successful in very small sections. Most dialogue in novels and plays is a kind of concentrated, tidied-up form of speech.

Some actual speech in a story can offer variety and a sense of immediacy, as you can see in this passage:

This was just after the war and he had left the army with a demob suit and malaria. Everybody knew about the suit because it aged before our eyes and was quite dead within a few weeks. But it was Israel Hands who discovered the malaria.

'Ere,' whispered Israel to a clutch of us in the playground one evening. 'Come and 'ave a dig at old Walrus. He's gone off 'is cradle.'

Eager for novelty, we followed him through the gym, up the back stairs to the bathroom landing. Israel hushed us and projected one eye around a corner.

'Cor,' he breathed, 'ave a dekko now.'

We did with a caution we forgot as soon as we saw him. He was standing in the middle of the corridor, his wide face a waterfall of sweat, his steps like an elephant's on a dark night.

'Biscuits,' he cried out. 'Get the biscuits.'

'Wot's 'e want bleeding biscuits for?' asked Hands.

'Biscuits for the tank crews,' said Walrus as though answering the question. 'Biscuits for the men. Come on. Steady now.'

Leslie Thomas, *This Time Next Week*

Notice how the dialogue is interwoven with the narrative. One sentence is enough to move the action from the playground to the house. Israel's surprise and excitement are summed up by 'Cor'. The words put into a character's mouth are appropriate to both the person and the situation. Israel drops his aitches, uses 'dekko' instead of 'look', and 'bleeding' as a mild swear word.

Dialogue is used sparingly; we hear just enough of Walrus to realise he is raving. Similarly, no one is given a long speech; most natural dialogue consists of short exchanges. Your characters need to *react with each other*, not *make speeches*. Don't get carried away and write more dialogue than is really necessary.

When using dialogue or direct speech, the temptation is to introduce all the spoken words with 'said'. This can be very monotonous. Remember that there are lots of other 'saying words' to choose from: in the above extract the author uses *'answered'*, *'cried'*, *'breathed'* and *'whispered'*. But don't go to the other extreme and over-emphasise your dialogue by trying to introduce too much variety.

When you use dialogue you must also set it out correctly. Look again at the extract above. The most important things to note are that the words actually spoken are placed inside *inverted commas* (or *speech marks*, as they are sometimes called) and that you start a *new line* each time a different person speaks. What happens if you want to quote *inside a quotation*? The usual device is to use both single *and* double inverted commas, as here: *'He said, "I won't be long," and that was the last time I saw him,' she explained.*

◀ Direct speech, Play script ▶

DIARY FORM

For some people, a diary is merely a list of appointments and reminders, which would not provide you with a very interesting piece of writing. However, many people at some time in their lives try to record their *feelings* and *thoughts* in a diary – and often they don't manage to keep it going for very long. This in itself should warn you that interesting diary writing is not easy and requires concentration. There is, however, a long history of personal writing in both autobiographical and fictional forms. You may have read *fictional* diaries, such as those of *Adrian Mole* by Sue Townsend. *Z for Zachariah* by Robert O'Brien is a story told entirely in diary form. *The Diary of Ann Frank* is an edited version of a *real* diary. You may wish to record some of your *own* experiences in diary form as a version of **autobiography**.

In fictional form, a diary provides a special way of telling a story. It gives us a first-hand and **first person** account of events. If you are going to use this form, then you really have to become the person whose imaginary diary you are writing. This doesn't mean you necessarily have to *agree* with all that your character says; we laugh at Adrian Mole's pride in being an intellectual, for example. Becoming the writer of an imaginary diary also involves using the appropriate language. For example, Adrian Mole uses the French term, *déja vu*, in one entry to show how intellectual he is, but he also gives himself away by using less than intellectual language, such as 'hang out' in this sentence: 'I should have written to the British Museum, that's where all the intellectuals hang out.'

As diaries are very *personal* records we get a special insight into the mind of the person writing the diary. It is almost as though we are being taken specially into their confidence or are even 'eavesdropping' on their thoughts. Entries are rarely limited to recording events alone.

Diary form does affect the way in which a story can be told. We experience the events step-by-step, as they happen, and so narrative devices such as hindsight or **flash-back** cannot be used; rather a simple **chronological** sequence has to be followed. This can still create a very effective simplicity and directness of communication.

If you come across diary form in your reading for understanding, remember that what is recorded will be *selective* – what is *not* recorded may also be significant. A diary will only contain the 'truth' as the person writing it sees it.

DICTIONARY

All students need access to a dictionary, preferably one of their own. Little 'pocket' dictionaries have the advantage of being easy to carry around and are inexpensive, but a larger dictionary will provide you with a greater range of words and give much additional information.

The **Examination Groups** underline the importance of dictionaries by saying that they may be consulted in the written examinations. Take advantage of this provision. You will need to check with your teacher precisely what the arrangements are.

When you open a dictionary you will see either a word or a group of letters in heavy type at the top of each page. These *head words* help you to scan quickly through the pages until you find the alphabetical sequence which contains the word you are looking for.

If you are checking on a word which is made up of more than one part, then you look for the key or significant word. For example, the phrase '*taking stock*' will be found under '*stock*', as will '*stock taking*'. When you have found your word, you may simply want to check the spelling, but the dictionary provides a lot more information than that. Look at the sample entry shown here.

²**reply** *n* sthg said, written, or done in answer or response

¹**report** /ri'pawt/ *n* **1a** (an account spread by) common talk **b** character or reputation ⟨*a man of good* ~⟩ **2a** a usu detailed account or statement ⟨*a news* ~⟩ **b** an account of a judicial opinion or decision **c** a usu formal record of the proceedings of a meeting or inquiry **d** a statement of a pupil's performance at school usu issued every term to the pupil's parents or guardian **3** a loud explosive noise [ME, fr MF, fr OF, fr *reporter* to report, fr L *reportare*, fr re- + *portare* to carry – more at ¹FARE]

²**report** *vt* **1** to give information about; relate **2a** to convey news of **b** to relate the words or sense of (sthg said) **c** to make a written record or summary of **d** to present the newsworthy aspects or developments of in writing or for broadcasting **3a** to announce or relate (as the result of examination or investigation) ⟨~ed *no sign of disease*⟩ **b** to make known to the relevant authorities ⟨~ *a fire*⟩ **c** to make a charge of misconduct against ~ *vi* **1a** to give an account **b** to present oneself ⟨~ *at the main entrance*⟩ **c** to account for oneself as specified ⟨~ed *sick on Friday*⟩ **2** to make, issue, or submit a report **3** to act in the capacity of a news reporter – **reportable** *adj*

reportage /,repaw'tahzh, ri'pawtij/ *n* **1** the act or process of reporting news **2** writing intended to give a usu factual account of events [F, fr *reporter* to report]

reportedly /ri'pawtidli/ *adv* reputedly

Source: *Longman Concise English Dictionary*

First, notice that there are two entries for REPORT, numbered 1 and 2. This is because '1Report' deals with the word as a NOUN and '2Report' deals with it as a VERB. As you read on you will see other letters and numbers used to separate out the different meanings and uses. For example, '2a – a detailed account or statement' is different from '2d – a statement of a pupil's performance at school'. Uses of 'report' in various phrases and expressions are shown in ITALICS.

When you look up a word, read the *whole* entry and check the meanings and uses given with the **context** in which you have found it before making up your mind which meaning is appropriate.

You can see that dictionaries make use of a lot of *abbreviated terms*. There will be a list of them, generally at the front of the book, and they are usually similar in all dictionaries. In the entry shown, *n* = noun, *vt* = transitive verb, *vi* = intransitive verb, *adj* = adjective, *fr* = from, *ME* = Middle English, *MF* = Middle French, *OF* = Old French, *usu.* = usually. The symbol ~ indicates that the head word is used in that space. For example, *a man of good report*. After '1Report' you will see /ri'pawt/. This represents the pronunciation. The ' shows you that the second syllable is stressed.

Look at the square brackets after '1Report'. These contain an explanation of the origin or history of the word. You will find that 'report' came into English from French at a time when our language was called *Middle English* (before 1500). The word was originally Latin and meant 'to carry'. If you then turn to 'fare' in the dictionary, it will give you some more information about this.

To summarise: a dictionary can be used to check on spelling, to check on meaning and to check on usage. It will also tell you about the history of a word and how to pronounce it.

Larger dictionaries also contain other kinds of information which may be of use to you: lists of **abbreviations** and what they stand for; lists of foreign words and phrases; and sometimes you even get lists of first names and their meanings.

DIRECT ADDRESS

Direct address is the technical term for talking directly to your reader. You may use it, for example, in some kinds of instructions, where you don't want to seem too distanced from your audience. 'For this recipe you will need two eggs and three ounces of sugar . . .' seems less formal than writing 'Take two eggs . . .'

Because it seems more personal, direct address is often used in **advertisements**. 'You'll be amazed at the improvement . . .' All you have to do is fill in the enclosed coupon . . .'

Very occasionally, you may come across direct address in fiction; you, as reader, are specifically addressed by the writer. This can have the effect of reminding you that you are reading a work of fiction, about events and people existing only in the writer's imagination. This kind of direct address will often contain some comment on character and events or put forward a particular interpretation – 'Now you may think our hero was wrong to do this, but . . .'

DIRECT SPEECH

Direct speech involves using the actual words spoken, as in: 'Mr Brown shouted, "Get out of my garden this minute!"'

Well-chosen direct speech can illustrate character and mood, but you should resist the temptation to use long stretches of direct speech. It is a very difficult form of narrative to sustain, and all too easily deteriorates.

There may be times when it is not appropriate to quote actual words. If, for instance, you were telling someone else about Mr Brown, then you would use **indirect** or *reported* **speech**: 'Mr Brown ordered us to get out of the garden that minute.'

Since you are usually telling your reader about events *after* they have happened, you can fall into the habit of putting *everything* into indirect speech. This will tend to make the exchange of words seem much more distant from the reader.

◄ Dialogue, Play script ►

DISCUSSION

Putting your thoughts into words and having to share them with other people in discussion is a very effective way of getting your ideas clear and straight. In discussion you can 'bounce' your thoughts off others who may not agree with you. The term 'discussion' is also used to refer to writing which involves a detailed examination of a given topic.

DRAFTING

Drafting a piece of writing means making two or more versions so that you can improve it each time. One of the main differences between writing for an examination and writing a coursework assignment is that you usually have the opportunity to draft and re-draft your coursework. If you take advantage of this opportunity, you can make sure that your coursework shows the best that you can produce.

There is little point in writing out your coursework again and again, however, if all you are concerned about is the neatness of your handwriting! It is the *changes* you make that are important. The work of spotting what needs to be changed is called *editing*. You expect your teacher to comment on your work, for example by saying if it is too long or too short, interesting or dull, and by pointing out mistakes in spelling and punctuation. When teachers mark work in this way, they are editing it. However, you cannot expect your teacher to edit your coursework until you hand in your final draft, because **examination groups** require coursework to be your *own unaided efforts*. To be successful in drafting, you therefore have to *become your own teacher*. You have to be **objective**, in other words able to look coolly and clearly at your own work, as if you were looking at someone else's, and see what has been done well and what has been done badly, and work out how to change it.

It is not easy to criticise your own writing like this. To be able to do it at all you must first know your own *strengths* and *weaknesses*. This is where all your previous work comes in useful. People sometimes say that English is a subject

DRAFTING

which you do not need to revise for. *This is not so*. Re-reading your old work will show you how successful you have been in the past, and what you need to watch for as you are writing. Do you write too little? Do you organise your work well? Can you choose the best words and use them imaginatively? Can you use a variety of sentence shapes, and punctuate them appropriately? What spelling mistakes do you make? The answers to questions like these lie in your past work, and it is up to you to find them.

When you are working on an assignment, you will have done your thinking, talking, research and planning by the time you are ready to sit down on your own to write in earnest. Before you begin, remember to leave some *space* on your draft, so that when you come to revise it, there will be room for your notes and comments. So, if you are handwriting, choose paper with widely spaced lines (if you are typing, double-space your lines). Leave a wide margin on both sides of the page, and at the top and bottom. Ghosts of your old teachers may arise at this moment complaining of waste of paper, but ignore them and carry on.

▶ THE FIRST DRAFT

When you write your first draft, your chief job is actually to *create* the piece of writing. All your energies should be devoted to trying to put your thoughts into words. You don't have to be too worried about whether your spelling and punctuation are totally accurate or whether your writing is neat and tidy. This is not to say that you should make careless or silly mistakes – you are only making more work for yourself if you do. Since this is the first draft, however, you know that you can concentrate on putting your thoughts into words, because you will have the opportunity to polish up your work at the next draft.

As you write, there will be times when you will need to pause. As you do, look back over what you have written and you will naturally begin to *edit* it. All pieces of writing have to go through this process. Do not be afraid to cross things out and re-write them. At this stage, neatness is not important. Your first draft may be covered in comments and notes of all kinds, but in the end it will be discarded like the crumpled chrysalis from which a brilliant butterfly emerges. When you are crossing things out, don't try to obliterate the words with thick lines or correcting fluid. It is often useful to know where you started from before making alterations – and you will sometimes find you were right the first time after all!

After the first draft is finished, it is a good idea to put it away for a while and to do something completely different. If you start to edit straight away, your head may still be full of what you meant to say, and this can often blind you to what you actually have said. When you *do* start to edit it, there are one or two things you should think about before you begin. First, remember those strengths and weaknesses you identified when revising your previous work. Second, think again about the *title* of the assignment you were given. Read it again and review what you have written. How does it fit the bill? What were you trying to achieve? You may discover as you re-read your work that there is something missing, or that you went off the point, or misunderstood what you should have been trying to do.

EDITING

Use a pencil when you are editing, as it contrasts with the original without obliterating your text. If you need to re-draft longish passages, it is better to write them out on a separate piece of paper, number them, and then use the numbers to key them in to the right place in your original text. Of course, if you can use a **word processor** it is then much easier to add to, or delete from, your original piece.

If you are making small changes, such as correcting spelling or adding a word or short phrase, it may be helpful to use an *editing code*. Your teacher may already use a code when marking your work, such as writing *Sp* in the margin to indicate a spelling mistake. You could make up your own codes, but here are some of the more commonly used ones.

Code	Example	Meaning
/	He was very very unhappy	Delete
S	It was a sory sight	Spelling mistake
[	[Next day the sun shone	Begin new paragraph
	... to use an editing code.	No new paragraph here
	Your teacher may	Run on the sentences
ʌ	She lost her yesterday	Something to be added
R	(in margin where needed)	Re-write passage indicated.

 FINAL STAGES

Now you move on to your next draft. If you think it will be your *final* one, now is the time to concern yourself about neatness of presentation, clarity of handwriting and anything else which will make your assignment pleasant to read.

Do not copy out this draft in an *unthinking* way. If you care about your work, you will go on seeing ways to improve it. Of course, you will have to work out changes carefully at this stage to avoid spoiling your final copy. It's a good idea to have some scrap paper handy so you can try things out *before* putting them in.

Drafting is demanding work, which can be laborious and time-consuming. But if you do it willingly, you are much more likely to produce a successful assignment than if you try to get it all right first time. Remember, professional writers have to draft and re-draft all the time.

DRAMA

◀ Acting, Play script ▶

DUAL CERTIFICATION

Dual certification examinations enable students to gain certificates in English *and* English Literature, without having to sit separate examinations. The first such scheme was introduced by the Northern Examining Association and is based on 100 per cent coursework assessment. The most important feature of the examination is that a number of assignments are assessed *twice*, once as examples of skill in English and once as evidence of literary understanding. Two separate certificates are awarded, but if one element does not reach the required standard it is still possible to gain a single certificate in either English or English Literature.

EDITING

◀ Drafting ▶

EMPATHY

Empathy describes using your imagination to enter into another person's personality and experience. You are most likely to need *empathic* skills in those questions which follow up the reading of a text by asking you to imagine you are one of the characters, and then to tell the story, or what happens next, from that character's **point of view.**

ENDINGS

Endings, like **beginnings,** are vital in writing. The ending of your work will be the last words an examiner reads; your last chance to impress and gain credit. There are two key issues here – knowing WHEN to stop and knowing HOW to stop.

You need to recognise the point in your writing when you have said enough. **Planning** is important in this respect. In personal or imaginative writing you must know the 'shape' of a piece – how it is all going to fit together – *before* you start writing. Don't – particularly in timed examinations – embark on a piece without having some clear idea of how it is going to end. Inspiration *may* come while you are writing, but you could find yourself driven to a very feeble kind of ending, or even be quite at a loss to know *how* to end.

In discursive or factual writing you need your planning to give you the confidence to be able to say to yourself, 'That's enough – I've made all my points clearly.' Padding the account with irrelevant detail or tacking on extra points or afterthoughts at the end is always very obvious. Writing just one more paragraph can often blunt the impact of what else has been said and give a feeble last impression.

▶ ENDING TECHNIQUES

And what about knowing *how* to end? Let's look at the problems of ending *imaginative* writing first. Offering illustration here is not easy since you need to know the whole story to be able to judge the ending.

Try looking carefully at the endings of books which you know well or which you are reading at home or for GCSE. How successful do you think the endings are? Can you identify what *techniques* are being used? Here are some which might be useful and which you could try out yourself.

Neat endings

Endings where all loose ends are sorted out can be very satisfying and give an air of completeness or of 'living happily ever after'.

This is the neat ending of *A Glass of Blessings* by Barbara Pym.

> The coach drew up outside St Luke's church hall.
> 'Very well,' said Father Bode, smiling his toothy smile. 'All very satisfactory, I think. Ransome should do well there.'
> I turned into the street where our new flat was, and where I knew Rodney would be waiting for me. We were to have dinner with Sybil and Arnold that evening. It seemed a happy and suitable ending to a good day.

This can also seem very contrived or unnatural, particularly as the real world is rarely so tidy!

Circular endings

A circular ending is where the events at the 'end' of the story have not really changed anything and the circumstances which sparked them off still exist. This is certainly one way of getting over the problem of ending a description of a state of affairs which does not itself actually end, as in this example from *The Secret Diary of Adrian Mole Aged 13¾*, by Sue Townsend:

> . . . I put my nose to the undercarriage and sniffed for five seconds, nothing spiritual happened but my nose stuck to the plane! My father took me to Casualty to have it removed, how I endured the laughing and sniggering I don't know.
> The Casualty doctor wrote 'Glue Sniffer' on my outpatient's card.
> I rang Pandora; she is coming round after her viola lesson. Love is the only thing that keeps me sane . . .

Descriptive endings

You might end with the picture of a scene which evokes the kind of mood or atmosphere you want your reader to go away with (perhaps also the same scene that you began with). Or perhaps with a description of a character whose life has been changed (or not) by the events.

This is the ending of Emily Brontë's *Wuthering Heights* – a novel full of turbulent emotions:

> I sought, and soon discovered, the three headstones on the slope next the moor – the middle one grey, and half buried in heath. Edgar Linton's only harmonized by the turf and moss creeping up its foot. Heathcliff's still bare.
> I lingered round them, under that benign sky; watched the moths fluttering among the heath and the harebells; listened to the soft wind breathing through the grass; and wondered how any one could ever imagine unquiet slumbers for the sleepers in that quiet earth.

Endings with a surprise or a twist in the tail

I must have slept on that bare hill. In the morning the flashing brilliance of the town was like the eye of an explosion. It was as bright as the sunlit iceberg. The brightness must have woken me.

For one moment I hoped. All the buildings stood as firmly as before. I could see them like a town plan in the Surveyor's office, small, distant but perfect and very clean. Not a speck of dirt. All white . . . and not a soul stirring.

R.W.Mackelworth, *Cleaner than Clean*

Open endings

Where everything is not really tidied-up, and you have to use your imagination on what you have found out in the story to work out what might happen after the story is over, you have an open ending. This is the ending of *Sumitra's Story* by Rukshana Smith.

She closed the door and took the small bag in her hand. It contained her nightclothes, radio, toothbrush and make-up. Anyone glancing at her would have seen a young, smartly dressed Indian girl, going off to work. But behind the smooth face, beneath the careful make-up, was a woman making a small step into the unknown.

Sitting opposite a middle-aged man who was hiding behind a copy of the Telegraph, reading about guerillas in Latin America, was an urban freedom fighter. And as the train followed its customary and prescribed route – East Finchley, Archway, Camden Town, Warren Street – Sumitra knew that when she stepped for the last time off the Northern Line, she would be stepping into a new life.

Another kind of open ending is when you are left with **ambiguity** – with an ending which allows more than one possibility of interpretation. This is the end of a science fiction story by Algis Budrys, *The End of Summer*.

He climbed into the car and drove quietly away, leaving the dog behind. Somewhere outside of town, he threw the cancelling generator outside, onto the concrete highway, and heard it smash. He unchained his memory vault and threw it out, too.

There had to be an end. Even an end to starlit nights and the sound of a powerful motor. An end to the memory of the sunset in the Piazza San Marco, and the sight of snow on Chamonix. An end to good whisky. For him, there had to be an end – so that others could come after. He pointed the car towards the generator's location, and reflected that he had twenty or thirty years left, anyway.

He flexed his curiously light arm.

Endings that seem like beginnings

Sometimes an effective way of ending is to leave your reader still 'working' and involved in the story. A word of warning – this is not an easy way out of a story which you cannot really resolve. Not knowing how to end is not the same as an *open ending*.

Endings to be avoided

Don't use 'and then I woke up . . . it was all a dream.' Such endings are predictable, and are worn-out clichés, which will not leave a good impression. Examiners are all too familiar with 'Things went black' . . . or 'I knew no more'.

Discursive Writing

Now, what about the problems of ending *discursive* or *argumentative* writing?

- Always aim for a strong finish. Leave a good point until last. Planning will help you here. Don't choose to end with a minor point, or leave the impression that your ending is some kind of afterthought, tagged on.
- Try to finish with a positive statement or something which will stick in your reader's mind, such as a challenging question.
- Avoid final paragraphs which summarise all you have said. This kind of repetition always gives the impression that you have run out of steam.
- Don't lamely repeat the question in a summarising sentence.

ENGLISH/ENGLISH LITERATURE

The National Criteria recommend that English and English Literature are studied as parts of a *unified* course. It is a requirement that the English course should include reading a *whole* literary text. However, there are separate examinations and certificates for English and for English Literature. If you are entered for English Literature you will need to study more texts than if you are entered for English alone. The introduction of the **dual certification** scheme does away with sharp distinctions between work for English and work for English Literature.

◀ Dual certification ▶

EVALUATION

◀ Drafting, Gathering information and ideas ▶

EVOCATION

Evocation, which means 'calling to mind', usually refers to a scene or an atmosphere. Sometimes, particularly in descriptive passages, authors *evoke* or suggest a feeling without actually describing it directly. The opening of George Orwell's *1984*, for instance, evokes a feeling of bleakness:

It was a bright cold day in April, and the clocks were striking thirteen. Winston Smith, his chin nuzzled into his breast in an effort to escape the vile wind, slipped quickly through the glass doors of Victory Mansions, though not quickly enough to prevent a swirl of gritty dust from entering along with him.

The beginning of the novel not only sets the scene and introduces the main character, but evokes a sense of the grey, depressing world of 1984. When reading a text you must be alert to what is being *suggested* or *evoked*, as well as to what is being directly *described*.

EXAGGERATION

◀ Figures of speech ▶

EXAMINATION

In the past, almost all examinations consisted of written papers only. In GCSE English at least 20 per cent of the marks are awarded for **coursework**. In some cases the *whole* examination is made up of coursework.

The term 'examination' is used in this guide to include the complete means of assessment – either coursework or coursework and written paper.

EXAMINATION GROUPS

The GCSE examinations are administered by six examination 'groups'. Except for the WJEC, these are groups of the separate regional GCE and CSE boards. The WJEC (Welsh Joint Education Committee) has always administered all examinations in Wales.

London and East Anglian Group (LEAG)
The Lindens
Lexden Road
Colchester CO3 3RL

Midland Examining Group (MEG)
Robins Wood House
Robins Wood Road
Aspley
Nottingham NG8 3NR

Northern Examination Association (NEA)
Devas Street
Manchester M15 6EU

Northern Ireland Schools Examination Council (NISEC)
Beechill House
42 Beechill Road
Belfast BT8 4RS

Southern Examining Group (SEG)
Stag Hill House
Guildford GU2 5XJ

Welsh Joint Education Committee (WJEC)
245 Western Avenue
Cardiff CF5 2YX

International GCSE (IGCSE)
Cambridge University Local Examinations Syndicate
1 Hills Road
Cambridge CB1 2EU

Although the groups are regionally based, they accept candidates from all over the country, so you may find yourself entered for an examination set by a group based outside your area.

EXAMPLE

The phrase 'for example' is used time and time again in this guide. Sometimes we refer to *illustrating* a point with examples. Examples are important when we want to make a point clear. It is easier for most people to grasp an idea if they can relate it to something they can picture or easily imagine. If you were discussing the question of nuclear power, you might wish to consider the issue of safety. You may know a great deal about the theoretical side of the subject or you may feel very strongly about the case for and against nuclear power. You are unlikely to make much sense to the average reader, though, unless you include clear examples. They might include *statistics* about the levels of risk or references to *particular circumstances*, such as the accidents at Three Mile Island or Chernobyl. Equally, you might wish to refer to the other side of the argument by introducing the matter of acid rain as an example of one of the risks of non-nuclear power.

Take care not to confuse a *particular example* with a *general truth*. The fact that Mr Brown crashed his car into the gatepost is not evidence that all people called Brown are bad drivers.

Remember, too, that examples really must *illustrate* something. A list of facts about nuclear power is not much use unless they are supporting a clear point of view. You may find it helpful to consider point of view and example together.

EXCLAMATION MARK

◀ Punctuation ▶

EXPANSION

◀ Amplification ▶

EXPLICIT MEANING

Explicit meaning is the clear, plain or literal sense of words, conveyed without any need for interpretation or 'reading between the lines'.

When giving instructions or presenting facts, it is usually most important to be explicit, so as to avoid confusion or ambiguity. It would not be very helpful to give someone a shopping list asking for 'something to lighten our darkness' when you needed three 60 watt pearl light bulbs. By contrast, when Lord Grey of Falloden wrote 'The lamps are going out all over Europe; we shall not see them lit again in our lifetime', he was not referring to a power cut. He was writing on the eve of Britain's declaration of war on Germany in 1914 and *implying* the terrible nature of what was to follow.

Factual information needs to be explicit. Weather-forecasters may not always be the most popular people, but they do try to make their meaning as explicit as possible:

> A frontal system is crossing the country. The south-eastern half of England will start dry and bright but cloud will increase with some rain before evening.
>
> Northern and western parts of England and Wales will have a cloudy day with outbreaks of rain or sleet, and some snow on high ground at first, turning drier after dusk.

Not a very pleasant day! But whatever we may feel about the weather, the forecasters must stick to the *explicit* facts as far as they can know them.

Those other popular forecasters, horoscope writers, on the other hand, may write in a way which looks positive and explicit, but leaves most to our individual fantasy:

> Life is most certainly taking a turn for the better. New friends will have an especially powerful, fortunate impact on your life. Holidays abroad are a must as they will bring idyllic experiences.

Perhaps there isn't so much difference after all!

Remember that, like the horoscope, most speech and writing has both explicit and implicit meaning. Literature, in particular, requires the reader to respond to both levels of meaning. The explicit meaning of Wordsworth's famous lines 'I wandered lonely as a cloud . . . That floats on high o'er vales and hills' is that he was out walking on his own, but the words convey as much about his mood and state of mind as they do about his activity or what he thought about clouds.

◄ **Implicit meaning** ►

EXTERNAL ASSESSMENT

External assessment is assessment of your work by an *outside* examiner as opposed to your own teacher. Written papers are externally assessed, while **coursework** is generally internally assessed by your teacher, although it may later be reviewed by an external moderator. One or two **Examination Groups** provide for external assessment of coursework and of **oral English** in special circumstances.

◄ **Internal assessment** ►

EXTERNAL CANDIDATE

This term applies to candidates who are not able to attend any centre or classes which prepare a candidate for GCSE, or to students whose centres are not able to send their teachers to attend standardising meetings. In this special case, individuals have to write to the appropriate **Examining Group**, which will give them guidance about how to enter the examination.

FACTS

A fact is a piece of information that can be tested or proven in some way. Remember:

- See that you recognise the difference between fact and opinion.
- Make sure that you get your facts right.

◀ Knowledge ▶

FAIR COPY

If you make several **drafts** of a piece of writing, the final draft is sometimes called the fair copy. Naturally, you will want your fair copy to be free of irritating spelling and punctuation errors and to look as attractive as possible. It is perfectly permissible to use a **dictionary** or any other guide to ensure that your writing is accurate. It is NOT permissible to *re-write* your assignment in any way AFTER it has been marked by a teacher. Sometimes, at an early stage, your teacher or tutor may suggest that improvements may be possible, but any corrections must be *your own* work.

◀ Checking, Drafting ▶

FANTASY

Fantasy is a very popular form of fiction; many young people find the imaginary worlds and extraordinary events described in fantasy fascinating. It is, however, a difficult form of fiction to write successfully. Examiners find that students tend to rely very heavily on what they have read and offer very predictable versions of *Dungeons and Dragons* plots, *Doctor Who* stories, or various forms of science fantasy borrowed from the cinema. So, unless you are really confident that you can do it well, it is a kind of fiction to be avoided.

FIGURES OF SPEECH

Figures of speech is the term which embraces a number of different techniques which can help to make our language more vivid or effective. Despite the name, they apply to *writing* as well as to speech. They are also known as *rhetorical* techniques.

They only work if they are used well. Sometimes students think that using figures of speech is an end in itself. The individual entries which follow outline some of the pitfalls as well as the advantages of figures of speech. But the general message is: experiment, where appropriate, but don't overdo it.

▶ ALLITERATION

This is the technique of repeating the same sound of a consonant at the beginning of a series of words. It is used to draw the readers' or listeners' attention, and to link together key ideas or words.

- It can be used to *link pairs of words*. For example, *cool* and *cloudy*; 'bonnet and brooch, bombazine black' (Dylan Thomas, *Under Milk Wood*). It is particularly effective when linking *rhythmic pairs*, such as 'text and trinket'.
- The *contents of lists* can be highlighted by using alliteration, as in this extract:

   Lots of folk live on their wits,
   Lecturers, lispers,
   Losels, loblolly men, louts . . .

   Philip Larkin, Toads

- It is a technique often used in *advertising*: 'Cruise the continent this summer' (P&O Ferries); 'Finish first with Indesit Omega'.
- You will frequently find it in *newspaper headlines*: 'French Girls Flown Back to Freedom' (*The Guardian*).

In skilful hands, alliteration can work well, but it can also sound contrived, and needs to be used sparingly.

▶ HYPERBOLE

This is the use of deliberately exaggerated language for emphasis. In *speech* we may use hyperbole almost unconsciously – 'There were millions of people waiting' . . . 'I've got tons of homework to do'. If a speaker uses this device very frequently, they may give the impression of being affected or possibly insincere – as in 'I'm eternally grateful to you. A million thanks for all your help. You're an angel!'

In *writing*, hyperbole can be useful for emphasis, particularly in helping to state arguments forcibly or in provocative openings. For this reason it is also a favourite technique of advertising language: 'You'll never find a more responsive partner'

The use of superlatives such as 'the most', 'best' or 'greatest' is another form of hyperbole; 'The world's most popular computer in the world's most popular range . . .'

▶ METAPHOR

This is a comparison, where we say that one thing is something else, when this is not literally true or possible, or where a comparison is *implied* rather than *stated*. For example:

Rage burned in his heart.
Wave upon wave of emotion crashed over him.
Black despair.

Some kinds of cliché are actually *worn-out metaphors*. For example, 'keeping our noses to the grindstone'; 'a sea of troubles'; 'swimming against the tide'. These phrases should be avoided unless you use them for a purpose, such as to suggest a very conventional or trite response.

Metaphor is a natural part of our language, often used unconsciously; we 'sail into a room'; athletes 'smash records'; we 'grasp meanings'; we have 'package holidays'.

Try to use metaphor in your own writing, if it is original and will genuinely make the work more interesting. But it is not obligatory to use metaphor. Always ask yourself whether the metaphor is really doing anything. In some kinds of writing, especially those which do not call for an imaginative treatment but for clarity of expression, metaphor is rarely appropriate.

You must also be aware of metaphor in responding to other people's writing. In tests of understanding you may be asked to pick out and comment on certain metaphors. It will not be enough to identify what is being compared with what. You will need to think about *why* this comparison is being made; what *point* is the writing emphasising?

The kind of writing where the most concentrated use is made of metaphor is probably poetry.

 ONOMATOPOEIA

This is the name given to the device in which the *sound* of a word in some way echoes the *sense*, for example, *sizzle, hiss, murmur, moan*. The words do not really re-create the sound; bells go 'Ding dong' in England but 'Bim bam' in Germany!

In your own writing, you may particularly want to think of onomatopoeic words in passages where evoking sounds is important. Look at this example:

> There's the clip-clop of horses on the sunhoneyed cobbles of the humming streets, hammering of horse-shoes, gobble quack and cackle, tomtit twitter, from bird-ounced boughs, braying on Donkey Down . . . curlew cry; crow caw, pigeon coo, clock strike, bull bellow and the ragged gabble of the beargarden school as the women scratch and babble in Mrs Organ Morgan's general shop . . .
>
> Dylan Thomas, *Under Milk Wood*

When you identify onomatopoeia in other people's writing, take care not to suggest it has more significance in creating the meaning than it really has. This is particularly important if you are looking at *poetry*.

PERSONIFICATION

This is a special kind of metaphor, in which an object, an animal or an idea is given the qualities or feelings of a human being. For example, 'The sun smiled down'; 'The wind whipped up the leaves into a frenzy'; 'The snow crept in under the door'.

 SIMILE

A simile is a figure of speech in which two or more things which have some quality in common are compared. The key words which identify simile are 'like' and 'as . . . as'. What distinguishes simile from metaphor is that the comparison is clearly stated. For example, 'The kettle hissed and spat like an angry cat'; 'Without his glasses he was as blind as a bat'.

Some similes are so well-used that they lose their impact and become clichés. Avoid similes such as 'pleased as Punch', 'sharp as needles', 'like a herd of elephants' and the like. Any frequent use of simile can become very tedious – except in very skilful hands, as in this passage:

> The playground roared like a rodeo, and the potato burned through my thigh. Old boots, ragged stockings, torn trousers and skirts, went skating and skidding around me. The rabble closed in; I was encircled; grit flew in my face like shrapnel. Tall girls with frizzled hair, and huge boys with sharp elbows, began to prod me with hideous interest. They plucked at my scarves, spun me round like a top, screwed my nose, and stole my potato.
>
> Laurie Lee, *Cider with Rosie*

 UNDERSTATEMENT

This is in some ways linked to hyperbole, but in this case the sense is deliberately *underplayed* to draw attention to what is being said. It may be used to create a kind of wry humour or irony. For example, 'At seventeen stone, she was not exactly a featherweight'.

 EXAMPLES OF FIGURES OF SPEECH

The winter evening settles down
With smell of steaks in passageways.
Six o'clock.
The burnt-out ends of smoky days.
And now a gusty shower wraps
The grimy scraps
Of withered leaves about your feet
And newspapers from vacant lots;
The showers beat
On broken blinds and chimney pots

And at the corner of the street
A lonely cab-horse steams and stamps.
And then the lighting of the lamps.

T. S. Eliot, 'Prelude'

The poem begins by *personifying* evening as if it is behaving like the people settling down for the evening, which seems an ordinary, comfortable thing to do. Further on, the shower 'wraps' paper about your feet as though this was a conscious, deliberate action on its part.

The first two lines establish a pattern of *alliteration* on the letter 's' which repeats throughout, giving a sense of unity and coherence, especially as 's' is part of many of the rhyming words. Further alliteration pairs are 'broken blinds', 'steams and stamps' and 'lighting of the lamps'.

Metaphor is used in comparing this rather depressing and in some ways squalid evening with (possibly) used-up candles or cigarette-ends, or both – using deliberate **ambiguity** of reference.

FILM SCRIPT

◀ Play script ▶

FINAL DATES

◀ Deadlines ▶

FIRST PERSON

First person refers to the use of 'I' and 'We' in narrative. There may be occasions when you are invited to imagine you are the person in a story or describe a situation in which you are involved. The use of the first person will be inevitable.

However, there are times when you might choose the first person as a **point of view**. It does have certain advantages; it involves the reader directly with the narrator; thoughts and feelings may be more convincingly displayed; you can experiment with *interior monologue* or *stream of consciousness*, where you write things down as they occur in the mind of your character; you can give the narrator a distinctive 'voice' or style of expression.

There are also some things to beware of: first person limits our range of vision, and you can only include information or events involving the narrator; it can be difficult to sustain – often students get so caught up in telling the story that they forget to use first person and revert to **third person**; you must have a clear picture of *who you are* when writing in the first person ... and it can be very difficult, for instance, to change sex and country and go back a hundred years! Endings can sometimes be tricky – it is very difficult to die at the end of first-person narrative, without using **clichés** such as 'then it all went black . . .' or else resorting to very elaborate devices; the passage of time can also be difficult to handle.

◀ Diary form ▶

FLASH-BACK

Flash-back is a term more usually associated with films where the main narrative sequence is interwoven with events which took place in the past but which we now see happening as though in the present. In your own writing, flash-back can offer you the chance to tell a story in a more varied way than simple **chronological** order. You can start in the middle of events and then use flash-back to relate what has led up to this. You can move from one time sequence to another, simply by starting a new paragraph and giving your readers enough **clues** so that they can realise what is happening. You can also clearly signal what you are doing by using such devices as 'It all started when . . .', 'My thoughts went back to the day when . . .' or 'Six months earlier . . .'

Flash-back can help you to *guide your readers' response or understanding*. If you first know what happened later, you read the circumstances leading up to the event differently. There is no suspense, but a *heightened awareness* of significance.

FLOW CHART

A flow chart, sometimes called a flow diagram, is a way of showing the order in which a series of events or sequence of ideas takes place. It can be very useful to sort out your ideas in a way which your eyes can easily follow. We often jot down ideas as we think of them in a very rough fashion, and then miss out something when we come to use the notes because they are so disorganised. A flow chart can help you get your ideas into a logical order, and even to decide what should go in each paragraph.

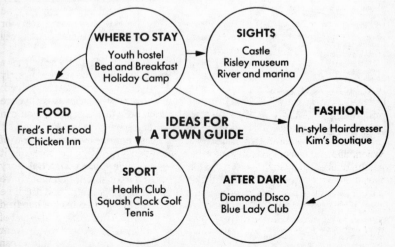

In the following example, a flow chart has been used within a dictionary to illustrate the various possibilities of meaning conveyed by the word 'alphabet'.

Types of script

The several hundred writing-systems of the world are based on many different principles. This diagram classifies and illustrates the various possibilities in terms of a sequence of choices.

1 Is the system an independent 'language' in its own right? **YES**

Or is it a means of transcribing a spoken language? **YES**

2 Do the elements of the script stand for meaningful units? **YES**

Or for units of pronunciation? **YES**

3 What size are the pronunciation units to which script elements correspond? **SYLLABLES**

PHONETIC FEATURES

SEGMENTS

Many primitive tribes have evolved subtle writing-systems for transmitting messages graphically without reference to spoken words. This letter from a girl of the Yukaghir tribe of Siberia to her errant lover expresses a complex message through stylized pictures:

Western mathematics is another such system; a formula such as $\sqrt{100} > 3^2$ is understood in the same way by people who speak different languages. This kind of 'writing' is on the increase at present, to create internationally-recognizable signs in areas such as clothes care and traffic information.

Chinese script has a separate written symbol for each word or 'morpheme' in the language. (Morphemes are the minimal meaningful elements out of which complex words are built.) Chinese words vary greatly in pronunciation in different regions, but their written form is constant.

筆 墨 相 副 曰 豐
brush ink co- operate is-called rich

'For brush and ink to co-operate is known as richness (in calligraphy).'

Because there are fewer different symbols in the script than Greek has syllables, pairs of consonants were written by 'borrowing' a following vowel, and consonants at the end of syllables were ignored: thus *mnon* became *mo-no*.

a ga me mo no 'Agamemnon'

The Linear B script was used to write Greek before the fall of the Mycenean civilization about 1200 BC.

In the Han'gul script of Korea, separate features of a sound are symbolized independently.

airstream interrupted
hissing between tongue and teeth
tongue-tip touches teeth-ridge

조 cho
선 son

Choson 'Morning Fresh' (ancient name of Korea)

Pitman's Shorthand uses a similar system to represent the sounds of English.

Mixed systems

Many scripts involve more than one of the principles displayed here. For instance, Japanese writing uses both the morpheme-symbols of Chinese and syllabic script comparable to Linear B. English orthography can be regarded as a mixed system; it is approximately phonemic, but the many 'irregularities' tend to provide distinctive spellings for meaningful units, as in Chinese writing. (compare *sign* with *sign-ature*; or *right*, *write*, and *wright*.)

4 'Segments' are individual consonant and vowel sounds. Does the script include signs for vowels as well as for consonants? **YES** **NO**

5 Are the vowel and consonant symbols grouped together into syllables? **YES**

Or written in a linear sequence? **YES**

Semitic languages are mostly written in vowel-less scripts. In Hebrew some vowels may be indicated by consonant-letters (w for long *u*, h for long *a*) but most vowels are ignored. The script reads from right to left:

ברוך אתה
h t ' k w r b

barukh atta 'Blessed art Thou . . .'

A system for indicating vowels exactly by adding small marks to the consonant-letters has been invented, but is not normally used in practice.

In Indian scripts such as Devanagari (used for classical Sanskrit and modern Hindi), groups of consonants are indicated by amalgamating the symbols for single consonants, and vowels are shown by strokes above and below the consonant letters:

म ब म्ब बे म्बू   जाम्बूनद
m b mb mbe mbu   jambunada

He vencido al ángel del sueño, el funesto alegórico

Spanish is a good example of a language with a 'phonemic' spelling system (one sound = one symbol).

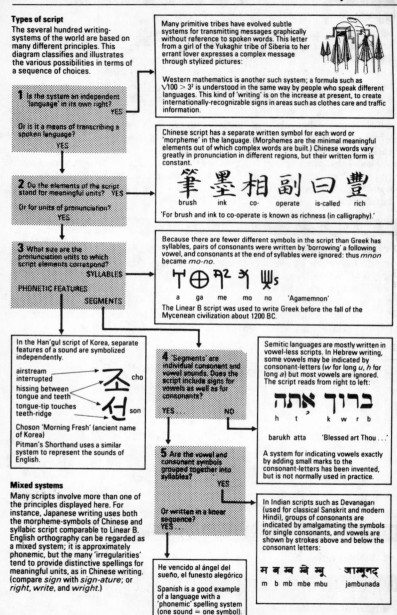

Source: *Longman Concise English Dictionary*

The following is a flow chart prepared by a pupil after reading *To Kill a Mockingbird* by Harper Lee. He wanted to write about prejudice, and began by putting his ideas down quickly as they came to him.

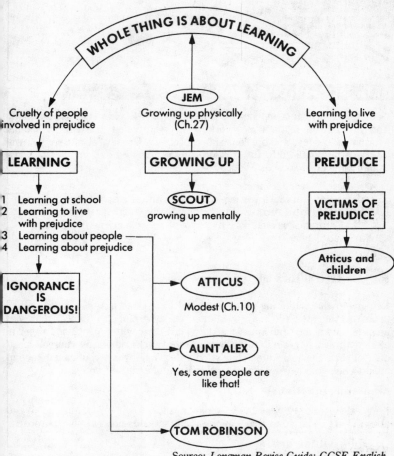

Source: *Longman Revise Guide: GCSE English*

FOOTNOTE

◄ Bibliography ►

FULL STOP

◄ Punctuation ►

GATHERING INFORMATION AND IDEAS

Gathering information and ideas is closely linked with **planning: assignments.** You must have material to work with, whether it consists of factual information or ideas and opinions about a subject. Usually, of course, you will be concerned with both. Information can be gathered in a number of ways from a number of sources. These may include:

- **research** – using a variety of sources;
- **discussion** – in which you explore ideas with another person;
- **brainstorming** – recording everything that you can think about a subject. 'Brainstorming' is best done by a group of people in a fairly rapid and intense manner.

▶ TECHNIQUES

Remember that gathering information and ideas does not only include other people's thoughts. You may well know far more about a subject than you imagine, and some time spent having a hard think with a pencil and paper is often surprisingly profitable. Although there is value in letting yourself loose on a subject, there are a number of considerations which you should keep in mind to help you avoid ending up with a pile of confused notes.

Aims and objectives

Keep asking yourself what the information is for. Review your aims as you go along. Don't be afraid to reject information that does not suit your purposes.

Consider all the angles

A single source, such as a newspaper article, may present a narrow view only. You may, for example, agree with an argument against the use of live animals in research. But what do the scientists say, and what does the issue look like from the point of view of, say, an AIDS sufferer hoping for a cure?

Be selective

This may seem to contradict the previous advice, but while you need to consider all angles, there is no point in piling up huge amounts of information about only one or two basic points at the expense of all the others.

Positive, negative or neutral?

As you gather information, think about whether it is positive and *supports* your point of view; whether it is negative and *opposes* your point of view; or whether it is neutral and has *no effect* on your argument either way.

Consider your priorities

Not all points are equally important. If you were writing about a transport system which included road, rail and air, what would be the most important considerations – cost? speed? comfort? pollution? private transport? public transport? going on holiday? getting to work? Decide on the most important aspects of your chosen topic.

Evaluation

All the considerations listed above involve a degree of *evaluation*. Effective gathering of ideas and information involves a constant process of evaluation. You should learn to pause for thought at all stages. There is no point in gathering information for its own sake. Try to follow a sequence on the following lines:

- choose your subject
- gather information
- evaluate
- reject and/or gather further information in the light of your evaluation
- repeat the process as necessary

When you think you have sufficient information you will need to review it and move into the detailed planning stage which begins with *organising your information*.

Even when you are working on your first draft, you may find you don't have all the information you need. If so, you have a choice: you can spend more time finding the extra information, or you can write your assignment in a different way so as to avoid having to use the missing material. For example, suppose you were tackling an assignment on transport and found you didn't have as much information on the development of railways on the Continent as you expected. If you felt the **data** to be essential to your plan, you would have to decide whether there was sufficient time to find the extra information. Otherwise, you would have to modify your essay plan, perhaps by limiting its scope to transport in the UK. You should *not* simply leave out the information and carry on writing as though it were there. That would only result in a badly imbalanced assignment.

◄ Drafting, Planning, Assignments, Research ►

GENERALISATION

The ability to form generalisations is a very important skill. To generalise is to take a step back and to see matters in a broader perspective. For example, if you are discussing the topic of popular television soap operas, rather than describing them *individually*, you can try to see what *general* qualities they have in common. You might identify features such as the escapist element, the nature of the content, the stereotyped characters and situation . . . Generalisations often involve a degree of abstraction, so that instead of talking about cars, buses, trains, ships and planes, you talk instead of 'transport systems'. Generalisations often involve putting information into categories and thereby making it easier to understand. For example, if you were designing a careers brochure, you might like to group a number of jobs together because they demand the same sort of practical skills.

Take care to avoid wild generalisations unless you are deliberately exaggerating. 'Classical music is boring' is a generalisation with which many people would agree, but it is certainly not true for all people, as the statement appears to suggest.

Where a generalisation is not an absolute truth which applies in all circumstances, it is wise to tone down your statement with such words as 'often', 'on the whole', 'usually', 'probably', 'tends to..'. You will notice words and phrases of this type used frequently in this guide.

◄ Assertion, Opinion ►

GRADES

Grades for GCSE are awarded on the scale A to G, with U indicating that the candidate has been ungraded. Grade C is described as being at least the equivalent of the old 'O'-Level Grade C or CSE Grade 1.

The grades for **oral communication** in English run from 1 to 5. Assessment of oral communication is compulsory, and a candidate must achieve at least a grade 5 (the lowest grade) to have a grade in English recorded on the certificate.

GRAMMAR

◄ Acceptability, Correctness, Standard English ►

HANDICAPPED CANDIDATES

All the **Examination Groups** have special arrangements for handicapped candidates, but the groups must be informed well in advance of the nature of the handicap. If you have a problem, you should consult your teacher so that possible action can be taken, and help given where appropriate. Special consideration is sometimes possible for candidates who fall ill during the period of the written examinations.

HANDWRITING

Clear, attractive handwriting is always pleasant to read, and teachers and examiners are always grateful if they don't have to decipher difficult scrawl. They are essentially concerned, though, with content, not appearance, and there are *no marks* for neat handwriting. If concern for your handwriting makes you lose sight of the content of your writing or makes you work very slowly, you are not enhancing your chances of success. If writing quickly but clearly is a problem, why not *practise*? After all, handwriting is a skill to be learned like everything else.
◀ Presentation, Typescript, Word processors ▶

HOMEWORK

Traditionally homework has been seen as something separate from classwork. The kind of work required for your GCSE coursework blurs this boundary, so that work started in class may be partially or wholly completed at home. The time taken to produce a piece of work does not fit very easily into the traditional homework slot, but may spread over a period of weeks.

HUMOUR

In English – no matter how serious the studies and examinations – you often have the opportunity to write and speak in a *variety* of **contexts** and styles. Do not assume that humour is out of place; touches of humour can make serious points very effectively, and not all language is used to discuss serious issues. This is not to say you should adopt an *inappropriately* jokey approach, but your readers and listeners will appreciate some use of humour.

HYPERBOLE

◀ Figures of speech ▶

HYPHEN

A sign (-) used to join two words together. It is often used to join the separated syllables of words which are broken at the end of a line. Another use is to divide words into parts or to signify a short pause between syllables in speaking.

A hyphen can also be used to create a new word out of existing words, a process sometimes called 'compounding'. For example, *no-frills*; *cook-chill*; *walk-in*; *up-front*; *bolt-on* are all recent additions to the language formed with hyphens (*Longman Register of New Words*, 1989).

It is not always easy to know precisely when a word needs to be hyphenated, when it should be two words and when it should be written as a single word. If you are uncertain, check in an up-to-date dictionary. At GCSE you will not be marked down for not hyphenating two words, but it's good to be in the habit of looking words up.

◀ Dash ▶

ILLUSTRATION

Illustration is a word often used to refer to the practice of offering specific examples to back up theoretical points. Such illustrations are an important way of making your ideas clearer to the reader and, indeed, of proving the truth of your point.

◄ Example ►

IMAGE

◄ Advertising/advertisement, Figures of speech ►

IMAGERY

◄ Figures of speech ►

IMAGINATIVE WRITING

You may come across this term used to indicate certain kinds of writing, such as short stories, poems and play scripts – as against more factual pieces, such as instructions on how to decorate a room or a report on a committee meeting. The term does, however, create an *artificial distinction*. All writing is imaginative, in that you have to think about the words you want to use, what you want to say, what will be appropriate for your audience, and so on. Very little language is totally factual; even a recipe will use words like *quite thick* or *white and frothy*. (How thick is *quite* thick? How many bubbles do you need before something counts as *frothy*? Use your imagination!)

IMPLICIT MEANING

The **National Criteria** require candidates to 'recognise implicit meaning and attitudes'. In other words, you have to 'read between the lines' and see what is suggested as well as what is stated.

Being able to recognise implicit meaning is essential if you are going to have a full understanding of literary texts and materials which appeal to our hidden emotions, as **advertising**, for example, so often can. However, implicit meaning is a common feature of *all* communication, and in many everyday situations we recognise it and respond to it with ease.

COMMON USES

Sarcasm is a familiar example of the use of implicit meaning. If someone says to you, 'You really are clever,' you may be flattered, but you are just as likely to realise the speaker is being sarcastic and means precisely the opposite of the literal meaning of the words used. We could say, therefore, that the literal meaning is that you are intelligent, but that the implicit meaning is that you are rather stupid. Obviously, which sense you take depends on the situation and tone of voice, or the **context**. If you do not take these factors into account, the implicit meaning will be lost.

When you are reading a text, it may not be so easy to spot implicit meaning. You may need to make a conscious effort to tease it out, but the process is much the same. You must explore the context and look for the **clues**. If you are dealing with dialogue, listen to the voices in your head or speak them out loud. (In the case of a dramatic text, you may perform it anyway.) Try to catch the tone of voice and the feelings that are being suggested.

If the text is narrative or description, think in particular about the **connotations** of the words used.

Consider this very brief short story, 'I Used to Live Here Once', by Jean Rhys.

She was standing by the river looking at the stepping stones and remembering each one. There was the round unsteady stone, the pointed one, the flat one in the middle – the safe stone where you could stand and look around. The next wasn't so safe for when the river was full the water flowed over it and even when it showed dry it was slippery. But after that it was easy and soon she was standing on the other side.

The road was much wider than it used to be but the work had been done carelessly. The felled trees had not been cleared away and the bushes looked trampled. Yet it was the same road and she walked along feeling extraordinarily happy.

It was a fine day, a blue day. The only thing was that the sky had a glassy look that she didn't remember. That was the only word she could think of. Glassy. She turned the corner, saw that what had been the old pavé had been taken up, and there too the road was much wider, but it had the same unfinished look.

She came to the worn stones that led up to the house and her heart began to beat. The screw pine was gone, so was the mock summer house called the ajoupa, but the clove tree was still there and at the top of the steps the rough lawn stretched away, just as she had remembered it. She stopped and looked toward the house that had been added to and painted white. It was strange to see a car standing in front of it.

There were two children under the big mango tree, a boy and a little girl, and she waved to them and called 'Hello' but they didn't answer her or turn their heads. Very fair children, as Europeans born in the West Indies so often are; as if the white blood is asserting itself against all odds. The grass was yellow in the hot sunlight as she walked towards them. When she was quite close she called again, shyly: 'Hello'. Then, 'I used to live here once,' she said.

Still they didn't answer. When she said for the third time 'Hello' she was quite near them. Her arms went out instinctively with the longing to touch them.

It was the boy who turned. His grey eyes looked straight into hers. His expression didn't change. He said, 'Hasn't it gone cold all of a sudden. D'you notice? Let's go in.'

'Yes let's', said the girl.

Her arms fell to her side as she watched them running across the grass to the house. That was the first time she knew.

At first reading, this beautifully written story may seem unremarkable. Not much appears to happen, and if you were asked what it is about, your summary might read like this:

- A woman crosses a river by some stepping stones that are described in some detail.
- As she makes her way, she notices the changes that have been made to the roadway.
- The day is fine but the sky strikes her as 'glassy'.
- She approaches a house and observes that it has changed somewhat.
- It strikes her as odd to see a car parked outside; she watches two children playing in the grounds.
- She calls them three times but they do not appear to notice her.
- Eventually, feeling suddenly cold, the children go indoors.
- Finally, the woman realises something for the first time.

When reduced to its basic, *explicit*, subject matter like this, the story doesn't seem very impressive. So what is the point? You have to delve below the surface facts and uncover its *implicit* meaning. There are a few clues.

First, the territory, although it has changed, is remembered in intimate detail. Notice how the stones are described as old familiar friends. Their exact characters are known from innumerable crossings in all seasons. They are identified by the definite article, 'the', and are described individually. How would she have gained such knowledge except in childhood? Ponder, too, the possible significance of this attention to the stones – suggestions of age? permanence? primeval nature? ancient roots?

Now let's look at the story stage by stage and think about any features that seem significant or unusual.

In the second paragraph she is *extraordinarily* happy because the road is still the same despite the changes. Why should this be? Why is she there anyway?

In the next paragraph one feature stands out. The sky is 'glassy'. The word is repeated and emphasised by having a minor sentence of its own. Is it significant because it is the one thing that she does not remember? Why should she forget such a striking feature? Is it a failure of memory, or has something changed? Is your impression of the scene altered in some way? Do you think of a somewhat unreal, dreamlike appearance?

By this time, you may have sensed that the woman seems to have an urgent desire to find the place *as it was*. The 'road was much wider, but it had the same unfinished look.' The screw pine and summer house have gone, but the clove tree remains *'just as she had remembered it.'*

The sight of the car parked outside the house strikes her as strange. Does this mean that, when she knew the house, the family did not own a car . . . or does it suggest that she lived there before cars had been invented? How long ago was that? Why has she returned? What is she seeking?

Then we come to the section in which the 'action' takes place. But it is very strange. The woman calls to the children three times but they act as if they do not see her. If a stranger suddenly appeared in your back garden, would you not take any notice? Perhaps they are used to strangers, or they are being very rude. Neither seems a very likely possibility, especially when the boy's 'grey eyes looked straight into hers'. How could he not respond in some way to her presence?

It is at this point that the woman stretches out her arms towards the children with a *longing* to touch them. Longing is a powerful emotion. What deep-seated need is revealed here, bearing in mind that she seems not to be a naturally outgoing woman? (Remember, she addresses the children 'shyly'.)

The key to these mysteries and to the underlying meaning of the story may lie in two final details. Notice that as the woman approaches the children, they feel cold *all of a sudden*. We have been told, however, that it is a fine blue day. Then, finally, we are told in the last sentence, 'That was the first time she knew.' Knew what? Think back to the children's failure to recognise her presence and the glassy appearance of the sky . . . you will see that what at first seems a simple narrative turns out to be strangely disturbing. *She knew* that she was a ghost, that the shining world of her memories no longer recognised her; she no longer had any existence.

When you have arrived at this stage, you will find that the story will grow with re-reading. Tiny details will take on new significance as layers of implicit meaning are uncovered. For example, you may now see the full importance of the stones at the beginning. They seem so substantial. They seem to confirm that she is home and she can return to childhood security. But their very permanence and solidity serve only to emphasise how fragile her dream really is.

Much more could be said about this story, but the crucial point here is that its true meaning is almost entirely implicit.

◀ Clues, Comment, Short story ▶

INDEX

An index is an alphabetical list of key words and/or ideas printed at the back of a book. It provides you with a detailed breakdown of topics covered in the book, and the page numbers where they are found, whereas the *contents page* will only give you a much more general outline of chapters and sections. Heavy print in an index usually indicates the main entry. The book you are now consulting does not need an index because it is *already* in alphabetical order, but learning to use an index can save you a lot of time searching through pages for the information you need. Consulting the index should give you an immediate guide as to whether a book is going to be useful to you or not.

INDIRECT SPEECH

◀ Direct speech ▶

INFERENCE

◀ Close reading, Clues, Implicit meaning ▶

INFORMATION GATHERING

◀ Gathering information and ideas, Research ▶

INK

Examination groups require you to use blue or black ink (or ballpoint) in written examinations. This is not because they want to cramp your style, but because other colours are used in the examining process for marking, and need to be seen easily. Remember that *pale* blue ink is very difficult to read.

INTENSIVE READING

◀ Close reading, Clues, Implicit meaning ▶

INTEREST

It is in your own interest to interest your reader and examiner! To be effective, any kind of writing must keep the reader's interest, and examiners will always generously reward a piece of writing which does this. If you read some of the examples of student assignments beginning on page 161, you will see this principle illustrated in the examiner comments.

INTERNAL ASSESSMENT

Coursework and **oral communication** are assessed internally by your teacher. Examination Groups appoint 'moderators' to oversee the process of internal assessment and to ensure that teachers mark to a common standard. In some cases, an individual's coursework may be marked *several times*, by various people concerned in the examining process.

INTERVIEWING

Interviewing can be a useful way of gaining first-hand information for either a magazine article or a biographical piece of writing. But you do need to prepare carefully before interviewing someone. After all, if they are prepared to give up some of their time to you, you must do them the courtesy of being well organised.

■ Write down a list of the questions you would like to ask, but also be prepared to improvise and to develop new questions from what your interviewee says.

- Give your interviewee time to talk; don't interrupt unless the interview is going seriously off-course. Beware too of putting words into your interviewee's mouth. Sometimes people are so anxious to be helpful, they will say what they think you want them to say.
- Decide how to make notes of what is said. It can be difficult to listen and write at the same time, so you could perhaps ask a friend to come along and take notes for you, or you could record the interview – but *only* if your interviewee agrees. In any case, some people feel awkward when being interviewed, and the presence of a tape recorder will only increase this feeling, so always give your subject time to settle down before you start the questioning in earnest.
- In all cases, be polite!

You may also be involved in interviewing, or being interviewed, as part of your oral assessment. In this case, you are unlikely to be taking notes, and your interaction with the other person will be especially important. You need to show that you can listen and respond appropriately to questions and answers.

◄ Biography and autobiography, Oral communication ►

INTRODUCTIONS

◄ Beginnings ►

ITALICS

Italics are a useful means of highlighting *key words* in a text. (They are regularly used in that way in this guide.) Italics may also be used to indicate that a word or a phrase is stressed. In this way they can be the written substitute for what in speech is achieved through pitch or tone of voice.

Italic type is often used for words in English which we somehow feel are foreign and still belong to the language from which we borrowed them – often French or Latin. For example: *Le mot juste* – a French phrase meaning 'the precisely appropriate word'. You are quite likely to come across this sort of word in your reading.

Italics also help to separate out parts of a text. For example, in play scripts, stage directions and guides to performance are italicised, as here:

DAVIES He's friendly, he's friendly, I didn't say he wasn't . . .
MICK (*taking a salt-cellar from his pocket*) Salt?
DAVIES No thanks. (*He munches the sandwich*) I just can't exactly . . . make him out.
MICK (*feeling in his pocket*), I forgot the pepper.

Harold Pinter, *The Caretaker*

Remember this use of italics if you are asked to take part in reading a play out loud.

Using italics to separate out some of the words is not limited to play scripts. You may find examples or additional comment italicised in books, as in this passage from a textbook:

Notice, finally, that each question has the same number of marks, so that your answers should be roughly equal in length and detail. *There is also a fuller Tutor's Answer to these questions from section A on pages 396–398. There is also a Tutor's Answer to the question from section B.*

JARGON

Jargon is a specialised form of vocabulary which people outside a particular occupation or social group are not able to understand easily. In your own writing and talking, you may occasionally want to use technical language or jargon. The **audience** here is all-important – if they are also familiar with this kind of language, then there is no problem. But if you are writing for a more *general* audience, then you need to exercise great care. The simplest rule is to ask yourself, 'Do I really need to use this word?' If the answer is 'no', then don't! If the answer is 'yes', because there is no alternative which can be understood more easily, then use it, but with an explanation of what it means. After all, your aim is to communicate, not to confuse.

You may come across the word 'jargon' being used critically, applied to unnecessarily complicated or clumsy language (as in the phrase, 'official jargon'). The aim of this kind of language may be to impress, or to make something seem more dignified or important than it really is.

◀ Slang ▶

JOINING WORDS

Joining words, or *conjunctions*, provide one of the ways in which we join ideas together to make longer, more interesting stretches of language. For example, no one wants to read page after page of writing like this: 'My alarm went off. I got up. I went downstairs. I could smell bacon cooking.' There is nothing wrong with short sentences; they can be very effective, but they do get tedious if used too frequently. The example would be appreciated more by the reader in the form of one sentence: 'After my alarm went off I got up and went downstairs, where I could smell bacon cooking.'

The most often-used conjunction is 'and'; it was probably the first conjunction you learned to use. It simply acts as a link, expressing no relationship between the ideas which it joins. Other joining words can introduce such elements as time, condition, or reason, as in these examples.

- I went to bed early because I was very tired (reason)
- A letter was waiting for me when I arrived home (time)
- I will certainly come if I am feeling better (condition)

Look at some of your own writing. How often do you use 'and'? Next time you write, stop to think each time you are tempted to use 'and'. Try to think of other words which you could use to join your sentences together. Further variety can be achieved if you remember that the joining words do not always have to fit *between* the sentences being joined; they can come *in front*.

- When she heard the scream, she was terrified.
- Although he can be rude at times, he is usually a very pleasant, easy-going man.

There are nevertheless times when a series of 'ands' *can* be effective. For example, if you want to stress a never-ending sequence or list: 'He went on and on and on'; 'I have to go to town and do the shopping and then come home and do the housework and cook the dinner.' Despite what you may have been told, 'and' can come at the *beginning of a sentence*, particularly if you want to emphasise the idea of adding yet more information: 'And that's not all'; 'And one other thing . . .' Other joining words which can effectively be used at the beginning of a sentence are 'but', 'so', 'or'. In each case they help to guide or prepare the reader for the next stage in the writing. 'But' immediately alerts you to the possibility of contrast or contradiction. 'Or' signals that an alternative is coming. 'So' introduces a conclusion or consequence.

A word of warning. 'Then' is not a joining word. 'I came in, then sat down,' is still a sentence with two parts – and the comma doesn't join the parts together either. It may improve the style of your writing if you try to avoid 'and then . . .' It is easy to fall into the habit of over-using this phrase, particularly when you are describing a series of events.

As a reminder, here is a list of commonly used joining words:

and	because	despite
but	although	where
for	while	before
since	after	so that

JUSTIFICATION

When you make statements, you will often need to justify them by providing **examples**. Not *all* statements need specific justification, but when you are answering questions on texts, for example, you should bear in mind that you have to justify what you say by referring to the text. Generally speaking, the only kinds of question which do not require you to justify what you say are those asking you simply to identify information or facts contained in the text. These questions usually come near the beginning of question papers, and normally do not carry many marks.

◀ Argument, Assertion, Comment, Example, Generalisation ▶

KEY INFORMATION

When you are skimming or scanning for information or reading closely, learn to separate the *essential* facts from the surrounding matter. Sometimes this may simply be a matter of separating the *points* which are made from their *illustrative examples*. Sometimes the essential information or the main points will be signposted by use of key words.

If you are reading a literary passage, it is less a matter of deciding what is important and what is not (you may safely assume that in a good piece of writing *everything* is important), than of finding the clues and significant details which will open up the story for you.

Deciding what are your priorities or your own key information is an essential aspect of planning. Although the word 'key' itself is not always mentioned, you will find aspects of the concept are explored throughout this guide.

◀ Close reading, Spider diagrams ▶

KNOWLEDGE

Unlike some of your other GCSE subjects, English is an assessment of your language and communication *skills*, rather than a test of how much you know. Nevertheless, you do need something to write about. Not every subject can simply come out of your imagination, so you are expected to take an intelligent interest in the world around you. Certain writing tasks will involve you in gathering information, research and collecting data.

◀ Revision ▶

LEAFLET

◀ Brochure ▶

LETTER-WRITING

Letter-writing is one area in which you are expected to conform to some set rules concerning layout, beginnings and endings, and so on. These rules are outside the scope of this guide, so if you are uncertain about them, consult your teacher, or refer to one of the many books on this topic. Students often get so involved in the details of layout that they forget that what is said in the main body of the letter is really of primary importance.

The **audience** and **purpose** of a letter are particularly important in deciding what it should contain and how it should be expressed. A letter to an insurance company giving details of a car accident will be very different from a letter to a friend describing the same accident. Letters are not always short! Sometimes students, particularly in examinations, do not do themselves justice because they write a letter which is just a brief note.

LINE NUMBERS

Passages printed on examination papers usually have the lines numbered, either in fives or tens, in the margin. These line numbers are put there for ease of reference, to guide you when you are relating the questions to the passage. It is surprising how many candidates fail to make use of them.

LISTENING COMPREHENSION

◀ Aural tests ▶

LITERATURE

◀ English/English literature ▶

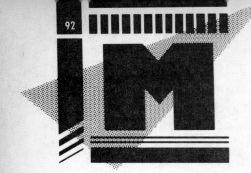

MAGAZINES

Magazines offer you models of a different kind of journalism from that usually found in newspapers. Try to familiarise yourself with magazines intended for different age groups and different kinds of audience. You may be surprised at the variety of styles used.

Writing a magazine article gives you a chance to entertain your readers and, at the same time, inform them on some topic or issue. However, be careful not to let the *information content* get out of proportion; magazines still have to *interest* their readers as well as supplying facts. Layout of the article also needs thought: how are you going to attract the reader's attention? Would the writing be helped by pictures, diagrams? How will you guide the reader's eye and divide up the information?

◀ Brochures, Persuasive writing ▶

MARK SCHEMES

A mark scheme is a set of rules for the assessment of students' work. Mark schemes identify what information or skills should be rewarded and explain the methods the assessors should use.

For GCSE there are *two* kinds of scheme. First, there are the schemes issued to the *examiners of written papers*. These are normally confidential and are not made available to the public. However, it is becoming increasingly common for the *Examiners' Reports*, which are issued to centres each year, to contain descriptions or summaries of the external assessment mark schemes.

The second type of scheme is the guidance issued to centres on the internal assessment of coursework. This guidance is usually contained in the syllabus and is of a more general nature than that used in written papers, because it has to apply to such a wide range of possible material. Normally, the mark scheme for coursework indicates what particular qualities are required to reach the various grade levels. The guidance is used in conjunction with samples of student work.

The fine details of mark schemes will probably not be of any interest to you, but it is useful to gain some knowledge of the general principles so that you have some idea how your work will be assessed. Your teacher or tutor should be able to give an outline of the basic requirements.

It is difficult to generalise, but the tendency in GCSE assessment procedures is to concentrate on evidence of skills such as those outlined in the **National Criteria**. Marking is positive, so you will be rewarded for what you do, with generally no specific penalties for making errors. But, if your expression is muddled or your punctuation is uncertain, you cannot expect to gain as many marks as a student who can write more clearly. The comments on the student assignments which appear on pages 161–220 of this guide will give you some idea of the sort of features examiners want to reward.

A final point about mark schemes. Your written examination papers will usually show the mark allocated for a particular question or section of a question. This information is designed to help you. Use it as an indication of the relative importance of the various questions; obviously a question worth five marks is not going to need as much as time and attention as one worth fifteen marks. Some candidates damage their performance by ignoring this useful guide, and spending too long on a minor question.

◀ Close reading, Spider diagrams ▶

MATURE STUDENTS

'Mature students' is a term covering a wide range of students who are over the usual sixteen-plus age range of GCSE. It includes students aged seventeen-plus who are still in full-time education, as well as older students. Because GCSE, like its ancestors CSE and GCE, is primarily an examination taken at the end of five years of secondary education, the majority of courses and syllabuses are aimed at that age group. This does not mean, however, that they cannot be followed by older people.

Many **Examination Groups** also provide separate syllabuses for mature students, where the nature of the stimulus material is more appropriate to the wider experience and maturity of the candidates. Some of these syllabuses have special provision for the different circumstances in which mature students are taught (at drop-in centres, adult education classes, and so on); some are even self-taught. These mature-student syllabuses are in every way comparable in standard to those designed for school pupils. All GCSE syllabuses must satisfy the same **National Criteria**. If you think a mature-student syllabus might suit you, the syllabus, and specimen papers, will be available on application from the appropriate Examination Group.

MECHANICAL ACCURACY

◀ Accuracy ▶

METAPHOR

◀ Figures of speech ▶

MODELS

A model is the term applied to an *example* of a particular style or form of writing, which you study in order to help you see the *key features* of that particular form.

In the work which you then produce, you should try to use similar techniques or features, but not to make a slavish copy of the model. An example of a model and the piece of writing which it stimulated is given on page 183 of this guide. If you refer to this, you will see that the student produced a genuinely original piece of writing; a model is not something simply to copy from.

When you are producing writing for your coursework file, it will often be a good idea to look at some models; for example, if you are drafting a leaflet or **brochure**, if you want to write some **advertisements**, a story for six- to seven-year-olds, or a newspaper report, you can benefit by studying a model. Looking at the model will help you to create 'real' pieces of work as they are in real life, not just examination exercises.

MULTIPLE CHOICE

Multiple choice in the context of GCSE English is the name given to a test of understanding in which you have to choose the correct answer from among a number of suggested possibilities. The **National Criteria** make provision for this kind of assessment, and you may come across multiple-choice questions in some older course books. However, it is not currently a very popular form of assessment. Examiners tend to be more interested in offering you the chance to respond as fully as you can in your *own words*. Even if you do not need to practise the technique, multiple choice can offer you a quick way of *assessing yourself* from time to time, since course books tend to give the correct answers at the end. Remember, though, that the *range* of understanding tested in this way is limited.

NAMES

◀ Character, Noun ▶

NARRATIVE

Narrative is the term applied to the re-telling of events or a story. We spend a lot of time in our lives telling other people what has happened elsewhere, and it is a form of writing to which we instinctively turn. But remember that it is not the only way of writing. In GCSE you are given the opportunity to express yourself in a *variety* of ways and sometimes it is left up to you to decide how you want to respond to a **stimulus**. At times that stimulus might even be a single word – 'loneliness', for example. You might choose a narrative response, but you could also write about the causes of loneliness in our society and the problems it brings. You might even write about the attractions of lonely places.

Narrative is not an 'easy option' – it requires a lot of skills which are detailed elsewhere in this guide.

◀ Beginnings, Close reading, Endings, Implicit meaning, Short story ▶

NATIONAL CRITERIA

The National Criteria set out the basic ingredients that *all* GCSE courses must contain, but they do not dictate the **syllabuses**. It is up to the individual **Examination Groups** to devise syllabuses, which can vary considerably in detail, but must satisfy the requirements of the National Criteria.

 OBJECTIVES

The requirements, or objectives, of the National Criteria are that you should be able to demonstrate your ability to:

- 1 understand and convey information;
- 2 understand, order and present facts, ideas and **opinions**;
- 3 evaluate information in reading material and in other media, and select what is relevant to specific **purposes**;
- 4 articulate experience and express what is felt and what is imagined;

- 5 recognise **implicit meaning** and attitudes;
- 6 show a sense of **audience** and an awareness of style in both formal and informal situations;
- 7 exercise control of **appropriate** grammatical structures, conventions of **paragraphing**, sentence structure, **punctuation** and **spelling** in your writing;
- 8 communicate effectively and appropriately in spoken English.

Put that way, the requirements may seem a little difficult to grasp, but the National Criteria recognise that the objectives are all related to one another and cannot be assessed in isolation. So you will not be expected to practise exercises in grammatical structure, but in the natural course of your writing it will become clear whether you have the necessary grammatical control.

Content

When we look at the content required by the National Criteria, the picture becomes much more familiar. You are expected to practise

- oral communication;
- reading;
- writing.

In each case, the emphasis is on working in a variety of situations.

There are five *special conditions* laid down in the National Criteria, to which all syllabuses and courses must adhere:

- 1 Coursework must account for at least 20 per cent of the marks.
- 2 There must be opportunities for students to read whole works of literature.
- 3 Where assessment is entirely by coursework, some of the work must be done under controlled conditions, such as a school examination.
- 4 Reading must include both literary and non-literary texts.
- 5 There must be a variety of work and activity in reading, writing and speaking.

Variations

The Examination Groups interpret the National Criteria in somewhat different ways, and syllabuses differ quite widely in such matters as numbers of written papers, and ways of testing the various skills laid down. However, the actual activities pursued by students entering different examinations will probably vary rather less. Consequently, if you move mid-course to a school or college which enters candidates for an examination under a different Examination Group, you should not meet undue difficulties. For example, what you may previously have done for coursework may now be tested in a written paper, but the kind of thing you have to do is likely to be similar.

NEWSPAPERS

Newspapers are a valuable resource for GCSE English. You should make an effort to read them regularly – the tabloids as well as the **broadsheets**. If you do not have a newspaper at home, you can usually read them in libraries. It is no use saying you don't need newspapers because you get your news from the television or radio; it may be true that newspapers are no longer our first-hand sources of news, but they do contain a lot of ideas, background articles and comment. They also contain many different types of journalistic writing, such as reviews, editorials and biographical features, which will provide you with **models** for your own writing.

Newspapers can also provide a **stimulus** for your own writing. A news item or a **photograph** could spark off an idea for a story or some other piece of writing. For example, an account of homeless people in London could give you material for a campaign leaflet on behalf of Shelter, the charity organisation.

Look carefully at the way a newspaper article is constructed. Study the headlines and how they relate to the rest of the item. Look at the way the information is divided up into short **paragraphs**, often using short sentences. Compare the ways in which the same story is reported in the *Mirror* and the *Daily Telegraph*, for example. You might attempt your own newspaper articles, with suitable headlines and layout. You could report real events – school or college news, local happenings – or fictional events, perhaps based on stories you have read. For example, you could report the witch trials in Salem in *The Crucible* or the trial of Tom Robinson in *To Kill a Mockingbird*.

The *letters page* of a local or daily newspaper also provides a real **context** for **persuasive** or argumentative **letter-writing**.

Newspaper articles are used in the written examination papers of some examination groups, so it will be to your advantage to familiarise yourself with a variety of styles.

◄ Argument, Persuasive writing ►

NOTES

Good note-making is a skill worth acquiring. Collecting and extracting information in a concentrated form is something you will need to do as part of the preparation process for a variety of both *spoken* and *written* tasks.

Before you start to make notes you must have a clear idea of what kind of information you are looking for, and what you are going to do with it. The notes you make before giving a talk on dogs, for example, will be different from those needed for an anti-smoking leaflet.

Notes are, as the word implies, very brief, abbreviated or condensed pieces of information or ideas. If you are making notes from *printed sources*, you should not be writing out large chunks! To save time and space, you can use **abbreviations**. But make sure your notes aren't so vague and sketchy that when you read them days later they do not make any sense! While you are making your notes, always keep in mind that you will need to use them later. Think about how to set them out, leave space, use underlinings, circles, arrows, anything which will be an aid to clarity and understanding. Not all notes need to be *words on a line*; try **spider diagrams**, boxes and so on. You might find that a highlighting pen, used sparingly, can be very helpful, but a page covered in bright yellow is not going to be of much use.

While many people will happily make notes for a piece of writing requiring information, they are often impatient of note-making before embarking on more personal or imaginative writing. But **planning** is just as important here.

Let notes *help* your work, though, not restrict it. If improvements and new ideas suggest themselves in the course of your writing, you shouldn't ignore them because they are not covered in your notes.

◀ Spider diagrams ▶

NOUNS

Son, tryst, pterodactyl, Scarborough, niblick, radiation, love, Winston Churchill and *multitude* all have one thing in common – they can all be used as nouns. As you can see from this list, the term describes the name of a person, an object, a place, an idea or a group.

Words representing people or places or titles are called *proper nouns*, and are given capital letters – for example, the Prime Minister: London: New Zealand.

Words for ideas or concepts are called *abstract nouns* – for example, independence, loyalty, hope, freedom. Writing which is handling argument or discussion is likely to use a lot of abstract nouns. They tend to sound very formal, and you should think carefully when using them in your own writing. Are they really **appropriate** to the content and style? Sometimes students use abstract nouns when they are inappropriate, in the mistaken impression that their writing is somehow more 'literate'. This is not so. 'The illumination levels were low' is not 'better' than 'There was very little light'. Indeed, using abstract nouns in the wrong **context** may be unintentionally comic. For example, 'His perambulations around the park occurred daily' is a pompous way of saying 'He went for a walk in the park every day'. Every noun has its place, though, and there may be occasions when 'perambulation' is the appropriate word!

Some nouns contain the sense of a group or a number of items – for example, team, government, crowd. So, do you think of these words as singular or plural? It all depends. You can say 'The team was top of the league.' Here, the team is being thought of as a single unit. But you can also say 'The team were outraged by the penalty given against them.' In that case the team is being thought of as a number of individuals. Remember also that some nouns are *plural* but refer to *singular objects* – for example, trousers, scissors, spectacles. In those cases you must use the noun in the plural.

You may have come across so-called *collective nouns*. Some of them are very familiar, such as *swarm* of bees, *flock* of birds and *herd* of cattle. Some are more rare, and these can be fascinating – a *charm* of goldfinches, a *sleuth* of bears or an *exaltation* of skylarks.

NUMBERS

Small numbers – one, two, three and so on – should be written out in full (in words) in most kinds of continuous writing. Leaflets and sets of numbered instructions are two obvious exceptions to this rule, however.

Large numbers should generally be left as numerals, since 'one thousand, nine hundred and ninety-seven' is very long-winded, and is only appropriate in very formal legal or official documents.

◀ Line numbers ▶

OBJECTIVE

An objective viewpoint is one where you do not allow your personal **opinions** and views to get in the way of making a judgement based on the facts or evidence. In most *arguments* you will need to try to be objective, unless a specifically personal response is required. So you have to be able to distinguish your personal feelings from objective views. It is often a danger signal if you find yourself using the phrase 'I feel . . .' or 'I think . . .' frequently.

When you read the arguments of others, try to make sure you identify what is objective and what is **subjective**. Writers, for example, of **newspapers** or **advertisements**, often try to convince their readers that feelings and opinions are objective assessments, when they are, in fact, no such thing.

An objective approach is not always the most appropriate one; there are many kinds of writing tasks in which reactions and feelings have a vital part, and your GCSE work will give you many opportunities for that kind of writing.
◀ Argument, Opinion ▶

ONOMATOPOEIA

◀ Figures of speech ▶

OPENINGS

◀ Beginnings ▶

OPEN WRITING

The term 'open' is used to describe writing for which there are no preconditions; that is the **purpose, audience** and form are not laid down. For open writing you may be given a subject or a title, such as 'Leaving Home', but how exactly you tackle it is left up to you. Usually, it is expected that the writing will be of a narrative or descriptive nature, though this need not necessarily be so.

◀ Closed writing, National Criteria ▶

OPINION

An opinion is a judgement or view which may or may not be supported by positive knowledge. Everyone expresses opinions, and it is vital that you should be able to distinguish between opinion and facts which can actually be checked. 'All doctors are lazy' may be a genuinely held opinion, but it is not a verifiable fact.

For certain types of work you may be specifically asked for your opinions; in other circumstances a more objective approach will be appropriate. Read the question carefully to check what sort of response is required.

When you are reading – particularly persuasive or argumentative pieces – check carefully whether the 'evidence' you are being offered is fact or opinion. A car might be advertised as 'the best hatchback in Europe'. Is that really a fact? What about 'Voted Car of the Year for 1989'? That could be checked, though you would need to be sure who voted; it would have a very different significance if it was the manufacturer and sales representatives! Beware, too, of the 'Everyone knows that . . .' or 'Most people agree that . . .' technique, with which people try to pass off opinion as agreed fact.

ORAL COMMUNICATION

Think of how many ways you can use a simple exclamation like 'Eh' in spoken English. It is possible to suggest surprise, curiosity, suspicion, bewilderment, anger and a host of other emotions by using only this simple utterance in different contexts. That is just one example to show the flexibility, adaptability and power of speech in our lives. Until fairly recently, however, speech has been considered less important than the written language in English courses, partly because written skills may need more effort to acquire and because written language can convey more complicated information at greater length. GCSE recognises that the spoken word is not a crude version of written English, but a form of communication with sophisticated qualities of its own.

The assessment of Oral Communication is *compulsory*. The National Criteria require that you obtain a grade in Oral Communication in order to qualify for a certificate in English. The oral component is, however, separately assessed, and provided you gain the minimum Grade 5, your performance in oral English does not affect your final grade. Your grades for English and for Oral Communication will be recorded separately on your certificate. You could, for instance, gain Grade 1 in English and grade 2 for Oral Communication. Equally, you might gain Grade 4 for English and Grade 1 for Oral Communication. In theory, any combination is possible. Although a high grade in Oral Communication is not needed for a high grade in English, there are good reasons not to neglect the oral element.

 VALUE OF ORAL WORK

Employment

Your oral grade may be a sign to employers and others that you possess the skills they require. It could be especially important if you are not very good at written English generally. There are many areas of employment where oral communication skills are actually more important than written skills.

Coursework

Oral discussion plays a vital role in all aspects of the English course. Both teaching and learning are affected. GCSE puts demands on students' ability to talk and *listen* in a variety of situations. For example, you could find yourself discussing a piece of writing in a small group, without prior explanation by the teacher about the work's meaning, or you could become a member of a team planning a project and having to work with others in the production of a report. Obviously, in these examples you would need both to listen carefully and to make a positive spoken contribution as well.

You will find that learning is more effective and enjoyable if you take an *active* part in discussion. Ideas become clearer when you have to explain them to someone. You are made aware of how well you understand your material, and your own thoughts are often sharpened by 'bouncing' them off other people's ideas. It can also be more fun to share your thoughts.

Examination work

If you are entering for examination in English Literature, oral work is the central point of contact between the requirements of the two English examinations. Discussion of a poem, for instance, may be in preparation for an English Literature assignment, but for the purposes of the English examination, it can be a valuable contribution to oral assessment. You may already be following a course leading to **dual certification**, in which case this point is even more important.

 ORAL SKILLS

For oral assessment, your teacher will attempt to build up a rounded picture of your ability in as many situations as possible, because the skills cannot really be taken separately. So, while it is highly unlikely that they would be considered as separate items to be tested, your teacher will assess the following skills:

- giving instructions
- giving an account of events or telling a story
- arguing and persuading
- giving information
- describing
- interpreting, evaluating and summarising
- asking and answering questions
- expressing personal feelings, opinions and attitude
- explaining
- co-operating with others to solve problems, make plans and discuss.

A single activity will give your teacher the opportunity to observe a number of these skills at once. Imagine you are a member of a *group* which has to draw up a booklet about nuclear power. It is up to the group to decide what the booklet is for and what information it should contain. Straightaway you can see that the ability to talk and discuss with others is tested. If there is disagreement, the ability to *argue your case* will be important. In doing so you may need to *explain* some tricky technical detail and *answer questions*. You might also need to *summarise* information you have gathered. Suppose you are not very good at drawing, but understand the technical side of the subject. You might need to *give instructions* to a member of the group who is good at drawing. Throughout the exercise, you will also need to demonstrate *personal skills*, expressing your feelings in a way which avoids disagreement or quarrelling.

Process

You can probably think of many other oral skills which you need in group work. The need for these skills arises naturally from the situation, and several of them may be required at once. This natural, unplanned, speech – which is nevertheless productive – is sometimes referred to as *process*. One syllabus suggests that process work might include exploring a poem or story, discussing a topic, preparing a statement of findings, solving a problem, interviewing and so on. In many respects, process is the most important aspect of oral communication, because it most nearly corresponds with ordinary life. Most people do not perform in public by making speeches or reading aloud. Most of our talk is an unprepared, if not unconsidered, process. It is important that you should feel at ease with this kind of communication. Obviously, there are many aspects of your oral ability which it would be impossible for an outsider to know about, let alone assess. In private, you may well show process skills which would never be revealed in the semi-public context of the classroom. For this reason the assessment of your oral skills is likely to be relatively limited, which means that it is most important that you participate fully in classroom talk.

Product

You may need to take part in more formal oral activities, such as giving talks, reading aloud, reporting on an assignment and so on. These planned *performances* are referred to as *product*.

Sometimes the distinction between process and product is not altogether clear. In real life it can often be hard to decide whether speech is natural and spontaneous or whether it is planned as a performance. Would you consider politicians appearing on *Question Time* as showing evidence of process or product? The answer, most probably, is a bit of both.

 ASSESSMENT METHODS

Because speech is such a continuously varying activity, assessing a student's competence is very difficult. Unlike a piece of writing, speech doesn't stand still while it is marked. Consequently, teachers have to form a continuous impression of your talk by observing you as much as possible. Probably only a small minority of classroom situations will be set up with the specific purpose of assessing oral communication. For the most part, the assessment will be based on how you communicate with your classmates and, of course, with your teacher. It is unlikely that your teacher will want to *mark* you, rather the aim will be to *build up a picture* of the positive qualities which can be observed. Your teacher will keep notes and, at the end of the course, make an overall evaluation.

Do not imagine that you are on trial all the time and that you have to put on a performance. Act and speak naturally, and remember that oral skill can be demonstrated as effectively in *quiet talk* as in *showy speech-making*. One sign of good oral skill is the ability to listen. The student who is always ready to talk, and never short of a word, may not rate so highly as the student who listens quietly and *responds* to what others say. Strange as it may seem, you are likely on occasion to be demonstrating your oral skill by not speaking!

Teachers sometimes make video recordings of classroom work. This technique has the advantage that the assessment can be made more carefully, at leisure. It may also have the disadvantage, at least at first, that the presence of the equipment can make the students rather self-conscious and create an artificial effect. However, most people soon become used to the method, which can be a valuable way of making you aware of your own oral skills. Once the initial giggles are overcome, a group discussion of your own talk can be a helpful and enjoyable exercise.

 ## SHOWING YOUR SKILLS

Be natural

Try to be as natural as possible in the classroom. Of course, this is not always easy. It is difficult not to be nervous when you think someone is watching you closely, but remember that, apart from the occasional 'public' performance, you are not undergoing a test. The aim is to recognise your strengths, not to expose your weaknesses.

Consider the audience

Be aware of your **audience**. In a small group discussion, listen and respond to the others in the group. When addressing a larger group, perhaps the whole class, *look at your audience*, but don't speak at any one person, such as the teacher.

Remember that talk is about talking. Do not bury your head in notes. Oral work is not about speaking your words 'well' and in a 'good' accent, but you must make yourself clear.

Try not to speak like a 'Dalek' if you are giving a talk or a reading. Vary your voice and intonation. Don't speak too quickly; very often, when we are nervous, we speak more quickly, so you may need to make a conscious effort to slow down.

Planning

When you are engaged in a product such as a talk, plan the outline of what you want to say in advance, but *do not* read out a prepared speech, as it will sound stiff and unnatural. On the other hand, if you do not *plan*, your talk is likely to sound hesitant and unconvincing. Pay special attention to the **beginning** and **ending**. The opening should engage the audience's interest and set out your intentions, while the ending should be a satisfying conclusion. Avoid simply stopping by saying 'That's it!', or words to that effect. The audience will feel left up in the air and not know quite what to think.

Help the listener

It is important to try to guide your audience, whether it is small or large. Listening to speech is different from reading a book. The *reader* can refer back and check that everything has been understood; the *listener* cannot do that, and doesn't always have the opportunity to ask questions. It is up to you to provide the signposts and reminders where necessary. In product, put in markers, so as to provide your audience with a *framework*. It is much easier to understand an explanation if you are told to expect a specific number of points and each one is introduced with 'First', 'Second', 'Third' and so on. Little phrases such as 'You will remember' or 'To go back to my first point' are useful in guiding the listener through tricky detail.

You may find it helpful to remember the old advice, 'Say what you are *going* to say – Say it – Then say what you *have* said.' You don't need to apply that rule mechanically, of course – but you must always bear in mind that what is totally familiar information to you may be fresh to your audience, and they may not be able to take it in all at once.

Choose appropriate language

Match your language to your audience and **purpose**. You will need to judge the relative formality of the situation and the subject. It is probably not advisable to talk to a large audience about a subject such as nuclear war, in the same chatty way in which you might describe going to a disco. Of course, you may come across very skilled speakers who can appear very natural and informal when discussing serious subjects, but they do, in fact, choose their words very carefully.

Take an active role

If you are engaged in a small-scale, but relatively formal, exercise, such as chairing a discussion or conducting an interview, you should take an active role. Where others seem at a loss for words, you may need to fill in for them or offer prompts. If you find that a person is hogging the discussion, you may need to intervene and deliberately draw someone else into the conversation.

Use gestures

If you have ever waited outside a telephone box, you may have noticed how the person inside will carry on a conversation complete with the full range of gestures. We don't just communicate with our voices. Sometimes you can guess what someone is talking about without hearing a word. Gesture, facial expression and even the way you sit or stand can be an important part of oral communication. Sometimes words take on a quite different meaning according to the 'body language' being used. A simple greeting such as 'Good Morning!'

can take on quite different senses depending on whether the speaker is looking at you or not. Skilled communicators use all these resources to reinforce their message. You may not be able to master all the techniques with ease, but try to put a little liveliness into your speech, for example, by using your hands to emphasise an important point. Don't *overdo* your gestures, however, or you can make yourself appear nervous or twitchy.

◄ Aural tests, Internal assessment, Video recording ►

ORIGINAL WRITING

Original writing is a term which used to be popular as a way of describing work which originated in the student's imagination, as opposed to **understanding exercises**, for example. GCSE defines more clearly the kinds of writing which you are expected to do, but you may come across the term *original writing* in some older course books.

PARAGRAPH

A paragraph is a convenient way of marking out a stage of development or a new idea in a piece of writing. The fact that the words start a new line helps to guide the reader through the text. If you look at some of the longer entries in this guide, you will see that they consist of many paragraphs, some quite short.

So, how long should a paragraph be? There is no simple answer to this question, except, perhaps, *as long as it needs to be*. That idea may seem little help at first, but if you think about it you will see that sometimes you need space to develop an idea, whereas at other times a single sentence standing on its own will have most impact. Try looking at a popular tabloid **newspaper**. There you are likely to see many short paragraphs, often only a single sentence long, which help the reader to glance quickly through an item. Compare that with something like a history text book, where the paragraphs may contain many sentences and run into twenty or thirty lines, and where the reader is expected to take time and look back over what has been read. You could also look at the example of narrative advertising shown as the model for the assignment on pages 182–7.

When you write **dialogue**, you should as a rule start a new paragraph each time there is a change of speaker. In a quick exchange of words, this can sometimes mean that every line is a new paragraph. Otherwise there are no rules to guide you. Sometimes students feel they need to start a new paragraph at regular intervals, such as every fifteen to twenty lines. This is not so. Paragraphs should develop naturally out of what you have to say, and thinking about them should be part of your planning and drafting processes. Three pages without a single paragraph, for example, would normally be a sign of rushed, unstructured work.

Paragraphs help you to build the overall structure of a piece of writing, but they in turn need some kind of structure. There are a number of ways in which you can construct a paragraph. It is possible to start the paragraph with a sentence which tells you what it is about: 'The first problem we encountered was . . .' Or, you could start with an anecdote, a question or an illustration of the point you are going to make: 'Last week fifteen items of junk mail fell through my letter box; why are we subjected to all this advertising?' It can also be effective to keep your reader waiting until the *end* of the paragraph for the key idea, or gradually build up to some kind of climax.

◀ Sequencing ▶

PARENTHESES

◀ Brackets ▶

PERSONAL WRITING

◀ Biography and autobiography, First person ▶

PERSONIFICATION

◀ Figures of speech ▶

PERSUASIVE WRITING

The term 'persuasive' can be applied to an enormous range of writing. Advertisements, posters, record sleeves, packets, newspaper articles, letters, political propaganda – these may all contain persuasive writing (also known as *rhetorical* writing). Much fiction is persuasive writing. Obviously, there is no *single* way of writing persuasively. There are, however, some features to look out for and to bear in mind if you are attempting to write persuasively yourself.

 SENSE OF PURPOSE

Persuasive writing should stick to the main subject and not introduce irrelevant information. An advertisement, for instance, might not be very convincing if the nature of the product was unclear because there was more information about the satisfied customers than about what they had bought. (Although one persuasive technique sometimes used in television advertising is actually to create interest by making you wonder *what* the advert is for.) Always make sure that your main point is clear to yourself. Examiners frequently come across the work of students who have failed to decide what their **purpose** really is, and who have as a result written something rambling and unconvincing. It is a good idea to write down your point of view and keep it in front of you. Often, it is a good tactic to begin a piece of writing with a forcible statement of your **opinion**. It is amazing how easy it is to lose your way, so that you end up saying the *opposite* of what you started with.

Linked with the purpose of your persuasive writing will be the nature of your **audience**. Your language and approach will have to be quite different, for example, if you are writing for old age pensioners, from the way you would write for teenagers. Make sure you have a clear idea of the people you are addressing.

 TECHNIQUES OF PERSUASION

Remember that being *persuasive* is not the same as being *fair and logical*. You need to win the audience over to your side, so you may need to emphasise and even distort the facts to suit your purpose. All the time you must try to influence the audience so they are *on your side*. There are many 'tricks of the trade', clever uses of language which you will find in all sorts of persuasive writing. Some are described here.

Bold assertion

'Everybody knows', 'It is a fact that . . .', 'Statistics prove . . .' Such phrases are used to suggest that the point of view expressed is unarguable. Care must be taken not to be too outrageous or the audience will become suspicious, but politicians, for example, use this technique frequently.

Reinforcing words will back up assertions. 'Of course', 'obviously', 'certainly', 'surely', 'definitely', 'It goes without saying' – all these words and phrases emphasise your point of view in such a way that it seems that the audience cannot possibly disagree with you.

Anticipating objections

You can pre-empt the opposition by anticipating their objections to your case. 'There will be some who argue . . .*but*', 'It is true that . . . *but*', 'Even though some figures suggest . . .' If you can dismiss the opposing arguments with quiet efficiency, your own arguments will seem all the stronger. However, simply saying 'I disagree with . . .' is not usually effective.

The rule of threes

Arranging ideas into groups of three seems to make a particularly strong impression on people. For example, you will probably remember Mark Antony's famous words in *Julius Caesar*, 'Friends, Romans, countrymen'. The fact that the opening of Jane Austen's novel *Pride and Prejudice* is so memorable seems to stem from the way the first sentence is constructed on a three-part basis: – *It is a truth universally acknowledged, – that a single man in possession of a good fortune, – must be in want of a wife.*

Look out for three-part statements; they are still much in use as a way of making opinions stick in the audience's mind.

Word association and connotation

The extract on pages 109–10 from Dr Martin Luther King's Washington speech makes use of Biblical language which would have had powerful *associations* for his audience, the majority of whom would have had a strong Christian upbringing. The effect is to draw into the issue of civil rights all the deeply felt religious conviction which he shared with his black audience. Whatever the purpose, persuasion often involves using word **connotation** to make information and facts appear attractive or unattractive. For example, depending on your point of view, a disagreeable choice might be seen as 'a challenge' or 'an imposition'. It has often been remarked that what one person calls a 'terrorist', another calls a 'freedom fighter'. You will rarely come across a piece of persuasive writing which doesn't make use of the connotations of words. Try to become attuned to the full meanings of words, including their **implicit meanings**.

Slogans and catch-phrases

If an idea can be wrapped up in a neat phrase, it can often be accepted as true simply because it *sounds* right. In the Martin Luther King speech shown below, the words *I have a dream* are a kind of slogan or rallying-call. Slogans and catch-phrases are often a feature of **advertising**.

Rhetorical questions

A rhetorical question presumes only one response – complete agreement – and does not require an answer. 'Who could refuse someone who has been through so much? Surely not any person in this audience?' If you were in the audience, would you have the courage to stand up and say 'Yes, I would refuse them'? This appeal to people's sympathies should not be overdone. Rhetorical questions are not a substitute for proving your point. They can also be used as a way of *involving* the audience once your argument is clear.

Human interest

Newspapers, in particular, often use examples of events involving individuals – so-called 'human interest' stories – to provide a focus for discussion of general issues. Often these examples 'colour' our point of view. One article on housing associations, for instance, began by introducing a tenant:

He sits crouched in front of a small gas fire in his flat in Handsworth, Birmingham shrouded in a woolly hat and scarf. 'I can't afford to heat this place so I keep wrapped up,' he says.

The article went on to examine the problems of housing associations in some length and detail, but the opening served to persuade the reader that this was a real human problem.

Repetition

Repeating yourself can be tedious, but when repetition is used positively to drive a point home, the effect can be extraordinarily powerful. The famous and impassioned Washington speech made in 1963 by the black American civil rights leader, Dr Martin Luther King, makes full use of repetition to stir the emotions. The speech pays re-reading, as there are many other skilful uses of persuasive techniques, which are worth full discussion.

. . . I say to you today, my friends, that in spite of the difficulties and frustrations of the moment I still have a dream. It is a dream deeply rooted in the American dream.

I have a dream that one day this nation will rise up and live out the true meaning of its creed: 'We hold these truths to be self- evident; that all men are created equal.'

I have a dream that one day on the red hills of Georgia the sons of former slaves and the sons of former slaveowners will be able to sit down at the table of brotherhood.

I have a dream that one day even the state of Mississippi, a desert state sweltering with the heat of injustice and oppression, will be transformed into an oasis of freedom and justice.

I have a dream that my four little children will one day live in a nation where they will not be judged by the colour of their skin but by the content of their character.

I have a dream today.

I have a dream that one day the state of Alabama whose governor's lips are presently dripping with the words of interposition and nullification, will be transformed into a situation where little black boys and black girls will be able to join hands with little white boys and white girls and walk together as sisters and brothers.

I have a dream today.

I have a dream that one day every valley shall be exalted, every hill and mountain shall be made low, the rough places will be made plains, and the crooked places made straight, and the glory of the Lord shall be revealed, and all flesh shall see it together.

◀ Advertising/advertisement, Connotation ▶

PHOTOCOPYING

There ought to be no objection to you photocopying material such as a diagram or chart for inclusion in your coursework, but the regulations regarding submission of the *whole of your work* in photocopied form are complex. Check, or get your teacher to check, the latest regulations. If in doubt, *don't*.

PHOTOGRAPHS AND PICTURES

Photographs and pictures may be offered as stimulus on GCSE papers. They are intended to give your imagination something to work on. A response which consists of simply describing what is in the picture will be regarded as very limited. Nor is it reasonable to use the picture only for your opening few lines and then move on to other things. The precise wording of the question may vary from one Examination Group to another, but generally the connection between your writing and the picture should be clear. This still leaves you with a wide choice of possibilities. For example, having looked at a photograph of a bicycle outside a dilapidated cafe, you could:

- develop the idea of a scene in the cafe;
- concentrate on the owner of the cafe or on the customers;
- weave a story around the bicycle and its owner;
- relate the setting, which suggests a rather run-down area, to the lives of the cafe customers.

PIE CHARTS

◀ Charts ▶

PLANNING: ASSIGNMENTS

Planning is crucial to almost every written task and many spoken activities as well. Examiners frequently find that otherwise good work is marred by poor planning.

Even everyday tasks can illustrate how planning is necessary, although we may be doing it without thinking about it. You may begin a holiday letter to your best friend without any clear idea of exactly what you will write, but you will certainly have thought about what news you want to pass on. If, however, you write a similar letter to an elderly relation, you are likely go about the task in a rather different way; your choice of news will be different, as will your *expression*. You will have *planned* the two letters.

Less familiar and more complex activities will require more conscious and detailed planning. What details you need to plan will depend on the nature of the task. An assignment on the question of animal *experiments*, for example, would probably involve considerable time gathering and arranging facts, before you could even begin to express a point of view. On the other hand, in order to tackle a story about *loneliness*, you could start by thinking about character, situation and the possible ways of telling the story.

Of course, good ideas sometimes come to you as you write or speak, and the finished article may turn out to be very different from what you originally plan, especially if it has been subject to revision and re-drafting. Even so, every task has its own special demands, and it is important that you identify them at the start. To help you, there are four *simple questions* that you should ask yourself:

- 1 What is the **purpose** of this piece?
- 2 Who is the **audience**?
- 3 What essentially *do I want to say*?
- 4 *How* am I going to say it?

How you set about tackling these questions and the order in which you take them will vary with circumstances. They are not really separate questions, in that the answer to one will influence the answers to the others. Take, for example, the following assignment, based on the true recollections of an old coalminer:

GINGER THE CAT

It is well known that until quite recently coal mines employed pit ponies who spent their entire working lives underground except for their annual 'holiday' when they were brought to the surface for a week or so.

They were cared for by a miner whose sole job was to see to their needs in the special underground stables. Unfortunately, the presence of the ponies and their food was an attraction to rats and mice and it is a less well-known fact that the mines also employed cats who lived and fed with the horses.

Most of the cats were quite happy to roam the tunnels in search of their prey. But Ginger was different. He yearned for the freedom of the surface and every day when Albert the Under-Manager went for his break in the mine canteen, Ginger ran into the cage beside him, only to be sent down again. The Under-Manager liked cats and would dearly have loved to give Ginger his freedom, but rules were rules and the mines were very strict.

Write a story for children about Ginger, Albert the Under-Manager, the ponies and all the other cats. Introduce any other characters you may need but remember to keep the outlines bold and the moral of the story clear.

In this case, the *audience* is provided for you and so is the *purpose*, which is to entertain, but also to offer some gentle instruction by way of a moral. Bearing these requirements (which cover questions 1 and 2) in mind, your planning will be concerned mainly with questions 3 and 4. See pages 211–13 for a student answer.

At this point it is worth looking at some examples of children's stories to find out how they are put together and what sort of language they use. While studying these **models**, you may form some clearer ideas about what might make an attractive story for children and the kind of characters you might include.

Further planning stages might include mapping out the main elements of the narrative and drafting ways of describing the *key characters*. As you reach the writing stage, you should keep a close check on the basic requirements of the assignment, so that you do not lose your way.

Most assignments can be planned using the four key questions as a starting-point, but the writing stages which follow may be rather different. In particular, assignments which involve *discussion* and *putting forward a point of view* require careful treatment. Consider this assignment:

ARMING THE POLICE

People are becoming increasingly concerned about the rise in crimes involving violence in our society. Some argue that our police forces should be better armed in order to protect themselves and to deter criminals. Others disagree and argue that to provide all police with weapons such as firearms would be dangerous; it would only encourage more criminals to arm themselves and innocent people could be killed or injured. Write a short article for a newspaper or magazine of your choice in which you review the arguments about arming the Police and present your point of view.

It is unlikely that an assignment such as this would have been presented without some preparation through discussion and the study of relevant information, but personal planning is still necessary.

In this case the purpose is to inform and to persuade the reader of your point of view. The audience is of your choice, depending on what kind of publication you imagine you are writing for. Once again, it will be helpful to study some models in order to get an idea of the appropriate style and language.

By this stage you should have gathered a fair quantity of information and you will have formed some ideas about the subject. Now you have to define exactly what you want to say, but you may find there is so much information that you are more than a little confused. If this is so, it is useful to lay out your work as clearly as possible, so that you can analyse what facts you possess and what ideas you have formed. **Spider diagrams** are especially useful, because they allow you to display all your information and ideas on one page. It is crucial that you *relate* your facts to your ideas. *Do not* decide to include information, however fascinating, unless it is related to a clear idea. Similarly, *do not* make statements which you cannot relate to experience, or support with reasonable evidence. For example, it may be reasonable to assume that if all the police were armed, at some time, a nervous police officer would shoot an innocent bystander. You cannot, however, treat such a possibility as a matter of proven fact. It is a good idea, therefore, to spend some time matching your factual information and your ideas. You could work on a spider diagram, or you could write the facts down one side of the page and then put the ideas to which they are connected opposite each entry. It does not matter precisely which method you use, as long as you give yourself every opportunity to master your material. An example of a simple spider diagram is shown here.

Spider diagram

Ask yourself which elements tie in closely with your point of view, which ones seem to lead to a different view, and which are neutral or merely interesting. Are there any supporting facts that you can use? As well as being prepared to add material, do not be afraid to *discard* information.

As what you want to say becomes clearer, you will be turning your mind to *how* you want to say it. It is important that you have a firm **beginning** and that it leads naturally forward. As this is a journalistic piece, you will need to think how you are to work in the appropriate style, say by adding 'human interest', if you have chosen a tabloid article. You will need some 'signposts' too, so that the reader is guided through the article in a helpful way. Some of these things may come to you as you write, but it is not a bad idea to work over some *key phrases* before you start. Even if you do not use them, you will have established the flavour of the article.

There are no hard and fast rules about how you should go about planning assignments, but thinking ahead and asking yourself questions about what you want to do and how to do it are essential. Planning is a skill which develops with practice and as you gain confidence. Do not neglect it, even if at first you do not always see the point of the preparatory stages. Never start writing before you have asked yourself all the necessary questions about *what* you are trying to do.

◄ Drafting, Gathering information and ideas, Notes, Spider diagrams, Story board ►

PLANNING: WRITTEN PAPERS

In examination conditions, your planning has to be precise. Check beforehand that you know exactly what you have to do, how many sections there are on the paper and how many questions you have to answer. See if the **rubric** gives you any advice about how long you can spend on the various sections. Make a careful note of it, and be strict with yourself about keeping to the timings. Clocks are provided in examination rooms, but it helps if you have a watch in front of you on the desk. Note the time when you should finish one section.

Examiners usually find that candidates who spend too much time writing an extra-full answer in one question cannot make up the marks they have lost by not writing enough in another. Use the mark allocation as a guide to the relative importance of sections or sub-sections.

In the written papers you do not have the opportunity to re-draft your work, but you must spend some time thinking about what you are going to write *before* you put pen to paper. Examinations can often make you feel pressured into starting to write as soon as possible; never mind if everyone is scribbling away – *you* take time to think! On the other hand, don't spend so long on planning that you have to rush the actual answer. Your notes should merely jog your memory, and they should not turn out to be almost an essay in themselves.

◄ Checking, Revision ►

PLAY SCRIPT

A play script is a special form of written **dialogue**. Although you can simply *read* play scripts, their primary purpose is of course to be *acted out*, with the words on the page translated into sounds accompanied by appropriate movement and gesture. If you decide to write a play script for your coursework, it is very important that you act it out if at all possible. Ask yourself, *Does it sound convincing*? If not, you will need to re-draft it.

A play script needs to provide more than just the words spoken. Think about what other information you need to give the actors who would use it: who is saying the words, the tone of voice or mood in which they are to be spoken; whether there should be any significant gesture or movement; and when they should pause or be silent.

With so much information to put on the page, clear layout becomes very important. However, it is *not* difficult, and there are some very simple guidelines which you can follow. Consider the following:

> FRED (*irritated*) Haven't you finished yet?
> PETER (*not looking up from his work*) What does it look like? I've been working non-stop since 8 o'clock. (*He rubs his eyes and returns to his work.*)
> FRED Nobody can get any further until you've got that ready. How much longer do you need, then?
> PETER (*trying to remain patient*) If you'd stop interrupting I should get on a lot better.
> FRED Alright! Alright! Keep your hair on. I'm going.

The name of each speaker is printed on the left. Stage directions in brackets can come next, in **italics** or underlined. Other directions can be given at the end of speeches. You could also use different coloured ink to mark out stage directions from dialogue. Avoid interrupting your dialogue with too many stage directions, though, as it becomes very difficult to read. Make sure they are genuinely *helpful* and *necessary*. For example, in the first line of the example, 'irritated' is necessary, since the question could be asked sympathetically. Fred's final speech has no stage directions, since the words themselves guide the actor.

You may also encounter play scripts or film scripts in your reading. Again your understanding will be increased if you can *act them out* – preferably out loud, but at least in your head. Don't skip over the stage directions – they are there because the writer thought they were important. Some dramatists are particularly aware that plays are read as well as performed, and write play scripts with a lot of extra detail about action and setting.

◀ Acting ▶

POETRY

Poetry may be offered to you as the **stimulus** for a piece of your own writing, probably with some class or group discussion, or it may appear on the written papers of some **Examination Groups**. In either case the main focus is likely to be on the *subject matter* and the *mood* or *ideas* which the poet conveys to you. A more detailed analysis of the language of poetry is appropriate to the English Literature paper.

You may wish to write some poetry of your own for your coursework. This is usually acceptable in terms of the **syllabus**, but you should recognise that writing poetry demands very special skills and presents a difficult challenge which you might be best to avoid unless you feel very committed to this form of writing.

POINT OF VIEW

The term point of view can be used to describe two quite separate concepts: the **opinions** you hold in a discussion – your *attitudes*; and the *standpoint* from which you describe a set of events or a situation. In the second sense, you may come across the term in film scripts or television **play scripts**, where it is sometimes abbreviated to POV.
◀ First person, Objective, Third person, Subjective ▶

PRECIS

◀ Notes, Summary ▶

PREDICTION

Prediction is the name given to the process of guessing what will come next. This is something which almost all readers do instinctively. In some cases, wanting to know what happens next is what keeps us reading. In your reading, a more conscious awareness of prediction can help you to understand more about the way a piece of writing is constructed. Are you deliberately led to expect one thing, only to find something else happening? Does the writer argue one point convincingly, and then suddenly face you with the opposite point of view? See the **short story** entry for an example of how prediction affects our understanding of what is going on.

You will sometimes be asked to use prediction in passages for understanding. You may be asked questions on part of an extract, and then be invited to read on and answer further questions, which may focus on the way in which your initial response or prediction has been modified.
◀ Clues ▶

PREFIX

A prefix is part of a word which is placed at the beginning and which affects the meaning of the whole word. For example, *ex*clude and *in*clude mean very different things, though the last part of the word is constant. *Post*-war and *pre*-war are actually opposite in meaning because of the prefixes.

A knowledge of the most common prefixes and their meanings can help you to avoid major misunderstandings of words, and can also extend your **vocabulary** range. You should know how to make words negative by using either *in*- or *un*-; and you should learn the difference between *anti*- and *ante*- or *hyper*- and *hypo*-. You will find a list of the most common prefixes (and their meanings) in any reasonably large **dictionary**.

PROCESS/PRODUCT

◄ Oral communication ►

PRONOUN

The term pronoun describes a word which we use in place of a **noun**, to refer to a person or thing already mentioned. 'Moira picked up the pen. She started writing.' – in the second sentence, we know that the pronoun *she* refers to Moira. Some of the most common pronouns are shown below.

this	he	we
that	she	you
it	I	they

PRONUNCIATION

◄ Accent, Dialect ►

PROOFREADING

Proofreading is the process of checking over a piece of writing for errors of spelling, expression or layout. It is a process used by all professional writers, and it is something which you should train yourself to do, both when **drafting** coursework and in written papers. In coursework it helps if you can let a little time elapse between the writing and the proofreading so that you can read your work more *objectively*. In examinations this time interval is not available – but you must leave yourself *some* time for checking. It is not easy at first to read your own work critically, but you can eliminate many careless slips of the pen, missing words, silly spellings, over-long paragraphs and so on by proofreading before the reader sees them.

◄ Checking, Drafting ►

PROVERBS

◄ Cliché ►

PUNCTUATION

Often we would dress up as doctors and nurses she would then flop out on the couch pretending to have some incurable disease we would race to rescue her quickly she would ask for her blood pressure to be taken and her arms to be checked As any mother would she made life as pleasant as possible for her children Making her children happy was very important to her

Why is this passage so difficult to read, even though all the words are correct and in the right order? The answer is that its meaning is obscured without punctuation. The principal use of punctuation is to help us to understand *written language* and to make it clear. Long stretches of writing without punctuation are very difficult to read.

Punctuation will not, however, help you to organise language which has been badly constructed; sprinkling full stops and commas around the page will not turn uncontrolled writing into coherent sentences.

How important is a good command of punctuation? The society in which we live tends to place a high value on being able to punctuate writing correctly. It is seen as part of being educated and literate, so you will find it in your own interest to master punctuation. Your writing for GCSE will be read by a number of people – it makes sense to try to make their task as easy as possible. Examiners will not usually *take marks off* for poor punctuation, but obviously work which is difficult to read straightaway because of poor or missing punctuation will *not gain as many* marks as writing which is clearly laid out. However, a properly punctuated piece of work which is dull is not likely to gain as many marks as a more lively piece of work with a few missing apostrophes or misplaced commas.

So the message is – be concerned about punctuation but get it in proportion.

PUNCTUATION MARKS

What follows is only a very brief guide to the various punctuation marks. If you would like more detailed help, you can consult your teacher, or use a specialised guide to punctuation. Apostrophes are dealt with in a separate section. Written forms of *speech* require special forms of punctuation, which are illustrated in the **dialogue** entry.

Full stop

The full stop is used to indicate the end of a sentence. Some people get into the habit of putting commas where they need full stops – avoid this. You may also find a full stop used after abbreviations – Esq., Rev., etc.

Comma

The comma has many uses. It can be used to split up parts of a sentence for easier reading:

- Although I was very tired, I did my homework before going to bed.

It is used to separate out items in a list:

- Papers, books, pens, a calculator and several used coffee cups lay on the desk.

The comma can also mark off a section of language from the main part of the sentence:
- Mr Jones, the Headteacher, began to read.

Exclamation marks and question marks

Exclamation marks suggest strong feeling. They should be used very sparingly, or they lose their impact and can merely irritate your reader.

Remember that both exclamation marks and question marks serve as full stops and therefore need **capital letters** after them to start new sentences.

Semicolons and colons

The semicolon is used between statements which are separate but related to each other:

- I am not quite sure what I am doing at the weekend; it all depends on the weather.

It can also be used instead of a comma to separate out items in a very lengthy list.

- The College has many facilities to offer: a newly refurbished library; a sports hall which is open to the community; separate student social areas; a well-equipped drama studio; excellent computing facilities.

The colon is used mainly to introduce a list or to precede an explanation or quotation.

◄ Apostrophe, Brackets, Capital letters ►

PUNS

Puns exploit the fact that in English there are many words which sound the same but have different meanings, and may even be spelled differently; *pale* and *pail*, for example. Puns work by drawing attention to themselves; the reader or listener is both *amused* by the invention of the writer or speaker and *flattered* that he or she has been clever enough to spot the dual meaning.

You will come across puns in all kinds of **context**; advertisements, T-shirts, car-stickers, newspaper headlines. The effect is usually to grab the audience's attention. Here is a brief selection:
'Manchester International – the airport that means business' (advert); 'The pot thickens' (soup advert); 'Avant Gardening' (headline of magazine article); 'It would foil most microwaves' (advert for microwave oven which doesn't react to foil); 'Ford Finance has your interest at heart' (advert for car loans).

Often puns produce a grim form of humour. In *Romeo and Juliet*, Tybalt is asked if he is badly wounded; he replies, 'Ask for me tomorrow and you will find me a grave man,' – meaning 'serious' or 'dead'?

◄ Figures of speech, Word-play ►

PURPOSE

All communication has a purpose. If they were described in detail, the possible purposes of speech and writing would probably be limitless, but, broadly speaking, they fall into four categories:
- to entertain
- to inform
- to instruct
- to persuade

In everyday communication you may have only the occasional need *consciously* to consider your purpose, but in formal situations you will need to think about what exactly you are trying to do. Lack of sense of purpose can lead to vague and uncontrolled speech and writing.

Try to keep your purpose clearly in mind as you work, so that you don't wander into irrelevancy. In written papers, *keep checking back to the question.* Remember that a sense of purpose is tied up with consideration of **audience** and *form,* so that before setting out on your task you should ask yourself three crucial questions:

- What is this for?
- Who is it aimed at?
- How is it going to be put across?

A satisfactory answer to any one of these questions will depend on consideration of the other two.

◀ **Audience, Planning** ▶

QUESTION

Question is a convenient term for the words on a written paper which inform you what you have to do, regardless of whether they are followed by a question mark. Some questions are, in fact, instructions.

The traditional advice, 'Read the question carefully', is still as important as ever. Every examiner has seen countless marks lost by candidates misreading questions.

Most questions for GCSE are likely to contain two basic elements:

■ the instruction – what you have to do;
■ the advice – what you should include, what you should think about, where you should look, how you should present your answer.

You should first pick out the *instruction* as precisely as you can and then see what *advice* there is about how you should go about your answer. Of course, some questions may be very plain and give you no further help beyond the basic question. Others may give you a great deal of background information and suggestions.

 SAMPLE QUESTIONS

Here are two contrasting styles of question. Question 1 is based on a reading of the short story by Jean Rhys 'I Used to Live Here Once', which is reproduced on pages 82–3 of this guide. Question 2 is an **open writing** question.

Question 1

Sometimes the meaning of a story only becomes clear when we have thought about it carefully and pieced the 'clues' together.

Now look again at the last sentence of the story.

What is it that the narrator knew for the first time? Give reasons for your answer based on detailed reference to the story.

It will help you if you think about:
■ *the way she described the scene and how she remembered it;*
■ *the strange appearance of the sky;*
■ *the behaviour of the children as she approached;*
■ *why they suddenly decided to go indoors.*

Commentary

At first this may seem quite a complicated task, but an attentive reading soon makes clear what the examiner requires.

- The first sentence alerts you to the fact this question concerns **implicit meaning** and may require re-reading the whole story.
- The second sentence draws attention to the immediately relevant part of the passage on which the question will be based.
- The third and fourth sentences give the specific *instructions*. It is particularly important to take notice of the instruction concerning a *detailed reference*, because that is a way of saying that a brief statement will not do.
- The remainder of the question consists of advice intended to help direct you to relevant parts of the story. It is not an instruction to write about each of these parts of the story in turn.

If you stand back for a moment, you will see that this question is asking you to interpret the last sentence by searching for **clues** throughout the passage and referring to them in your answer.

Question 2

It has often been observed that one does not need to be alone in order to feel lonely. Write about a time when you felt lonely although you were surrounded by people.

Commentary

This is a fairly typical two-stage question, in which the first part is designed to start you thinking, while the second part gives you your instructions. You must bear in mind that this question is requiring a piece of open writing, so you have a fair amount of choice about how you tackle it. Questions of this sort often avoid being too specific, in order to allow you scope. For example, there would be no objection to your interpreting 'surrounded' as freely as you wish. You could take it literally as being in a crowded room or you could take it more loosely as being surrounded by humanity at large. Similarly 'a time' could suggest a particular incident or a period in your life.

However, you should pay attention to the main focus of the question. It would not be satisfactory to write simply about being lonely. The essential ingredient, which is stressed in both parts of the question, is the fact that you are lonely when it appears you should not be.

▶ APPROACHING QUESTIONS

Before tackling *any* question, you should try to decide *what its purpose is.* **Understanding** type questions set on passages may require you simply to find information or they may require you to comment on stated details. More difficult questions, such as question 1 above, may ask you to look at large sections of text and select material and comment on it for yourself. Some questions may deal with **explicit meaning** alone, while others may ask you to deal with **implicit meaning** as well. It is customary for the simpler questions to be placed first but on some papers all the questions are of *equal difficulty*.

Where questions are of equal difficulty they are often *open-ended*; that is, they allow for any number of possible answers, ranging from the very simple to the most sophisticated. Usually these questions ask you for a personal opinion (such as 'Do you think this advertisement is successful'), or they offer you a free choice (such as 'Give as many ways as you can how this advertisement would appeal to young people'). Some questions like question 1 can in fact be essentially open-ended, even though they may appear very tight, because they leave so much up to the student's judgement.

Questions normally have an indication of the number of marks that may be awarded. These mark *tariffs*, as they are sometimes called, are there to give you some idea of the importance of each question compared to the others. Take notice of these figures and plan out your time, so that you write most fully in response to the questions which carry the highest marks.

Remember as well that if something is printed in **heavy type**, it is meant to be **important**.

◀ Explicit meaning, Implicit meaning, Understanding ▶

QUESTIONNAIRES

Questionnaires can be useful ways of collecting up-to-date information on particular issues or attitudes. People are often quite willing to fill in questionnaires; so much so, that magazines sometimes print them as a light-hearted form of self- analysis. Most of us are sometimes tempted to fill them in.

You may decide that some of the **data** you need for a piece of coursework could be provided by a questionnaire. So, how do you go about it?

▶ CHOOSING QUESTIONS

First of all, do you want to offer *yes/no/don't know* questions? These have the advantage of being simple to sort out afterwards, but you will be strictly *limiting* the response of your subjects. This kind of question also needs to be worded very carefully. For example, think how someone would answer the question 'Do you like holidays in England or do you prefer to go abroad?' It's impossible to choose one of only three answers, because the two issues are linked together.

Second, remember that the very nature of the *words you choose* in asking your questions can also cause problems. We have all been asked questions to which we can only reply: 'It all depends what you mean by . . .'

Third, avoid what are known as loaded questions. These are questions such as 'Don't you think cruelty to animals is wrong?', in which it is clear that there really is only one acceptable answer. Or they can be questions which ask the subject to accept something as true, *before* the question can be answered: for example, 'Given the very high level of street crime in this country, don't you think the police should have more powers?'

Fourth, decide if it is helpful to ask open-ended questions. Not all issues can be responded to at a simple *yes/no* level. How do you answer the question 'Do you like dogs?' The subject might want to reply that she doesn't mind *some* breeds of dogs, or well-trained ones, or perhaps that she is frightened of Alsatians, or she only likes her granny's dogs.

If you want to leave your subject plenty of scope to reply as he or she likes, the open-ended questions are needed. This kind of question usually produces more interesting answers, but they take a lot of sorting out and you may get an unworkable variety of responses. You also need to leave more space on the questionnaire form for a reply.

▶ TARGETING

Where possible, get your teacher's advice on your proposed questionnaire, or try it out for snags on a small group first.

Choose your *sample* carefully. When you have finally worked out your questionnaire, *who* are you going to ask to fill it in? There may be an obvious target in terms of age-group or sex; a questionnaire on teenage drinking habits defines its own target group. But many other issues are not so clearly directed. Ideally, the wider the range of people you ask, the more reliable the information you will receive, but there are obvious practical limits to the number of people you can ask. For an effective *sample* you need to identify the target age, job, sex, social status, location, religion, wealth, educational background and so on. Just nipping next door, or asking your auntie, isn't likely to give you very reliable data.

You should allow yourself plenty of time both to compose and carry out a questionnaire survey. Collecting the data and analysing it can be quite time-consuming. This last stage should not be forgotten. Sometimes a student can see a questionnaire as an *end in itself*; remember it is only a *means to an end*.

A word of caution – even the most carefully worded questionnaire, given to a very appropriate sample, will not necessarily provide accurate information. People do not always give honest replies. Sometimes they say what they think the questioner wants them to say. Smokers will usually under-estimate how much they smoke, for example, and are likely to admit cheerfully that smoking is bad for their health.

QUOTATION

Quotation is the term given to the exact reproduction of someone else's words, either in speech or writing. Quotation is normally marked off from the rest of the text by **quotation marks**. If you are not certain of the precise words, then you cannot fabricate a quotation, but must either *paraphrase* or use **reported speech**.

Why should you want to use someone else's words? You may want to use them to illustrate a comment you are making on the text. 'The writer expresses considerable disapproval by using words such as "disgraceful", "outrageous", and "scandalous".'

You may want to give a sense of authority to your arguments by using quotations from other people to support your ideas; 'As the Bible says . . .' Quotation can also add a sense of realism or ring of truth. Newspapers use quotation in this way – '"I didn't know where to look! I was so embarrassed," said 22-year-old Mavis.' "The lady's not for turning," said the Prime Minister.'

In your own writing, use quotation sparingly. After all, your English work is an assessment of *your* language skills, not of your ability to stitch together a lot of quotations from the language of other people. If you do quote someone else's words, they should always be *acknowledged* in some way or other.

◀ Authentication ▶

QUOTATION MARKS

Quotation marks – 'and' or "and" – are sometimes referred to as *inverted commas*. They are symbols which mark off the use of someone else's words from your own. For example: 'As the Bible says "Love of money is the root of all evil." '

They can also be used to indicate a *title* of a film or play. This use can in fact help prevent potential confusion, such as between Macbeth, the character, and 'Macbeth' the play.

Words under *particular discussion* or which are being used in a *special sense* may be indicated by quotation marks. For example, *It all depends what you mean by 'democracy'*.

Don't be tempted to use quotation marks in an effort to make an inappropriate or unsatisfactory word or phrase more acceptable. It won't! If you describe someone's behaviour as 'over the top' in the wrong context, it will still be inappropriate colloquialism, despite the quotation marks.

Newspapers sometimes use quotation marks to imply some kind of disapproval of a term currently being used. For example, a headline such as *Consumer 'watchdog' to get more teeth* would suggest that the newspaper thinks the organisation in question isn't really safeguarding the interests of the consumer.

◀ Dialogue ▶

RADIO

Radio is often undervalued as a source of ideas and models. BBC Radio Four in particular has a wide variety of speech styles and ways of addressing an audience. For example, the news, and other programmes, contain extracts from speeches made by public figures; many programmes use interviewing techniques; current affairs programmes may give you information for coursework.

You might consider writing a *radio programme* for your coursework. It involves less technical know-how than writing for television. You can even get some friends to help you record it, so you can see how effective it is. Remember, radio scripts are not simply words; you will probably need music and sound effects too.

Keep a look out in the press for special schools radio programmes which are designed specifically to help you with various aspects of GCSE. Don't just rely on your teacher to find and record them for you!

READING

Reading is an activity which many students take for granted. But it is important to recognise that there are several different kinds of reading. There is scanning through writing looking for some particular information. There is skimming to get a general impression or outline of a work. There is close reading for understanding exercises. Poetry and some other kinds of writing may demand the ability to read out aloud in your head (or silent acting).

It can be useful to know *how quickly* you read. It will help you to plan your work timetable if you know roughly how long it is likely to take you to get through some background reading or research.

READING ALOUD

◀ Oral communication ▶

RECEIVED PRONUNCIATION (RP)

◀ Accent ▶

REGISTER

Register is a term used to express the idea that different kinds of language are **appropriate** in different sets of circumstances. For example, we speak in a different register to close friends than to our employer or head teacher. We write to a relative in a different register from the one we use to complain of poor service from a mail-order company.

The term is also used to describe the special kinds of language used by particular professions or interest groups. The law has its own register; so have stamp-collectors or hi-fi enthusiasts.

In your GCSE work, you must be conscious of register, in order to choose the most appropriate language for your **audience, purpose** and **context**.
◄ Jargon ►

RELEVANCE

Relevance in the context of GCSE describes a clear connection between what you write and the **question** or task set. It is all too easy to get carried away by some issue on which you feel strongly. If, for example, you are discussing the advantages and disadvantages of having a part-time job, a long account of how difficult such jobs are to come by will not be relevant. Similarly, if you were writing about witnessing a serious accident, it would not be relevant to spend a long time explaining how you came to be in town at the time of the accident.

In reading for **understanding** questions and other tests of your ability to select appropriate information, examiners reward candidates who are able to select what is *relevant*. You will not be doing yourself a service if you write down a lot of material and hope that the examiner will select from it what is relevant. The examiner will not do your work for you!

REPETITION

Repetition – saying some word or words more than once – can be both good and bad.

In speech-making, for example, it can call the audience's attention to a key word or idea, as in 'This can only be good for Great Britain, good for Europe, good for the whole world.' Advertisers use a similar technique and also frequently repeat the name of the product so that it sticks in our mind.

In some kinds of writing, repetition can have an ironic or mocking effect. In his famous speech in Shakespeare's *Julius Caesar*, Mark Antony repeatedly describes Brutus and the other assassins of Caesar as 'honourable men'. The more the phrase is repeated, the more we realise that he thinks they are no such thing.

Sometimes students are tempted to repeat ideas as an **ending** to a piece of work. This is rarely successful, as it generally gives the impression that the writer has run out of ideas.

Repetition can also be a weakness. It may reveal a limited vocabulary or range of expression, which means that the writer is unable to avoid repeating the same word or ideas. It may also indicate poor planning, and suggest that the writer does not know when a point has been made. Sometimes students consciously repeat ideas in different words, hoping to make a limited number of ideas go further. This never works!

◄ Figures of speech ►

REPORTED SPEECH

◄ Direct speech ►

RESEARCH

Research is a term which can describe any form of information gathering.

Although English is not a test of your general knowledge, you do need to have something to write about, and this will sometimes involve you in some form of research. Well-researched pieces of writing will tend to attract higher marks. Here are some points to keep in mind.

■ 1 Be realistic about the time you can spend on research. Sometimes students get so involved with this stage that they leave themselves with too little time to sort it out.

■ 2 Decide in advance how much material you need or can handle.

■ 3 Have a clear idea of what kind of information you need.

■ 4 Keep an open mind – don't automatically discount any unexpected information that your research uncovers.

■ 5 Don't just think of looking in books; *people* can be useful sources of information, as are newspapers, leaflets, television programmes . . .

■ 6 Make sure your **notes** are clear; don't rely too much on your memory and write too little down.

■ 7 Keep a note of all your sources for your **bibliography**.

■ 8 Use your judgement on the accuracy and reliability of your sources. Remember that what you read may be fact or it may be only **opinion**.

◄ Gathering information and ideas, Interviewing, Questionnaires, Scanning and skimming ►

RÉSUMÉ

A résumé is a form of summary. It is a term you are unlikely to encounter for GCSE, but it is in general use for any kind of edited, concentrated version of something.

◄ Notes, Summary ►

REVIEW

A review is an evaluation of a book, film, exhibition or other piece of work, found either in print or on radio or television.

A review generally provides some information on the work in question, but also includes a good deal of comment and interpretation, so that the writer's own response to the work is clear. To demonstrate the extent to which the writer's views can influence the reader's response, here are some brief extracts from two reviews of the same play:

Review A

The West End is in desperate crisis. Coming cold on the heels of Mr Archer's droopy little piece we now have a ritual exhumation at the Duke of York's of Agatha Christie's 'And Then There Were None' which has the unmistakable aura of seaside weekly rep in the late Forties and which is so preposterously bad it has acquired the dubious status of camp . . . In Kenneth Alan Taylor's wooden production the characters enter one by one through the upstage french windows and then pause at the top of the steps to announce their credentials before doing a pantomime walk-down into the living room.
                                    Michael Billington, *The Guardian*

Review B

Both the novel and play are masterpieces of their genre, with a stunningly original plot, a cast of varied and believable characters (at least to Christie addicts) and a strongly generated mood of suspense . . . The current revival is all that the audiences for which it is intended could wish it to be. The curtain rises on an attractive art-deco set which, on the first night, won a round of applause . . .
                                    Charles Osborne, *The Daily Telegraph*

Which one do you believe?

If you consider writing a review for your coursework, look at as wide a variety of models as you can. This will help you see the tremendous variety of this form and appreciate how important a sense of audience is. The reviews in a film magazine are not intended for the same audience as those in a popular daily newspaper. The style of concert reviews is not the same in the *New Musical Express* as in *The Times*.

Sometimes the writer of a review adopts a particular style to suit the subject or content – perhaps deliberately 'way-out' language for an extreme pop group or, as in this extract from a student's work, a cult film.

RAT-A-TAT-TAT! RAT-A-TAT-TAT! Bang! Boom! Whiz! ARRGH! are about the only things that happen throughout the film 'Rambo' with the exception of the odd mutter and grunt and the infamous phrase of 'Don't push me!' from the main character of the film, Sylvester Stallone . . . or more commonly 'Sly' to his close friends – 'Hi Sly!' . . . Like all Stallone movies, he once again takes on an explosive (get the joke?) tall order – this time it's to defeat the whole of Saigon, at a big game of hide and seek.

◀ Argument, Newspapers, Persuasive writing ▶

REVISION

It is sometimes argued that you can't revise for English. This is not true. If you are preparing for written papers you can check that you know exactly what you will have to do. You should also look back over the work which you have done during your course, including your actual coursework drafts. Are there any recurrent mistakes or problems? Seek advice on how to tackle them. Learn the spelling of words you always get wrong.

Look at the work you have done specifically as examination practice. Attempt more practice in any areas you are unsure of. You might also swap work with your friends and take note of their comments or reactions (and do the same for them).

Read over your teacher's comments on your work, and try to act on any suggestions.

Practise handling a dictionary quickly and efficiently; make sure you understand how dictionary entries are organised.

◀ Planning: written papers ▶

RHETORICAL TECHNIQUES

◀ Figures of speech, Persuasive writing ▶

ROLE-PLAY

◀ Acting, Oral communication ▶

RUBRIC

The rubric is the technical term for the instructions given at the top of an examination paper. The rubric needs to be read very carefully; it is there to guide you.

All too often, candidates are so anxious to get started on the actual tasks set that they fail to read vital instructions, and lose marks because of it. Answering *two* questions where *one* is required is plain silly, as you will produce poorer, rushed work. Your work cannot gain high marks if you have not done exactly as the question asked or if, for example, you have written from the wrong point of view.

SARCASM

◄ **Implicit meaning** ►

SCANNING AND SKIMMING

Scanning is the technique of reading quickly through a text to find specific information; this is necessary where you have a question or predetermined purpose in mind and know what you are looking for. Scanning is therefore very useful if you are collecting information in preparation for a piece of writing. It is not a suitable technique for understanding assignments!

A related technique is skimming. This involves quickly looking through a page of text (or even a whole book) in order to get a general impression of its contents. If you are collecting information for coursework, skimming through a book, by looking at the contents page, the **index**, and a few sample pages, will quickly give you some idea of whether it is likely to be useful.

If you need to study a piece of writing in some detail, it is helpful to skim through it first to get an overall impression. Your second, more intensive reading will be easier because you already have an outline of the structure and contents.

Skimming is a skill which you need to practise if you are going to do it reliably and accurately. Try to incorporate it into your everyday reading, of a newspaper or magazine for example. Always go back, however, to check that your first skimmed impressions were accurate.

SCENE-SETTING

Setting the scene can be hopeful in a piece of writing. The place where events occur may itself in some way contribute to what happens; the nature of the scene may help to establish an appropriate mood or atmosphere. But *detailed* scene-setting is not obligatory. Sometimes the scene is not vital to the **purpose**, and a detailed description can actually distract the reader away from the central interest.

◄ **Beginnings** ►

SCRIPT

◄ **Dialogue, Play script** ►

SEMICOLON

◄ Punctuation ►

SENTENCE

What is a sentence? During your education you may have come across many different definitions of a sentence – a complete thought; something which makes sense; something which begins with a capital letter and ends with a full stop . . . and so on.

In English a sentence is most usually defined as a group of words containing a finite **verb**. The following are all *complete sentences*, with the finite verb in italics.

- He *was* at the bus stop hoping a bus *would come* soon.
- She *gave* him a wave as she *drove* past.
- He *felt* very angry.
- You *are* probably *able to tell* instinctively if you *have written* a sentence.

See if you can identify the complete sentences here:

- 1 Walking in the rain.
- 2 Turning the corner, we saw a huge crowd.
- 3 Come here!
- 4 Having completed two circuits of the track, the runner collapsed, exhausted.
- 5 Dust everywhere.

Numbers 2, 3 and 4 are complete sentences. As you can see, numbers 1 and 5 also 'make sense', but they are not actually sentences. Sometimes using a short sequence of words or a phrase can be very effective, as long as you know when you are doing it and why. The following passage is from the opening chapter of *Bleak House* by Charles Dickens. It consists entirely of phrases or groups of words, sometimes known as *minor* sentences.

Fog everywhere. Fog up the river, where it flows among green aits and meadows; fog down the river, where it rolls defiled among the tiers of shipping, and the waterside pollutions of a great (and dirty) city. Fog on the Essex marshes, fog on the Kentish heights. Fog creeping into the cabooses of collier-brigs; fog lying out on the yards, and hovering in the rigging of great ships; fog drooping on the gunwales of barges and small boats. Fog in the eyes and throats of ancient Greenwich pensioners, wheezing by the firesides of their wards; fog in the stem and bowl of the afternoon pipe of the wrathful skipper, down in his close cabin; fog cruelly pinching the toes and fingers of his shivering little 'prentice boy on deck.

This is a very concentrated, evocative piece of writing, moving rapidly from one point to the next, almost like a sketch. Technically, it does not contain a complete sentence. The technique used here by Dickens can be effective if used in *limited* quantities, especially for **scene-setting**, fast action and so forth. Using minor sentences, or even fragments of language, can also convey thoughts. The student assignment on pages 190–93 of this guide makes very effective use of these short phrases in putting across a character's state of mind.

LENGTH OF SENTENCES

A sentence can be a single word, like 'Stop!'. A short sentence coming after some much longer sentences can draw attention to an important idea or give a clear signal to your reader. For example: 'After many years of hard work and long hours in dangerous conditions, I was looking forward to a quiet and happy retirement. This was not to be.'

Look at a piece of your own writing. If all the sentences are about the same length, it can make your work seem very monotonous. Varying the length of sentences adds variety and changes of pace, and makes the writing more interesting to read. (See the entry on **joining words** to remind yourself of various ways of joining sentences together.)

Answering questions

What about answering questions in sentences? In passages which test your **understanding** you may be told to answer in *complete sentences* wherever possible. This instruction is intended to be helpful, to warn you against too short answers. Sometimes candidates write single-word answers, or even answers in note form, and as a result lose marks.

SEQUENCING

Sequencing is the placing of one idea in a clearly defined pattern in relation to other ideas. Whenever you have a number of pieces of information, points in an argument, or ideas, you have to decide in what order or sequence to put them. As a reader you instinctively look for **clues** in the text to help guide you through a piece of writing, and writing which has poor sequencing is confusing or difficult to read – it hides those clues.

The links in sequencing can simply be *implied*, but they can be made clearer by the use of certain key words which identify or 'signal' the sequence being used.

 SEQUENCING RELATIONSHIPS

Sequencing can depend on one or more of a number of possible relationships.

Continuous line of thought

This is where a number of points simply follow each other in logical order. You can use words indicating chronology, such as: *first*; *second*; *third*; *finally*.

Some other examples of other words which can be used to signal this continuity are: *furthermore*; *in addition*; *also*; *next*; *similarly*; *moreover*; *at the same time*.

Conclusion or summary of the previous points

The following words often indicate this sequence: *therefore*; *as a result*; *accordingly*; *consequently*; *in conclusion*.

Change of direction

The next point you want to make may be an opposite or contrasting one, which you might indicate by words such as: *but*; *on the other hand*; *on the contrary*; *conversely*; *nevertheless*; *however*.

Positive statement

This is a statement which you expect your reader to accept, perhaps indicated by: *obviously*; *of course*; *surely*; *without doubt*.

Consequence or cause and effect

The words which might be used to highlight this sequence include: *because*; *since*; *so that*; *accordingly*.

Apparent contradiction

Sometimes what you want to say next may run the risk of confusing your reader because it seems to contradict the previous point. You can guard against this by preparing your reader with such words as: *despite the fact that*; *even though*; *although*; *yet*.

Example

It is helpful for a reader to recognise that what you are saying is not a new point but rather an illustration of what has just been said. This can be indicated by: *for example*; *for instance*.

Extra or afterthought

This is not generally an advisable sequence, as it suggests informality of approach and a lack of pre-planning. However, there are occasions when it might be appropriate to indicate this relationship by using: *incidentally*; *by the way*.

◀ Paragraph, Argument, Persuasive writing ▶

SHORT STORY

A short story is not a condensed novel. You must be realistic about how much you can include in terms of action and plot. Short stories tend to focus on a single event or situation. **Dialogue** needs to be used very carefully, since you do not have much space for extended development of conversation. The challenge is partly one of **planning** and editing.

There are many different ways of attempting this task, but the following story, 'I Spy' by Graham Greene, helps to illustrate some ideas you should consider. At the end of each stage of the story are some comments on the writing and the techniques used.

▶ 'I SPY'

Charlie Stowe waited until he heard his mother snore before he got out of bed. Even then he moved with caution and tiptoed to the window. The front

f the house was irregular, so that it would have been possible to see a light
urning in his mother's room. But now all the windows were dark. A
earchlight passed across the sky, lighting the banks of cloud and probing
he dark deep spaces between, seeking the enemy airships. The wind blew
rom the sea, and Charlie Stowe could hear behind his mother's snores the
eating of the waves. A draught through the cracks in the window-frame
tirred his nightshirt. Charlie Stowe was frightened.

ommentary

he story starts without any preamble. No reason is given for Charlie Stowe
etting out of bed; curiosity is aroused by this and by the last sentence of the
aragraph. The shortness of this sentence adds to its impact. At the end of
aragraph one we have been introduced to the first character. We know the
ime of day and the historical setting. We are not sure what will happen next;
he opening sentence of the next paragraph keeps us guessing.

But the thought of the tobacconist's shop which his father kept down a
dozen wooden stairs drew him on. He was twelve years old, and already the
boys at the County School mocked him because he had never smoked a
cigarette. The packets were piled twelve deep below, Gold Flake and
Players, De Reszke, Abdulla, Woodbines and the little shop lay under a thin
haze of stale smoke which would completely disguise his crime. That it was
a crime to steal some of his father's stock Charlie Stowe had no doubt, but
he did not love his father; his father was unreal to him, a wraith, pale, thin,
indefinite, who only noticed him spasmodically and even left punishment to
his mother. For his mother he felt a passionate demonstrative love; her
large boisterous presence and her noisy charity filled the world for him;
from her speech he judged her the friend of everyone, from the rector's
wife to the 'dear Queen', except the 'Huns', the monsters who lurked in
those enemy airships in the clouds. But his father's affection and dislike
were as indefinite as his movements. Tonight he had said he would be in
Norwich, and yet you never knew. Charlie Stowe had no sense of safety as
he crept down the wooden stairs. When they creaked he clenched his
fingers on the collar of his nightshirt.

Commentary

We have now found out something about Charlie's character, what he is going
o do, and why. His relationship with his father has been contrasted,
unfavourably, with his feelings for his mother. We are told of the uncertainty
of Mr Stowe's movements, but think that this is only the explanation for
Charlie's nervousness.

At the bottom of the stairs he came out quite suddenly into the little shop. It
was too dark to see his way and he did not dare touch the switch. For half a
minute he sat in despair on the bottom step with his chin cupped in his
hands. Then the regular movement of the searchlight was reflected through
an upper window and the boy had time to fix in memory a pile of cigarettes,
the counter, and the small hole under it. The footsteps of a policeman made
him grab the first packet to hand and dive for the hole. A light shone along

the floor and a hand tried the door, then the foosteps passed on, and Charlie
cowered in the darkness.

Commentary

The searchlight of paragraph one is used again. We are led into thinking that
the plot (concerning the policeman?) is about to begin, but this is a false alarm,
leading to an anti-climax. Notice how events are telescoped; the action moves
directly from locating the cigarettes to having some in his hand as he dives for
the hole. The word 'cowered' tells us both his position and his feelings.

At last he got his courage back by telling himself in his curiously adult way
that if he were caught now there was nothing to be done about it, and he
might as well have his smoke. He put a cigarette to his mouth and
remembered that he had no matches. For a while he dared not move. Three
times the searchlight lit the shop, while he murmured taunts and
encouragements. 'May as well be hung for a sheep,' 'Cowardy, cowardy
custard,' grown-up and childish exhortations oddly mixed.

Commentary

A little more is added to our understanding of Charlie's character, and we are
reminded of his age. There is another anti-climax when we think he is actually
going to light a cigarette and then is frustrated by having no matches.

But as he moved he heard footfalls in the street, the sound of several men
walking rapidly. Charlie Stowe was old enough to feel surprise that anybody
was about. The footsteps came nearer, stopped; a key was turned in the
door, a voice said: 'Let him in,' and he heard his father, 'If you wouldn't
mind being quiet, gentlemen, I don't want to wake up the family.' There
was a note unfamiliar to Charlie in the undecided voice. A torch flashed and
the electric globe burst into blue light. The boy held his breath; he
wondered whether his father would hear his heart beating, and he clutched
his nightshirt tightly and prayed, 'Oh God, don't let me be caught.' Through
the crack in the counter he could see his father where he stood, one hand
held to his high stiff collar, between men in bowler hats and belted
mackintoshes. They were strangers.

'Have a cigarette,' his father said in a voice dry as a biscuit.

One of the men shook his head. 'It wouldn't do, not when we're on duty.
Thank you all the same.' He spoke gently, but without kindness: Charlie
Stowe thought his father must be ill.

Commentary

At first we don't feel that his father's return to the shop is unusual – we have
been prepared for the possibility – but some of Charlie's comments now alert
us to the fact that something is wrong: *note unfamiliar, voice dry as a biscuit,
thought his father must be ill.* The reference to his father's hand on his collar
now reminds us of the earlier reference, in paragraph two, to Charlie showing
fear by clutching his collar. The two strangers are not characterised – except
by bowler hats and belted mackintoshes – but their reference to 'being on
duty' sounds a warning note. The focus of the story still seems to be on
whether the boy will get caught doing something wrong.

'Mind if I put a few in my pocket?' Mr Stowe asked, and when the man nodded he lifted a pile of Gold Flake and Players from a shelf and caressed the packets with the tips of his fingers. 'Well,' he said, 'there's nothing to be done about it, and I may as well have my smokes.' For a moment Charlie Stowe feared discovery, his father stared round the shop so thoroughly; he might have been seeing it for the first time. 'It's a good little business,' he said, 'for those that like it. The wife will sell out, I suppose. Else the neighbours'll be wrecking it. Well, you want to be off. A stitch in time. I'll get my coat.'

'One of us'll come with you, if you don't mind,' said the stranger gently.

'You needn't trouble. It's on the peg there. There, I'm all ready.'

The other man said in an embarrassed way, 'Don't you want to speak to your wife?'

The thin voice was decided, 'Not me. Never do today what you can put off till tomorrow. She'll have her chance later, won't she?'

'Yes, yes,' one of the strangers said, and he became very cheerful and encouraging. 'Don't you worry too much. While there's life . . .' and his father tried to laugh.

ommentary

he **details** of Mr Stowe's 'caressing' the cigarette packets and his long look ound, plus the short exchange of dialogue, help us to imagine how he may be eeling. We are also given some inkling of what he has done and what might appen in the future. The conversation helps to characterise Mr Stowe and at his stage we, as readers, may link his use of proverbs and cliche with that of is son in paragraph four. Now the story skips to after his father has left. We lo not need a description of their departure.

When the door had closed Charlie Stowe tiptoed upstairs and got into bed. He wondered why his father had left the house again so late at night and who the strangers were. Surprise and awe kept him for a little while awake. It was as if a familiar photograph had stepped from the frame to reproach him with neglect. He remembered how his father had held tight to his collar and fortified himself with proverbs, and he thought for the first time that, while his mother was boisterous and kindly, his father was very much like himself, doing things in the dark which frightened him. It would have pleased him to go down to his father and tell him that he loved him, but he could hear through the window the quick steps go away. He was alone in the house with his mother, and he fell asleep.

ommentary

We are perhaps a bit surprised that Charlie goes back to bed. We now realise hat his understanding of the events he has just witnessed is more limited than urs. 'He wondered why his father had left the house again so late at night . . .' The story now moves in a different direction as Charlie realises that he and his ather are in some ways alike (we as readers have been prepared for this) and is feelings towards him change. The irony comes from the sad fact that he is ust too late. This is the end of the story.

'I Spy' has been set for a GCSE understanding paper. Some candidates assumed that it was only an extract. How stories should end is in some ways a matter of taste. In this case the writer leaves us with a number of clues about what might happen later. As we look back over the story, for example, the reference to his good-natured mother's hostility to 'Huns' takes on new meaning if we now think that his father really is a German spy. When we have read the whole story and look back at the title, we have to reassess how it is intended to affect our interpretation of the text.

SIMILE

◄ Figures of speech ►

SKIMMING

◄ Scanning and skimming ►

SLANG

What is slang? It is not always easy to distinguish between slang and **colloquial** speech. One person's colloquialism may be another person's slang. Typical cases are when a footballer says he is 'over the moon' or 'sick as a parrot', or when someone uses 'booze' for alcoholic drink.

Slang is essentially limited to speech but, unlike colloquialism, is only used in very informal situations among people who know each other well. Sometimes it is so specialised that only that particular group of people can understand it (as with **jargon**). For example, thieves' slang, where 'half inch' means 'steal', or cockney rhyming slang, where 'apples and pears' means 'stairs'. Using slang in the wrong circumstances can be thought of as 'uneducated' or vulgar.

Slang sometimes goes out of date very quickly, and the words disappear from the language. Using slang from another period or social class can therefore seem amusing or quaint – for example, referring to a man as a 'blighter' or referring to a person's legs as 'pins', or using 'ripping' to mean 'very good'. Sometimes slang does become accepted in **standard English** – one example is the word 'mob', which was a slang word in the seventeenth century.

How do you know if you are using slang? You must be aware of your own language uses. If you are not quite sure whether a word is considered slang, consult a good, up-to-date **dictionary**, which should give not only meanings but also the history and derivation of words (an *etymological* dictionary).

Is the use of slang ever appropriate in GCSE work? *If in doubt, don't* is a good rule of thumb. Some kinds of slang may be used in dialogue and play scripts when they are **appropriate** for that character. In fact, very careful, limited use of slang can add realism and may help to highlight some facet of personality.

What if you see what you think is slang in a piece of reading for understanding work? Again, check in a dictionary, if you have one available,

hough it needs to be an up-to-date one. Think carefully why the writer has
hosen the words; they will be there for a purpose.

◀ Colloquial, Jargon, Standard English ▶

PEECHES

A speech is a prepared formal talk, usually to a large audience. There may be
ccasions when you have to make a speech for GCSE, but it is unlikely. What
s more likely is that you will have to prepare to talk to your fellow students
bout a topic, generally of your own choice, as part of your **oral** assessment.
he emphasis here will be on *talk* and communicating with your audience, and
ot on the very specialised skills of formal speech-making.

You may wish to produce a written speech for your coursework folder as a
ample of persuasive or informative writing. This is quite a demanding task.
ou should find or listen to examples of speeches to use as **models**. As with all
oursework tasks, you must have a very clear idea of your **audience** and the
ontext of the speech you are writing. Where possible, you should try it out,
r at least tape record yourself so that you can assess its effectiveness.

◀ Direct speech, Play script ▶

PEECH MARKS

◀ Dialogue ▶

PELLING

pelling causes a lot of anxiety to people writing English; those who cannot
pell some words often feel somehow guilty about the problems they have. It
s probably more socially acceptable to say that you can't add up than to say
ou can't spell. It is certainly true that our society tends to place a high value
n being able to spell, and spelling errors often attract critical comment about
alling standards' in English. Everybody, however well educated, makes
pelling mistakes from time to time. Why, then, does the spelling of our
anguage cause us so many problems?

First of all, we have far more *sounds* in our language than we have *letters* in
he alphabet. Second, we do not have a consistent system of using the same
etter, or combination of letters, to represent the same sound. Bernard Shaw
rovided a famous example of this by saying that 'fish' could be written as
ghoti'! (*f* as in *cough*; *i* as in *women*; *sh* as in *nation*.) Similarly, '*ough*' in these
ve words represents quite different sounds: cough, bough, through,
iccough, ought. Third, because of the complicated history of our language,
ve have more than one spelling system at work. For example, 'qu' to
epresent 'cw' came to us from French. Another cause of inconsistency is the
act that at one time certain spellings *represented the sound*; the way we say
hese words has changed, but the spelling hasn't. Some of the most everyday
vords have been affected in this way, for example: *name, knife, stone*.

All this means that, while you will be able to find many text books giving you
he 'rules' of English spelling, these rules have so many exceptions that in
ractice they are not very useful.

So where does all this leave you if you *are* worried about your spelling? Most important, *don't give up* or take refuge in saying 'I'm a poor speller'. If you work at it, you will improve and, in turn, this will make you feel much more confident.

▶ HOW TO IMPROVE SPELLING

There is little evidence to suggest that *reading* will, by itself, improve your spelling. Spelling is a skill which has to be consciously learnt. The following activities might help: writing words down; looking at them on the pages; checking words for yourself in a **dictionary**, rather than asking someone to tell you; consciously learning words which you know you always get wrong. Look at some of your own work; do the same mistakes crop up again and again? If your teacher has written in the correct spelling, learn it! If not, make the effort to look it up. Research has shown that learning lists of words *out of their context* is not very effective, so use your *own writing* as part of the learning proces.

Remember that in all the writing tasks at GCSE you are allowed access to a dictionary. Spelling also improves when you *know more about* words. When you look up a word in the dictionary, read the whole entry; it will tell you about the various forms of a word, and how the spelling may vary. For example, *argue – argument; place – placement – placing.* Learning words in this way, in groups or clusters, is usually effective.

One curiosity of English is the number of words which sound the same but which are spelled differently (called *homophones*). Watch for words like *their/there/they're, were/where* and *whose/who's,* which have to be carefully distinguished.

Your spelling can sometimes benefit from *listening* carefully. There is a difference between *lose/loose, accept/except, off/of* and so on.

Remember to *check* your work. Some of the spelling mistakes which teachers and examiners come across are caused by speed or lapse of concentration rather than real ignorance. This is quite understandable; our thoughts often outrun our pens. But the solution is careful checking after you have finished writing. In fact, if you have read *this* entry carefully, you will have noticed a (deliberate) spelling mistake.

In examination conditions, do not be afraid to cross out an *incorrect* spelling; it has been known for candidates to be reluctant to do this because it might look untidy!

▶ SPELLING FOR GCSE

So how important an aspect of language is spelling going to be in your overall assessment at GCSE? Obviously, you should aim to be as accurate as you can; it is always satisfying to get things right. But you should not let anxiety about the correct spelling deter you from using what you feel is the *best* word. An examiner is more likely to reward the appropriate language than to criticise the spelling. (This is not an excuse for not trying to spell – the most successful candidates will have a wide vocabulary which they can spell accurately.) It is,

owever, in your best interests to master all the most frequently used words.
A *lot* is not one word, *'to'* and *'too'* have different functions, and *'thier'* does
ot exist.

Finally, if you can spell all or most of the words in the following list, then you
re well on the way to being a confident speller.

accelerate	endeavour	mattress	seize
accidentally	exaggerate	minute	separate
accommodate	exceed	miscellaneous	siege
acquaintance	except	mischievous	silhouette
acquire	excite	missile	skilful
acquit	exercise	necessary	slander
advantageous	exhilarating	neighbour	solemn
appalling	extravagant	obscene	splendour
assassin	extreme	occurrence	sprightly
awkward	favour	outrageous	stomach
behaviour	favourite	parallel	stripy
benefit	flavour	parliament	stubbornness
campaign	foreign	pastime	succeed
cannibal	forfeit	pillar	success
capital	fulfilment	possession	surprise
cellar	government	precede	sincerely
cemetery	grammar	privilege	tendency
clamour	grievous	proceed	terrible
commemorate	handkerchief	professor	tragedy
committee	harass	pursue	treachery
conscience	hindrance	quarrel	truly
conscious	humour	queue	tyranny
definite	hypocrisy	receive	vacuum
democracy	independence	recommend	visitor
develop	innocent	relevant	weird
different	irrelevant	resistance	wilful
disappear	jewellery	restaurant	withhold
disease	leisure	rhyme	woollen
dissatisfy	lightning	rhythm	woolly
eerie	listener	satellite	yield
embarrass	loneliness	scandal	
	manoeuvre	secondary	

Constructing a spider diagram is an effective way of making notes, planning
nd revising. The basic principle is that you place the *main idea or topic* firmly
n the centre, and then branch out as individual ideas come to you. This
pproach is more effective than the traditional *list* form because all the
nformation is clearly displayed in its relation to the main idea. New ideas are
easily added without confusion. Because it is a visual display, it is much easier
o find your way around the ideas and see the connections between them.

Here are some notes for an assignment on the subject of experiments on live animals written out in the traditional way:

- 1 necessary for research on disease
- 2 animals are sensitive to pain
- 3 there are other ways of carrying out research
- 4 humans more important than animals
- 5 we kill animals for food and sport
- 6 all life is sacred
- 7 too much unnecessary suffering
- 8 too much testing of cosmetics
- 9 humans need to be protected from possible harmful effects of drugs, etc.

Now look at the same ideas presented in the *spider diagram*. You can see how much easier it is to grasp the overall pattern. See page 113 for another example of the use of spider diagrams in planning.

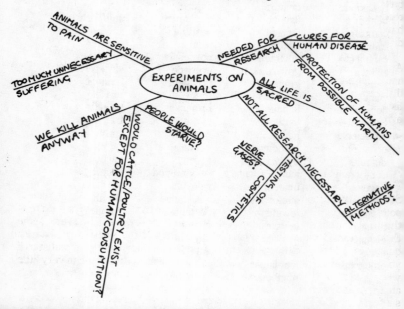

SPLIT INFINITIVE

◀ Acceptability ▶

STANDARD ENGLISH

Standard English is sometimes described as *good* or *correct* English, but this is really a shorthand way of expressing the idea that it is the kind of English which you normally see in print. It is the form of English taught to people who are learning the language, and everyone, no matter which part of the English-speaking word they come from, will understand it.

Standard English has nothing to do with **accent**. It can be spoken in any regional accent as well as Received Pronunciation. Certain kinds of word which are not acceptable in Standard English are often referred to as **slang**. For example, 'The concert was dead exciting' rather than Standard English 'The concert was very exciting', or 'He looked a right Charlie' instead of 'He looked very silly.'

How important is Standard English? The answer to this question really depends on whether you are thinking of talking or writing. If you come from an area with a strong regional dialect, you will be expected to use Standard English wherever possible in writing, otherwise people from other parts of the country may be confused, or misunderstand certain words or usages. Regional dialects vary from Standard English in two aspects – vocabulary and grammar. For example, in some parts of the country, an alley or lane between buildings may be called a *snicket*, or a *ginnel*. These words would mean little to readers from elsewhere. Similarly, 'I be' for 'I am', or 'I have for to go' for 'I have to go' would not be acceptable in writing, unless you were writing dialogue.

In **oral communication**, there is more flexibility about what is acceptable. At times Standard English can sound inappropriately formal, even unnatural, and **colloquialisms** add colour and variety to our talk. In your own work, some dialect forms are likely to be acceptable, as long as you are intelligible to your listeners. You should certainly not make yourself feel awkward or uneasy by avoiding all non-standard forms.

◀ Dialect, Slang ▶

STATISTICS

Statistics is a term which describes data usually collected by official bodies, polls and so on. Many people feel somehow distrustful of statistics – there is the famous phrase, 'lies, damned lies and statistics'. However, some **Examination Groups** do offer statistics as part of the **stimulus** or data for questions, and you will certainly find it useful to be able to interpret statistics if you encounter them when **researching** a topic. Sets of figures mean very little when taken on their own; what you need to do is compare one set with another, and then place an interpretation on the comparison so that it has some meaning. This means that you need to look very carefully at the *evidence* and work through the data very thoroughly before coming to an *interpretation*. Always check back with the question to make sure you are looking for the right information. It is quite possible that the statistics will contain information which you do not need, so you must exercise your judgement.

STEREOTYPE

A stereotype is a generally accepted, but by no means necessarily accurate, picture of a person or events. It is the picture which often first comes into people's minds when they hear a particular word. For example, *stockbroker* may conjure up a dark pinstripe suit; short, neat hair; middle-aged male; an umbrella and briefcase; bowler hat; 7.34 train each morning; the *Financial Times*; house in the leafy suburbs; boring routine; and so on. Try asking an older person what springs to mind when they hear the word *student*. Note that stereotyping involves making assumptions about attitudes, character and lifestyle.

Stereotyping occurs quite often in the media, particularly in **advertising**, where, for instance, a typical 'Mum' will be seen making her husband and regulation two children happy by using Oxo in her casserole. The son will be called in from the garden where he is playing football with his father while the girl is putting her teddy to bed. These stereotypes are based on sexist assumptions about family behaviour.

In your own writing, think about character and situation and avoid stereotypes – unless, of course, you want to use it for deliberate effect, perhaps to comment on predictability or 'averageness'.

In some kinds of **persuasive writing** you may find stereotypes used in an attempt to convince you of the strength of an argument – the 'everyone knows that . . .' type of **assertion**. This is obviously not a valid, logical argument, but it can be surprisingly effective in preventing people from challenging what has been said.

STIMULUS

Stimulus is a term which can describe any kind of information, model, photograph or television programme which may provide ideas for a piece of work. You may be offered stimulus material on a written paper or by your teacher as part of your coursework. This does not mean that you should not keep your *own* eyes open for potential stimulus material.

As its name suggests, this material is only intended to arouse ideas, to start you thinking, to give you **models**. It should not be slavishly copied, as the work you produce must be your own.

In an examination, the question will clearly state the extent to which you can use the stimulus material and how much must be of your own providing. It will also make clear how close you are expected to keep to the stimulus.
◀ **Authentication** ▶

STORY BOARD

A story board is a device used by film makers to break a film's action down into a series of shots or scenes – a bit like a strip cartoon. The **dialogue** for each scene is set down underneath it. You could devise a story board for a scene or an **advertisement** on television for your coursework. The example in the picture shows you how to set it out. You might also consider using a story board as a form of planning other kinds of **narrative**.

Middle-distance shot — sets scene.

Close-up of Clare:— looks worried.

C: Hi, Sam.
S: Watcha! Have you finished with the stuff I borrowed?
C: No, not quite.

S: What's wrong?
C: Oh, nothing. Just thinking about something.
S: What are you thinking about? You look as if you've done something really bad.
C: Not really.
S: Anyway, when are you going to bring 'em?
C: Soon
S: How soon?
C: Say in a week's time?
S: All right.

Middle-distance shot — close to school gates.

Middle-distance shot — at the disco.

C: Going to the disco tonight? It's going to be really good.
S: Yeah, I'm going, but guess who's taking me?
C: Who?
S: Clinton.
C: You mean Clinton Jones?

S: Oh, Clinton. This is great!
CJ: I can see that you're enjoying yourself.
S: Yeah. Oh, there's Clare

STRESS

◀ Italics, Underlining ▶

SUBJECTIVE

'Subjective' describes attitudes or reactions which are based on personal feelings or views. In some circumstances a subjective viewpoint is appropriate; if, for instance, you are asked to explore your feelings in a given situation. There are also many *issues* about which people tend to react subjectively – cruelty to animals or children, for example, or nuclear weapons. This is perfectly understandable, but a subjective approach may not be suited to many of the tasks you are asked to do for GCSE. People often find it difficult to recognise when their judgement is subjective in circumstances where this is not appropriate – you must at least be aware of the problem.

If you are asked to consider the points *for and against* proportional representation, that is what you must do, whichever side of the argument you are on. If you want to favour one side of the argument it must be done with *evidence*, not sentences full of 'I feel . . .' and 'I think . . .'

If you are assessing someone else's argument, keep a careful look-out for subjective views based on personal feelings which are being offered as *established truths*. Many kinds of persuasive language use this technique, including some kinds of *journalism* and advertising.

◀ Argument, Connotation, Objective ▶

SUBJECT MATTER

◀ Explicit meaning, Theme ▶

SUMMARY

Summary is a term which describes the technique of extracting the main points from one or more pieces of writing, and rewriting them using fewer words than in the original. This is sometimes also referred to as precis. You are not likely to be asked simply to write a summary as part of a written paper, but the ability to extract and select relevant ideas and re-present them for a specific purpose to a particular audience is contained in the National Criteria. These are skills which you will need to use in many tasks, whether in an examination or in coursework. A summary is a test of your understanding as well as of your language skills. Keep these points in mind when you are summarizing something.

- Make sure you have a clear picture of *what the task involves* – who it is for, what its purpose is, how much material it needs, what the most appropriate style of language and format will be.
- *Preparation* is important. Go through your material carefully, making notes. You may feel impatient at this, but it is impossible to write a good summary working straight from the original to your own version.

- Make sure your *own ideas* do not creep into your notes; write down only what is there, not your own opinions.
- Miss out *illustrations, examples* and so on.
- Think about the **sequencing** or *arrangement* of your ideas. Do you need to keep to the same sequence as the original, or will some new order serve your purpose better?
- Have you chosen the most appropriate *style*? You are not likely to be able to keep the words or style of the original.
- Check through your summary. Does it read fluently and sound like natural English, or does it read like bits of writing sewn together?

One idea of a summary is that it reduces the original material to one-third of its length. In many cases the judgment about how long a summary should be will be left to your discretion. It will obviously depend on what the audience and format are; a letter to a newspaper will be shorter than a leaflet or brochure. Occasionally you may be given a **word limit**. If so, you should remember that exceeding the specified number of words will lose you marks.

SWEAR WORDS

◄ Bad language ►

SYLLABUSES

Each **Examination Group** offers a variety of GCSE English syllabuses. They all conform to the **National Criteria**, but otherwise they vary quite considerably. You should check at an early stage what syllabus you are following and what its requirements are. Some are designed specially for **mature students**.

SYNTAX

Syntax is the name given to the order and arrangement of words within a sentence. Every time we put words together we make decisions based on the particular patterns, or syntax, of our language. 'Happy I am' may make sense but it is not 'English'. Sometimes you will read something that you have just written and think that it doesn't sound quite right. What you are probably responding to is *unconventional syntax*.

In the film *Return of the Jedi*, the Jedi Master's speech is made to seem alien by the use of unusual syntax: 'Sick I've become, Strong with the Force you are. Your father he is. When nine hundred years you reach, look as good you will not.' In your reading you may come across writing which *deliberately* uses unconventional syntax in a similar way. For example, poets often experiment with sentence patterns.

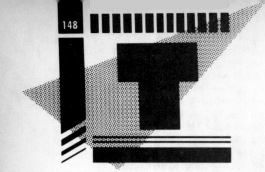

TABLES

Do you panic when you see a column of figures or words? Depending on which syllabus you are following you may be given information in *tabulated form*, as in the example. It may be offered for interpretation, as a *stimulus* for your own writing or as part of an exercise in **understanding**. Being able to handle material in table form is therefore a skill worth practising. In the example shown here, the tables were given as part of the data for a magazine article about setting up a new organisation to promote the views of young people.

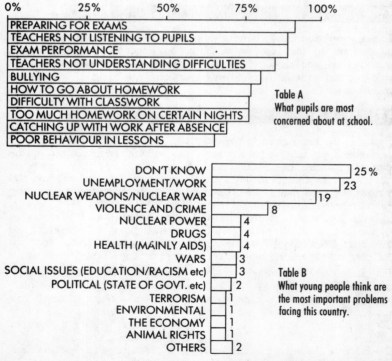

Table A
What pupils are most concerned about at school.

Table B
What young people think are the most important problems facing this country.

Source: *Northern Examining Associa*

You do not need to be a mathematical genius to follow a table – just use common sense. And in your own writing, you may find that columns of words or figures are a clearer way of presenting information than always trying to put everything into sentence form. If you supply tables as part of your coursework, they should not be a substitute for continuous writing. They will need paragraphs of comment or interpretation – you cannot expect your reader to do your work for you.

◀ Charts ▶

TABLOID

◀ Broadsheet ▶

TAPE RECORDING

◀ Audio recording ▶

TEACHER

Before you started your GCSE course you were probably used to your teacher telling you precisely what she or he wanted you to do, taking in your work and marking it, noting all the mistakes and possibly writing in the corrections for you. The role of teachers in GCSE is rather different. They will offer you stimulus material, give you opportunities for discussion, set you your task or tasks. When they 'mark' your work your teachers may suggest areas which need attention, discuss the strengths and weaknesses of a piece of writing, ask you to suggest ways of improving it. If the spelling is weak you will be told so, but the actual errors will not be pointed out or corrected for you. Only when you have finished **drafting** a piece of work will your teachers 'mark' it in the traditional sense. The teacher is not allowed to 'mark' a piece of work and then let you write a **fair copy** of it.

Remember that the teacher is there to help you produce the best work of which you are capable. Listen to what your teacher says and take advice. The most successful candidates are likely to make the best of all opportunities to discuss their work in a constructive manner.

TECHNICAL LANGUAGE

◀ Jargon ▶

TELEVISION

Television is often referred to as being a 'bad influence' on society, but there are several ways in which it can be of use to you. Keep an eye open for the programmes which are specially designed for GCSE. Watch current-affairs and general-interest programmes to widen your understanding of the world. Use discussion programmes and interviews to give you ideas for your own work. Well-scripted drama will help you to understand how a **play script** should sound. However, a word of warning. Avoid relying on the plots of films or plays on television as the basis of your own writing.

TENSE

The term 'tense' refers to the way in which the form of verbs in our language tells us *when* an action is taking place – past, present or future – and also whether it is *still continuing* or it *has stopped*.

In speech, we can move rapidly from one tense to another, and this is acceptable. For example, 'When he told me he was leaving, I says to him, "Whatever will you do?" but he doesn't know.' (Past/present/future/present.) In writing, different standards apply, and such abrupt changes of tense will not be acceptable, unless they are made consciously, for a particular effect.

Sometimes candidates get so involved in what they are writing that they forget that they started in the past tense and begin to use the present, as in this example:

> I was walking along the road. It was past midnight and no one was about. I was thinking about how much I had enjoyed the evening when, suddenly there are footsteps close behind me and the street lights go out. I'm terrified. Then I looked around and it was my friend John; I had forgotten my scarf and he was trying to catch me up. 'Oh, you did give me a fright,' I says.

Generally it is safer to keep to the *same* tense throughout a piece of writing, although it is possible to make constructive use of tense changes. For an example of writing which tries to create an effect by changing tenses, see the student assignment on pages 166–70.

▶ CHOICE OF TENSE

We instinctively tend to use the *past tense* in writing, because it is a record of ideas and experiences. At times you may feel your writing will be more vivid and dramatic if you use the *present tense*, and you may well be right. It is quite useful in some kinds of **first person** writing, for example. But the present tense is very difficult to sustain, and you need to take care not to slip unconsciously into the past tense. Some candidates also use what is called the *present continuous tense* as here: 'I am walking up the hill and it is getting dark.' This produces an effect in which you become a kind of commentator on your actions. If this is the effect you want, all well and good. Otherwise, avoid it.

THEME

The theme of a piece of writing is its overall *significance* or *meaning*. This is not the same thing as the subject matter. For example, in the **short story** entry you will see a story called 'I Spy'. Its subject matter is a boy deciding to steal some cigarettes from his father's shop so that he can stop being teased at school. He has to hide when his father unexpectedly returns with some other men, and he listens to their conversation which seems to suggest that his father is a spy. The *themes* of the story might be the problems of the relationship between father and son, childhood misunderstanding of the adult work, the problems of adolescence and self-awareness.

THESAURUS

A thesaurus is a special kind of **dictionary** in which the words are grouped together because they are similar in meaning and **connotation,** and not simply in alphabetical sequence. A thesaurus is useful if you need to use a number of words related in meaning for a particular effect or if you can think of a word which seems roughly right, but feel sure there is a more suitable one.

Take care, though, that when you choose a word from the selection in the thesaurus it fits the **context.**

THIRD PERSON

Third person is the term applied to writing in which the writer is a detached outside observer of the events. It indicates the point of view which is most frequently, almost instinctively, used. If you were describing a football match you might write something like, 'The game was very fast-moving and the goalkeeper had to work hard.' Sometimes you might feel that a more *involved* point of view is required. In that case, you could use the **first person.** The sentence would then come out something like this: 'I was playing in goal and was rushed off my feet; the ball seemed to be coming at me all the time.'

◄ First person ►

TIMING

◄ Planning: written papers ►

TYPESCRIPT

A common question is: 'Can my coursework be typed?' Ask your teacher or check the syllabus, but the answer is generally *yes*. You may, however, have to submit the original as well as the typescript to prove that it is your own work.

Is it to your *advantage* to type your coursework? There is no doubt that a neatly typed page is easy to read and does look pleasant. If you have writing which you know is difficult to read, then typescript may make the task of assessing your work easier for your teachers or moderator – who are only human after all! However, marks are awarded on the *quality* of what you say, so you will *not* be at a disadvantage if you use handwriting, as long as it is legible.

Bear in mind that:
- typing will not make poor work better;
- poor or badly spaced typing, with mistakes and corrections, is not pleasant to read;
- the typist is not allowed to correct someone else's work.

◄ Authentication, Word processors ►

UNDERLINING

Underlining is the customary way of identifying headings and subheadings in handwriting, and so its use in your GCSE work is quite appropriate.

Sometimes students use underlining in a piece of work to indicate an important idea which they want to stress. In **dialogue** it is sometimes used to represent the emphasis of speech. But underlining should be used very sparingly, otherwise the writing takes on an exaggerated, over-emphatic tone. If you think carefully about the way you construct your **sentences** and **paragraphs**, you should not need to resort to underlining. If you have access to a **word processor**, you may occasionally want to use *italics* for the same purpose as underlining, but the same warning applies.

UNDERSTANDING

All syllabuses contain references to understanding as part of their assessment objectives. For example, here is a passage from the LEAG syllabus.

Candidates will be expected to demonstrate their ability to:
1 understand and convey information;
2 understand, select, order and present facts ideas and opinions;
3 evaluate information in reading material and in other media and select what is relevant to specific purposes . . .

How your understanding is assessed will vary from one **Examination Group** to another, and from syllabus to syllabus. If the assessment is by written paper, the actual title of the paper may link understanding and *response*. This is an important idea. As you can see from the LEAG example, your understanding is most fully displayed when you can reuse or reorganise the material which you are given to study, and is not simply a question of copying out the right words. Understanding therefore is closely linked to the idea of **implicit meaning**, or reading between the lines. Demonstrating understanding is rarely limited to *single-word* or *single-sentence* answers.

Understanding is also assessed in your **oral** work. The NEA, for example, expects a student who achieves a grade 1 to be able to demonstrate 'competence in understanding and conveying straightforward and complex information . . .'

You may come across the term *comprehension* in some older course-books. A comprehension test is similar to an understanding exercise.

UNDERSTATEMENT

An understatement is a form of words which deliberately under-plays the intensity or significance of what is being said. Understatement can be a permanent characteristic of someone's expression – perhaps *reflecting* their unassuming personality. For example, someone who had been badly injured in a car crash might say that the experience 'wasn't very pleasant'.

Understatement can also be used as a device of *style*. A writer may deliberately choose a very simple style, with minimal use of adjectives or description. This style is sometimes described as *understated*, and it places great weight on the words which *are* used. One example of this approach is the passage by Hemingway reproduced in the adjective entry on page 6.

◀ Figures of speech ▶

VARIETY

You are expected to be able to write and speak in a variety of styles and situations. However good you may be at one kind of writing, for example, your coursework will not be highly rated unless you can show competence in the required variety of forms. Similarly, your oral assessment will be based on your ability to speak and listen in a number of different contexts.

VERBS

In the following sentences all the italicised words are verbs.
- He *played* football all morning.
- The wind *had been blowing* fiercely all night.
- She *was sitting* by herself.
- I *am* hungry.

As you can see, a verb may be a *single word* or a *whole group of words*.

Remember that many words which you might think of as **nouns** can also function as verbs. For example:
- Three little pigs went to the market.
- The advertising agency *markets* a wide range of products.
- She had a little smile on her face.
- She *smiled*, nodding her head.

Most of the **sentences** we write need a verb; in fact they can contain a verb and nothing else – 'Stop!'

 CHOICE OF VERB

Here are some points to keep in mind when choosing a verb.

Try to choose a verb which really 'says' something. For example, 'He loitered on the street corner' suggests the reason for standing there, something about his posture, and even his possible mood. 'To pore over' suggests more concentrated effort and attention than 'to read carefully'. A verb plus **adverb**, as in 'read carefully', generally does not have as much impact as a *single* verb. 'To saunter' is more effective than 'to walk slowly'.

Do you want to concentrate on *action* in a piece of writing? If so, the writing will tend to have lots of short sentences, to add pace, and you will be using a lot of verbs. Make sure they are well-chosen, as in the following extract from *Cider with Rosie*, by Laurie Lee:

> The flood water *gurgled* and *moved* thickly around us, *breeding* fat yellow bubbles like scum, *skipping* and *frothing* where the rain hit it, and *inching* slowly towards the door. The drain *was* now hidden beneath the water and we *swept* at it for our lives, the wet candles *hissed* and *went out* one by one. Mother *lit* torches of newspapers, while we *fought* knee-deep in cries and thunder, *splashing* about, wet-through, *half-weeping*, *overwhelmed* by gigantic fears.

The verbs in this extract are all in italics. You will see that some end in *-ing*. These are called *present participles*; they are particularly effective in suggesting movement which is actually happening, giving a sense of immediacy.

Do you want to emphasise a particular *quality of action*, for example, haste? Choose verbs which all have this idea as part of their meaning. A **thesaurus** is useful for this purpose.

Try to avoid weak or over-used verbs such as get or go. It is not usually difficult to find an alternative:

- I got the bus – I caught the bus.
- I went home – I returned home.

Sometimes 'got' is simply redundant:

- I got dressed – I dressed.

Active and passive verbs

A verb is described as 'active' if the subject of the verb *is actually performing* the action of the verb. For example, 'The girl ate the banana.' A verb is described as 'passive' if the subject of the verb *is on the receiving end* of the action – 'The banana was eaten by the girl.' Sometimes with passive verbs we do not know who has actually performed the action. For example, 'A meeting has been arranged for tomorrow'; 'It has been decided to close the youth club until further notice.'

The passive is useful at times when you wish to avoid clearly linking an action to the person who has done it, or when you may not actually want to admit that you don't know. In your own reading, keep a look-out for the passive, and ask yourself why it is being used. It occurs quite a lot in news reporting, for example. Passive verbs tend to sound much more formal than active verbs, and are also often used in text books and official notices, such as 'Trespassers will be prosecuted.'

There are some occasions when it is appropriate or effective *not* to use a verb. For more detail on this, consult the entry on **sentence**.

◀ Sentence, Tense ▶

VIDEO RECORDING

Video recording is not a resource which is available to everyone, but if you do have an opportunity to be recorded in this way, you may find that it helps you to make a clear assessment of yourself in a variety of **oral** situations. A video recording may show that you need to look at your audience more, handle display material more confidently, or even smile a bit more. It may also reassure you, since we often under-estimate our own abilities, or imagine that our nervousness is written all over our faces.

Even though the pictures may be fascinating, remember that it is your language and communication skills which are being assessed, not your appearance!

In some cases video recording may be used to provide your teachers with a permanent record of some of your oral tasks.

◀ Audio recording ▶

VOCABULARY

A wide vocabulary can only be to your advantage. The greater the range of words you can choose from, the more appropriate your choice is likely to be.

Try to become actively conscious of words. When you read it is all too easy to skip over a word you don't know and hope it won't matter. It is not always convenient to consult a **dictionary** there and then, but you can make a note to do so later. When you come across an unfamiliar word, use it to incorporate into your natural vocabulary. On the other hand, avoid using 'long words' for their own sake.

If you know you over-use some words, look up possible alternatives in a **thesaurus**, and try them out in your writing to check their use in **context**.

◀ Connotation, Register ▶

WHOLE TEXTS

The **National Criteria** require you to read whole texts as part of your course. The different Examination Groups and syllabuses have varied ways of satisfying this requirement.

A whole text is not necessarily an extensive piece of writing. It could be a complete **short story**, for example.

WORD LIMITS

Generally speaking, word limits are rare in GCSE English. As far as coursework is concerned, a piece of work needs to be as long as is appropriate. This may seem a big vague, but if you consider the wide range of writing which exists in the real world, then to set artificial limits on the length of your work would not be in the spirit of *real writing for real situations* which lies at the heart of much coursework. For example, the number of words appropriate to an **advertisement** is radically different from that appropriate to a magazine article, or again, to a short story. And remember also that *more* does not necessarily mean *better*, and you should not write at length for the sake of it.

Occasionally you may be asked to confine yourself to a set number of words, probably on a written examination paper. Check with your teacher on precisely how such word limits should be interpreted; in particular, find out if they are a *guide* or an *absolute maximum*.

WORD-PLAY

Word-play describes a similar concept to a **pun**. Word-play exploits the fact that words can sound similar and can be used with more than one meaning at once. Word-play often makes assumptions about the level of knowledge of the reader, since it involves all the possible meanings of a word or phrase, and relies on the reader to supply the linking ideas or information rather than stating the connections directly. It is in this quality that part of the effect of word-play arises. The reader *feels clever* in being able to make the connections and *admires* the writer's ingenuity and wit. Since it is a kind of 'show-off' language, drawing attention to itself, word-play frequently appears in newspaper headlines and advertisements, where it is used to grab attention. Can you guess what the newspaper article with this heading was about?

Wok on, Wok on, with hope in your heart

It was an account of how the writer averted a kitchen disaster when the oven broke down by using a wok. To appreciate the word-play, you have to recognise the song popular with certain football fans – 'You'll never walk alone' is the next line – as well as the reference to the Chinese cooking pot. As you can see, if you have to explain word-play, then – like many other forms of humour – it loses its effect.

Try to work out all the allusions in this very brief advertising slogan for a well-known glucose drink promoted by a popular Olympic athlete: DALEY CAN.

WORD PROCESSORS

Being able to use a word processor (WP) is a useful skill to have, particularly when it comes to **drafting** your coursework. Some **Examination Groups** already accept final drafts produced on word processors. The situation is under constant review, and you must check your particular Examination Group's attitude. If work produced on a word processor is not accepted, there is still nothing to stop you using the word processor in the first instance to take the donkey work out of drafting, and then producing by hand your final draft.

ADVANTAGES OF WP

So, in what ways can a word processor help you?

- It takes the labour out of copying your work, which means that you will not be put off making changes because you have to write the whole piece out again.
- You can easily make corrections without the need for crossings-out or correcting fluid.
- You can move large sections of text around until you get the sequence right, without having to keep copying it or shuffling pieces of paper.
- You can produce typed text of pleasing quality without being an expert typist.

Not everyone, of course, has access to a word processor, and if you are not able to use one you should not feel that you will be disadvantaged. What is ultimately of prime importance is the *quality* of your work, not what it looks like. Word processors are simply a useful *means to an end*.

◀ Typescript ▶

WRITE-ONS

This term refers to tasks where you are invited to continue a given passage in some way, so as to demonstrate your ability to show **empathy** with the situation or character, to write in an appropriate style and to predict what might happen next, using the given text as a **clue**. A write-on is often indicated by instructions such as *'Imagine you are the child in the story. Write an account of what happened when you returned home.'*

WRITTEN PAPERS

◀ Examination, Planning: written papers ▶

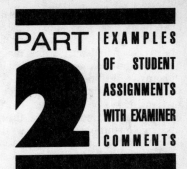

All the writing in this section is by students in the fourth or fifth year at secondary school. Most of the pieces were done as coursework assignments, but some of the writing was done under examination conditions. The work has been chosen to demonstrate a range of subject matter, approaches and styles. Small errors have been corrected but otherwise no attempt has been made to improve the students' work.

Assessment is ultimately made according to the overall impression the writing makes on the reader, but the examiner comments which follow each assignment attempt to pinpoint and describe in some detail some of the most positive features found in the writing. In many cases, the comments refer to the aspects of GCSE work discussed in the A–Z section of the guide.

You may well find that you disagree with the examiner comments – if so, it will be helpful to work out *why* you disagree.

VISITING UNCLE GEORGE

INTRODUCTION

The purpose of this assignment was to describe a visit to an old people's home without introducing undue sentiment or stereotyping. It was also an exercise in **empathy**. One problem was the difficulty of maintaining interest in a likely narrative structure.

My Uncle George, or to be more precise, Great Uncle George, had recently moved into an old people's home. He had lived on his own in a small house a few miles from us, but had eventually become incapable of looking after himself. The protests he made were ignored, and he finally agreed to stay in a home. He had been in Springvale Home For The Elderly for over a month now, and having put the event off for as long as possible, I was going to visit him.

I had bought a box of chocolates for Uncle George, remembering his sweet tooth, and then set off with the box pushed down inside my coat. I wasn't looking forward to this visit, and so I did not rush to the home. However, it didn't seem to take long to reach my destination, and with some trepidation I found myself cycling up the drive of the old person's home.

The gravel underneath my wheels crackled as I rode between the neat rows of bushes and flower beds. When I reached the building itself I stopped and locked up my bicycle, resting it against a wall. The home wasn't nearly as imposing as I had imagined. It was fairly modern built in pale brick and was all one storey high. Taking a short breath, I opened the door and stepped inside.

The first thing I noticed was the large doormat I found myself standing on. It was fairly worn in the middle, but the message painted on the mat was still clearly decipherable. 'Welcome', it said in big red letters. The sentiment did nothing to comfort me. I carried on briskly, heading for a desk a little further down the corridor.

Sitting at the desk was a prim nurse shuffling through papers and trying to look business-like. My footsteps echoed as I walked, disturbing the quiet, but the nurse didn't look up once. I shuffled to a halt at the desk and looked around feeling very uneasy.

'Can I help you?' questioned the nurse, no expression in the tone of her voice. Still she did not look up.

'Erm, yes,' I replied, still uneasy. Still the nurse didn't lift her head.

'Well how can we help you then?' She looked up. A hint of irritation in her voice now.

'I'd like to see Mr Holway, please,' I said quietly, wishing I hadn't come at all.

'Oh, him. Very well,' said the nurse, stressing the word 'him' ominously. She rose, pushed the chair back under the table tidily, and strode off down the corridor beckoning me to follow. I did so. After going through several more narrow passages we entered a spacious room in which about fifteen old people were sitting around a large television. I spotted Uncle George sitting in an armchair directly in front of the television. He hadn't noticed our arrival and was avidly watching the screen. The nurse sighed and walked over to him.

As he received the news, he eagerly turned round and signalled for me to come over. I hurried to him. Meanwhile, the nurse stood up and asked in a loud voice if everyone was happy. The reply came as a chorus of non-committal mumbles. 'Good!' she shouted, and without further ado, left. I suddenly felt very lonely.

'Hello,' called Uncle George as I approached, 'I'm glad you came.' I stopped and stood in front of him, smiling nervously. 'There's nothing to do here,' Uncle George carried on, almost ignoring me. 'I hate living among old bags, and all those pestering nurses.' He sighed as he ended his sentence. For a few seconds I didn't know what to say or do. I settled on a sympathetic sounding 'um'. I looked around at all the other old men and women, and finally at my uncle. He didn't really look younger than the rest of them, yet he obviously considered himself so.

'I've brought you some chocolates,' I said suddenly, remembering the box wedged down in my coat. I had said that rather louder than I intended. I could feel everybody looking at me. I squirmed, again feeling very uneasy and out of place.

'Oh, good,' replied Uncle George. 'All for me!' He said it loudly. He was hoping the others would be jealous. I handed the box over.

'Will you be giving us one?' called a lady hopefully from the back of the room. Uncle George ignored the call, and rested the box on his lap. 'I'll have them later,' he decided aloud.

'Were you watching something on the television?' I asked, anxious to change the subject.

'What? Oh yes, the television. Yes indeed, I was. Sit down and we can both watch it. There really isn't much else to do here. At least these nurses can't interfere,' answered Uncle George in a sudden burst of conversation. I obliged, and pulled up a spare chair, and started to watch. The sound was turned down quite low. I doubted that my uncle could actually hear the words. The programme was all about farming and was very boring, but when I turned round Uncle George seemed to be quite enjoying it. I settled back in the chair and tried to think of some excuse, so that I could leave.

I glanced around the room in desperation, only to find one man staring intently at me. I found the penetrating gaze unnerving so I returned to the television. I was trapped, so I just waited.

After a few minutes I turned to my uncle, and to my

surprise found him snoring quietly. Seeing my chance for
escape, I carefully got out of the chair. Uncle George
hadn't noticed, so I made my way out of the room. When he
wakes up he'll probably forget I even visited him, I
thought to myself — with only the chocolates to remind
him.

I walked towards the exit, weaving my way through the
chairs. Again, everybody looked at me, making me feel
very uncomfortable.

'Have you brought any presents for me, boy?' an old lady
asked, reaching out towards me. I dodged the hand, and
carried on, slightly more quickly.

'Nasty boy,' the lady shouted. I speeded my walk a bit
more.

'Wicked boy,' joined in another lady. I started to run,
only slowing down when I came to the exit. I speedily
unlocked my bike, and cycled away.

▶ EXAMINER COMMENTS

The most striking aspect of this writer's work is its restraint. There is no
attempt to heighten the interest with sensation. Nobody dies. There are no
twists in the tail or overstated outrage.

Features worth noting

1   The scene is very well observed and has the ring of truth. It is a very
difficult subject for a young person to write about because without some
personal familiarity or sense of empathy, it is likely to be a largely alien world.
Do not write about subjects you have little knowledge of because the result is
not likely to be very convincing.

2   The story is full of interesting **detail**, but there is no attempt to lay on
effects by using a self-consciously wide range of colourful vocabulary. How
many students would not be able to resist the temptation to write about
hag-like old ladies, wizened and wrinkled as walnuts? Occasionally, the
narrative is pointed up, but the words are carefully chosen and very precise.
Furthermore they always perform a function within the overall plan. 'The neat
rows of bushes', the 'prim' nurse, Uncle George 'avidly' watching the
television, the old man's 'penetrating' gaze, all have a particular contribution to
our overall understanding. Nothing is highlighted or described for its own
sake. Remember that while you are rewarded for range and variety of
expression, whatever you write should have a point, and 'rich' vocabulary can
be totally unconvincing.

3   There is a touch of **humour** that helps to underline the hopelessness of the
old people's situation. For example, Uncle George is 'avidly' watching a boring

farming programme which he cannot hear and probably has no real interest in.
4   The narrative is a simple **chronological** sequence of events. The writer tells the story very straightforwardly and makes no attempt to 'liven it up' with false excitement. However, it is not a boring series of dull happenings. The story is not enlivened by action but by *significance*. There are a number of intertwined themes running through the story which leave the reader thinking. The writer has obviously considered the **purpose** of the story and what qualities, emotions and ideas need to be incorporated.

There are the feelings of the narrator, which are largely to do with understandable teenage discomfort and embarrassment. The narrator's feelings are made explicit at a various points in the story where there are comments such as 'wishing I hadn't come'. The sense of the narrator's unease is **implicit** from the start, however. When the box of chocolates is 'pushed down' inside the coat, the awkwardness of the action is an effective mirror of the narrator's feelings.

Other factors also emerge; the home's neat and efficient appearance but unsympathetic feel; the enforced communal spirit in the television lounge emphasised by the nurse's empty enquiry about the inmates' well-being; the stifling sense of confinement and unvarying, mindless routine; the disturbing encounter with senility illustrated by the old man's 'penetrating' gaze and the grasping old lady. The details are chosen to speak for themselves. The *author's* sympathies obviously lie with the plight of the old people, but the *narrator* stays in character, as a rather reluctant observer who is not a little frightened.
5   The **ending** is simple and ties up neatly with the moment of arrival; the reluctance to enter the home is matched by the anxiety to escape. The avoidance of any stated moral or comment at this point gives the story force and strength. Some might be tempted to have Uncle George die in a few months, but anything so specific would hinder the workings of our imagination. Far better that we are kept wondering.

A WOMAN'S PLACE?

 INTRODUCTION

This piece developed out of a discussion of ways of putting across strongly held views in fictional form. There was to be a conscious attempt to focus on a single episode and to make the writing as pointed as possible.

 THE STUDENT ASSIGNMENT

I sat in my kitchen, surrounded by pots, pans, cups, plates and 'Elizabeth Ann' kitchen fittings. A pile of grubby dishes lay lifeless on the draining board. The pressure cooker was hissing away quietly on the hot-plate. The clock ticked quietly away on the wall and the baby was screaming quietly in the next room.

Sitting at the table polishing knives and forks I suddenly felt the urge to smash everything up, end this boring monotony which surrounded me every day. Smash the plates against the wall, throw food all round the kitchen, hack up the furniture with an axe and take a knife to the baby. Instead I make myself a cup of coffee and read a magazine.

I picked up a copy of 'Cosmopolitan' and turned over its glossy pages. 'Are you getting the most out of life?', 'Are you getting enough out of your man?', 'Are you getting the most out of your career?', 'Are you getting enough from your cooker?', 'Are you getting enough?' These were the titles that graced its glittery pages and my answer to all of them was 'No.'

The women in the magazine were brown, lean, glossy-haired and beautiful. I was white, pasty, dull-haired and worn. I looked worn like an old penny, once bright and shiny, now old, dirty and well-handled. I had given up all my life for him and his off-spring. Given up my career to sit and vegetate. I served him like an unpaid servant. I fed him, clothed him, cleaned and polished him and turned him out next morning when he went to his job.

A job? I rolled the thought round my brain and carried on peeling the potatoes. The door clicks. The digital clock bleeps six. He enters. We go through our evening ritual.

'Hello darling.'

'Had a good day at the office darling?' (Pause for quick peck on the cheek.)

'What's for dinner darling?'

It eats like a machine, the knife and fork flashing, shovelling the food into its greedy mouth. This will go on until the plate is cleaned and bare, sometimes pausing to say 'This is awful' or 'This is revolting'. Today it says neither.

'I want to go back to work,' I announce out of the blue. The machine stops. The knife and fork crash. The head falls back, roars with laughter. My face flushes red hot with colour like a beetroot that I frequently clean and prepare to eat.

'Going back to work,' he says, 'is a stupid idea. What about the baby?'

'A baby-sitter' I thought, but say nothing. 'What about the housework, my dinner, the washing, the ironing, the supper?' he said to me that night.

He announced that besides all that, a woman's place is in the home. Of course, I'm sorry, a stupid idea. The baby began screaming. I went to see. My throat tightened, my eyes pricked but instead of crying like an adolescent girl I crammed my mouth full of valium, drank a large scotch, lit a cigarette and much happier I was ready to face my boring world through new drugged eyes.

The evening over, we retire. Clad in stripy flannelette pyjamas he announces innocently, like a line from a comedy play, 'Not tonight love I've a busy day tomorrow.' Swallowing a snigger, I climbed into bed, closed my eyes and dreamed that the pounds of lard heaving gently next to me was Robert Redford. We did not live in Suburbiton but down-town Hollywood, but the dream was spoilt by nappies and Milton sterilising fluid bottles floating through the air crying 'We need washing, sterilising and ironing. Hurry up, your place is in the home.'

 EXAMINER COMMENTS

In many ways this student displays more vigour than control. The story lurches from tense to tense and does not have the rounded, consistent quality we can see in some of the other examples. However, there is a positive and individual quality to much of the writing. In particular, it is a good example of how language can be organised for deliberate effect.

Features worth noting

1   Tedium is established at the outset by effective use of a *list*. By itemising the reality she lives with in an almost matter-of-fact way, the writer has created a sense of the least glamorous side of domestic life pressing in on the narrator. The sense of ordinariness is **appropriate** and important to the theme of the story. It is especially important to establish the mood straightaway.

2   Detail is used in a telling way. The household objects are chosen and identified with care. We often form impressions of people and their status by noting their possessions. For example, we are very quick to relate people's characters and habits to the cars they drive. What would you think if your grandmother turned up one day in a Ferrari? Bear in mind that it is possible to

play upon our readiness to read meaning into objects. The point this writer stresses is that ownership is no longer a source of pride and sense of well-being. The 'Elizabeth Ann' kitchen fittings (once a status symbol) have lost their allure. The digital clock, which was once the very essence of efficiency and modernity, now only serves to signal the arrival of her uninterested husband.

3   There is some very effective use of repetition. In the first paragraph, the repetition of 'quietly' obviously stresses the deadening, numbing uneventful-ness of the woman's life, but it is using 'quietly' of the baby's screaming that brings us up sharply. It shows the student is alive to unusual possibilities and is trying to avoid a predictable track. The effect is obviously deliberate. Is she suggesting that even motherhood has ceased to be fulfilling? The baby's cry no longer stands out; it merges with the quiet monotony of her existence.

Another example is the insistent questioning of *Cosmopolitan* magazine (Are you getting . . .?). Here the writer has used a little licence for effect. The questions are plainly not direct quotations from *Cosmopolitan*, but they are typical of the kind of material that we associate with many of the newer, glossy women's magazines. Giving a well-known title produces a much sharper image than just a general reference to 'a glossy magazine'.

4   Contrast is used forcefully in conjunction with parallelism to make the effect especially sharp:

The women in the magazine were
BROWN   LEAN   GLOSSY-HAIRED   AND BEAUTIFUL.
I was
WHITE   PASTY   DULL-HAIRED   AND WORN

The strength of the effect comes from the arrangement of the words as much as from what they mean. This is an example of rhetoric, which is the art of using language eloquently and **persuasively**. Used in the appropriate context, this can give your writing a special kind of life – but you must know what you are attempting.

5   There is purposeful **variety** of sentence pattern. The succession of short sentences describing the husband's arrival seems to capture the predictability of the ritual.

6   The writer succeeds in creating an effect of distance between the narrator and her husband. This effect is created in a number of ways:

- The writer presents the arrival of the husband like a scene from a play that has been well rehearsed from long practice. The mechanical use of 'Darling' is effective here.
- The narrator turns into a detached observer of her husband's behaviour. This is achieved by using the present tense to give a sense of a running commentary on the action ('This will go on until the plate is cleaned.').

   A word of warning, however. The writer changes tense in mid-story – in fact, in mid-paragraph. Such changes can cause confusion and should normally be avoided. In this story the change could possibly be justified as suggesting a new episode, but it would have been better if a new paragraph had been started with the sentence 'The door clicks.' The abrupt changes of tense in the last paragraph are too chaotic and should not be imitated.

- The husband is dehumanised and viewed as an alien being; the personal **pronoun** 'he' becomes 'it'. Later, the husband's sleeping form becomes 'the pounds of lard', a compact and appropriately acid way of expressing total distaste.
- There is a vein of **humour** running through the story that saves it from being too earnest. For example, the stripy flannelette pyjamas conjure up a humorously unromantic image soundly rooted in reality. The role-reversal, 'Not tonight love I've a busy day tomorrow', is also quite a nice touch.

Summary

Although the writer doesn't quite succeed in giving the story an entirely convincing shape, examiners would generously reward the lively sense of style and the general quality of inventiveness. The subject lends itself to a cliché-ridden approach but, without resorting to the wholly improbable, the writer avoids being predictable. There are some rough edges, but the task was to get across a point of view and the writer is not diverted from the main **purpose** of the story.

LEAVING HOME

 INTRODUCTION

This story was written in examination conditions. Apart from the title, the only guidance was the suggestion that the experience might be a mixture of anticipation and sadness.

 THE STUDENT ASSIGNMENT

I woke up feeling excited, but at first I did not know why. I crawled out of bed to look out of the window, but on seeing the overcast, grey sky I huddled back into the warmth and comfort of my duvet. Then I remembered. Today was the big move! I was to leave home at last, to be my own boss. No more little brothers bursting into my bedroom while I was half-dressed, and no more parents nagging at me to do the washing up. I would be free at last!

Downstairs the atmosphere was strange. I knew that my mother was excited for me, but at the same time she was tearful and in a nostalgic mood. I felt very mixed up.

'The train leaves at two thirty,' my mother said.

'Oh,' came my reply. She had told me at least a dozen times before. Somehow I didn't want to tell her that. Today, I felt as if I didn't want to say anything critical to her in case she got upset. I felt uneasy as if I was handling a china doll, and the slightest wrong move would shatter it. My brother was watching me. I even felt a slight twinge of love for him as he gave me a sweet smile. Oh, why did everyone have to be so nice to me, today of all days? If I left home angry with them for something I would have felt much more independent and capable. At the moment I felt two inches small.

After breakfast I went upstairs to wash and change. I was quite excited now, and in a very good mood. As I started to pack my last few bits and pieces my brother came in.

'You know that tape you liked? Well, you can have it, as a sort of going away present.'

'Aah, thanks. That's nice of you,' I whispered, feeling weepy. All this 'niceness' was unbearable. I then had a chat with my brother and he was asking me every question you could think of. You would have thought I was going to the South Pole, not London to go to college! I continued packing, and then all I had to do was wait.

It was awful. My dad was to run me to the station, but it was far too early yet. I hated waiting. I didn't like the questions and doubts that began creeping into my mind. I was worried about getting the wrong train, or arriving at the wrong place in London and being all alone in a big, cold city. Alone — that word sprang back into my mind, and suddenly my self-confidence began shrinking. More doubts and 'what ifs . . .' came floating into my mind and I got very scared.

'Are you ready then love?' My father was stood up, smiling anxiously at me. I nodded, before bursting into a torrent of tears. In an instant the whole family was around me, fussing, cooing, whispering 'there, there' and generally making me feel two inches small again. I took a deep breath, asserted what was left of my independence, and said aloud, 'Right, I'm as ready as I'll ever be. Now don't worry, I'll be fine!' In my mind I was thinking, you could become an actress, you fibber. Well, why let them worry?

I walked out of the door, after many hugs and kisses,

with my head held high. Even the sun had come to see me off.
As we drove off in the car I waved to my family, and then sat
back in my seat. In no time at all we were at the station.

'Here love, have this,' my father said as he shoved a
bank note into my hand. The train was waiting impatiently, so I gave my father a firm hug and said goodbye.

'I don't know, my little girl . . .'

'Please don't start that again, Dad,' I pleaded
jokingly. As the doors were about to shut I ran on to the
train, jolting my luggage about. I shouted a tearful
goodbye through the window, and sat down. Although there
were still doubts nagging at the back of my mind, I felt
calm and confident. I was alone now, and this was it.

 EXAMINER COMMENTS

This story was rated highly because its simplicity disguised real subtlety. The story is a very good example of the fact that you don't need to invent an out of the way situation to show originality. The *storyline* is almost humdrum and reads like many a very ordinary attempt at the subject. In fact, you would be wise positively to avoid the way this student opens the story. Examiners' hearts sink when they read yet another essay that begins with waking up in the morning. At least in this case an overcast, grey sky is a welcome change from the usual streams of sunlight and fluffy white clouds! However, as we shall see, this student doesn't begin this way without a reason.

What proves so impressive throughout this story is the skill with which the writer *uses* a fairly standard situation. It is as though we are asked to take the outline of the plot for granted, so that we can concentrate on more important matters.

Features worth noting

1   The writer has the ability to characterise a whole situation with great economy. Partly it is to do with pinpointing the right detail, but the effect is also a result of combining observation with a sense of feeling for the moment. There are numerous examples. At the opening we read 'No more little brothers bursting into my bedroom while I was half-dressed, and no more parents nagging at me to do the washing up.' Apart from the amusing images conjured up by these words, the observations may seem unremarkable. However, the writer has taken the context into account. She has, after all, just come to and may instinctively groan at the thought of another uninvited visit from her brother. But no! That is all done with, and the sense of relief and release comes flooding through her.

If this were an isolated example, the examiner might justifiably be accused of making something of nothing very much. Time and time again, however, the narrative details allow us to chart the profile of the narrator's thoughts and emotions. A particularly effective example comes towards the end as she travels to the station. After all the nervousness and tension of the day, what would she be feeling? The disarmingly simple sentence 'In no time at all we were at the station', says it all. Caught up in thoughts of relief, sadness, anticipation and concern, her mind becomes numb with nervous excitement. The brevity and simplicity of the statement is *psychologically* accurate.

2 The **vocabulary** is entirely **appropriate** but it does not call attention to itself. It has a quality of rightness which, like the use of detail, helps to reflect the inner feelings of the narrator. A particularly interesting feature is the writer's ability to breathe new life into rather tired words. For example, you may have been properly advised against using the word 'nice'. It is quite true that the term is more often than not used as a substitute for proper thought. It is an umbrella term, used to indicate a sense of general well-being. This writer, however, is able to use the word exactly to convey the sense of a smothering desire to be pleasant: 'Why did everyone have to be so nice to me, today of all days' . . . 'All this niceness was unbearable.' The fact that 'niceness' is put into inverted commas indicates that the word is deliberately chosen, and that is a crucial point. Any word, however ordinary or stale, can work in **context** if it is used for a conscious **purpose**. 'Nice' exactly matches the sentiment and is entirely in keeping with the overall tone and style. A word such as 'deferential', which amounts to a similar idea, would be totally out of place in this context. It is very much a case of 'proper words in proper places'. Another example is 'It was awful', a totally unremarkable use of words until it is seen in the context which fills out its meaning. What more immediate word could there be to capture the awkwardness and embarrassment of waiting?

3 The sentence structures are varied and responsive to the writer's purposes. The writer is alive to the possibilities for flexibility in the English language, but always in the interests of registering emotions in a direct, compact manner. Observe, for example, how she compresses so much of the anxiety about going to London into the simple phrase, 'What ifs . . .' By turning the implied questions, such as 'What if I am ill and haven't anyone to turn to?', into a simple noun phrase, the writer has summed up the whole state of the narrator's mind without having to go into tedious detail.

4 The story has a clear sense of progression and shape. The form is in this case very simple. There is a sequence of five principal episodes: waking, breakfast, waiting, the journey to the station, departure. Nothing happens which may be considered anything other than commonplace. The writer's skill, however, is shown in the fact that the events of the story are in the right proportion. The story has mental pace. Very little which seems out of place with the feelings of the narrator is mentioned. Notice, for example, how the seemingly endless waiting is brought out, not by stating that it felt endless, but by stressing the embarrassing 'niceness' of everyone. However, when the moment of departure does arrive, time seems to speed up. Father breaks into her thoughts with the words 'Are you ready then love?', and suddenly she is on her way.

5 The **characters** are convincingly imagined. Notice that no one is actually described, but the snippets of dialogue and references to behaviour make it

easy for us to picture the family. Hours before her daughter is due to leave, Mother is anxious about being late. Father, who doesn't want to appear over-emotional, says nothing until he is finally alone with his daughter, when he shows himself to be as soft as the rest of the family. Little brother demonstrates embarrassed affection by the gift of the tape.

Summary

Given that this story was written in examination conditions, the writer demonstrated with remarkable control how to use simple means to rich ends. A word of warning, however. Some might argue that this story is too conventional and makes too much use of ready-made language. Certainly, it is very easy for this kind of writing to become over-casual and lacking in substance. To make the familiar interesting requires a deceptive degree of precision, as is illustrated by one weak spot in the story. You may find the conversation with the brother rather unconvincing. Here the single sentence 'I then had a chat with my brother and he was asking me every question you could think of' is too vague. Unlike the reference to the 'What ifs', it fails to provide a clear focus so that we can imagine what the conversation was really like.

Finally, the rather trite **beginning** is given a humorous twist in the provision of a matching conclusion, in which even the sun comes out to see her off!

EQUALITY

 INTRODUCTION

The task in this case was to produce a piece of discursive writing on the subject of equality for women. No particular audience was given, but it was suggested that the piece should be more **persuasive** than analytical.

There are various difficulties in tackling this kind of task. First, there is a vast body of fact and opinion to grapple with, so that a fairly short presentation such as this must be highly selective. At the same time, the selection must be *representative*. Being fair to the subject as a whole is not easy and requires careful planning. It is all too easy to become bogged down in a side issue and lose track of the main point. For example, students tackling this subject often concern themselves solely with the physical differences between men and women, and forget that only very few men are engaged in heavy manual labour. Consequently the wider issues are forgotten at the expense of a particular example.

Second, it is sometimes difficult not to confuse *fact* and **opinion**, especially when the opinions are in a sense the 'facts' you have to work with. This student refers to the **stereotyping** of women. Examiners would accept the stereotyping of women as having the status of fact, in the sense that most people accept that as a reasonable judgement. But an **assertion** that women have not the skill to be managers would be considered as opinion needing some proof. Deciding what you can say without having to explain can be tricky.

Third, there is the difficulty of organising the information into a reasonable order. It is very easy to become confused and even contradict yourself.

▶ THE STUDENT ASSIGNMENT

We live in an unequal world. A world in which half the population is thought of differently, treated differently, and is expected to behave differently. Women have not been equal to men throughout the ages, and as everyday life will inform anyone, they are not yet equal.

Inequality exists today in many different forms, some subtler and more difficult to detect than others. The most obvious are the rigid stereotypes that have been created — happy women at home, doing all the menial tasks. The typical woman of this type — that society is supposed to support — stays at home to care for her family in a typical loving manner, worrying about the latest fashions and washing-up liquids. These sort of stereotypes are built up from childhood, with girls playing at being concerned nurses whilst boys pretend to be protective cowboys. Even in literature, right from childish fairy stories, women are portrayed as inferior. How many helpless princesses have been rescued by dashing knights, or given as 'prizes' to brave heroes?

Inequalities also exist in the language, and many of us no doubt use them unwittingly. For example, people often refer to women as going 'out to work' — reinforcing the 'Woman's place is in the home' idea. A more subtle difference is hidden behind the associations of the words 'bachelor' and 'spinster'. Although they supposedly mean the same for each sex, the word spinster conjures up a very different image to that of bachelor.

Women are also sometimes blatantly treated as inferior, in such subjects as pay. Until recently many women were paid less for the same jobs as their male counterparts, and indeed, there are still some similar complaints. Even women who are paid the amount they deserve may have difficulty in gaining promotion. All of these things are grossly unfair to women, but why do they exist at all?

The main reason is probably that women have been treated as second-class citizens for so long. Men have been in charge for too long, and a male-dominated society is bound to suppress women. The stereotypes that have gradually built up over the years are still very powerful, affecting our views, even subconsciously.

There are also certain religious beliefs that could be blamed. Some religions actually do treat women as inferior. Even in the Bible women seem to be treated unequally; from the beginning Eve is thought of merely as a 'companion' for Adam. This hardly encourages equality.

And then there are the obvious differences — the very fact that women are different, physically and perhaps even mentally, may lead to a lack of understanding between the sexes. This leads on to an important question — will it ever be practical to consider women totally equal to men? Indeed, should there ever be total equality?

After all, as I have just said, women ARE different (though obviously not for things like washing-up). It has been proven that women are, in general, physically weaker than men — and there is therefore no reason why women and men should be considered equally able to perform jobs such as coal-mining. On the other hand, girls are generally more able at certain school subjects, for example languages (but this reasoning does not explain why more girls continue to study such subjects as Home Economics). Slightly more controversially, it is sometimes argued that women are different emotionally. As women do bear children, it makes biological sense that women should be caring — especially towards the young. But this does not explain why men should be any less caring.

However there clearly will always be some difference — and so why should women be 'equal'?

Solutions to some of the unfairer inequalities must be found though. So what can be done?

Of course, there are some claims to total equality already, for example communism. However, this can hardly be considered a real success. There are very few women in positions of power in the USSR (as far as we can tell). Real success will only come gradually, with changes to the society we live in. By changing certain discriminatory laws in our courts and even churches (or other places of worship), the views of people will surely change too. Indeed this can be the only way, by a slow re-education of everyone in their attitudes towards women. However this will take time. It will probably be decades, even centuries, before we hear the last of 'but it's a man's job,' or even 'women first!'

▶ EXAMINER COMMENTS

On the whole, this student avoids the most common pitfalls and produces a readable and persuasive argument that shows some sensitivity and balance.

Features worth noting

1   It begins strongly with a firm statement. The short sentence establishes a standpoint and gets the reader's mind working. Never begin with vague introductions, such as 'There are many sides to this question.' They don't say anything but the obvious and don't lead anywhere.

2   The opening statement is immediately reinforced by a *three-part statement* which turns our attention to the subject of discussion. The use of *repetition* is important here. Saying something in three parallel statements ('thought of *differently* – treated *differently* – and is expected to behave *differently*') is a very old but effective way of getting the audience on your side.

3   The writer begins with a *general* statement about an unequal world so as to give weight to the argument and to suggest that this is no mere temporary issue that will soon go away. Another way of tackling the beginning might have been to start with a vivid example and then show it to be typical of the wider issue. Either way, it is important to start firmly.

4   The writer then sets about reviewing the issue by describing categories of inequality. Clearer 'signposts' would have helped. Having stated there are obvious and subtle forms of inequality, the writer only mentions a subtler form midway through the third paragraph. If you introduce lists or varieties of points remember to signal each new stage clearly.

5   There is a reasonable balance between setting out the issue and putting forward a **point of view**. For example, the use of the word 'blatantly' in connection with the matter of women's pay establishes an attitude of disapproval at the same time as introducing the issue. Too often, students only offer an opinion *after* presenting the facts. Short persuasive arguments usually carry more force if the relevant information is tied in to the point of view throughout.

6   The writer is *aware* of the possible objections to the point of view put forward and uses them to advantage. Always try to anticipate what your

opponent might say to your arguments. Here the obvious objection is that there are differences between the sexes. The writer concedes this point, but goes on to note that the differences are not all to women's disadvantage. This is a ground-clearing technique. Rather than argue about the physical differences, the writer accepts that they exist, so that the really important matter can be dealt with. Unfortunately, the writer doesn't quite answer the question, 'There clearly will always be some differences – and so why should women be "equal"?' At this point, there should have been some discussion of the notion that the difference between the sexes does not rule out equality of status, opportunity and respect. This is a good illustration of how important it is to ensure that your argument contains no obvious gaps. A little more development would have led more effectively into the concluding consideration of what action might be taken in the future.

7 The vocabulary is **appropriately** formal and *consistent*. Lapses into a chatty style would have jarred. Once you set off using words and phrases like 'inform', 'rigid stereotypes', 'menial tasks', and 'portrayed as inferior', it is essential to continue in similar language.

8 Although the argument doesn't quite follow through as smoothly as it might, the writer has provided a neat concluding sentence. When most of your argument is of a formal nature, it is often effective to finish with something simple, to which the audience can relate. Here the writer has chosen to end by giving a twist to two familiar sayings.

AFTER THE LIGHT

 INTRODUCTION

The task in this piece of writing was to imagine some unspecified catastrophe and to see it entirely in terms of its effects on normality. Students were asked to think about how the realisation that nothing would ever be the same again could be conveyed through concentration on tiny everyday details. Descriptions of the exact nature of the catastrophe and physical horror were to be avoided.

 THE STUDENT ASSIGNMENT

After the light and the heat came silence.
  We waited hour upon hour for the silence to end.
  'Mummy?' a small voice said into my chest.
  'Yes dear,' I replied.
  'Mummy, I didn't like that, I was frightened.'
  'It's alright now dear, it's over now. Everything will be back to normal. You can go and see if Julie wants to stay for tea if you like.'
  Silence.

'Mummy, where's Daddy?'

'He went to Liverpool to get the car fixed, dear.'

I'd never regretted saying anything more in my life than that. A snippet from a recent news broadcast flashed through my recent memory. Or was it recent? I didn't know.

'The cities that the government think will be the main targets of the event are London, Portsmouth, Glasgow and Liverpool.'

'Don't worry love,' I replied, 'Daddy will be back soon, once he's got the car fixed.'

I doubted if I spoke the truth.

'Do you think it's hot in here, dear? I think I'll get up and turn the heating off. OK?'

'Mummy, I'm coming with you.'

We sat up and crawled from under our shelter. What a sight met our eyes. There was broken glass everywhere, smashed ornaments lay watching the ceiling and there was a covering of dust over everything.

My first thought was to get out the hoover. But it was still hot so I stood up and walked to the boiler picking my way through the mess. I reached the boiler to turn off the heating and to my surprise it wasn't on. It must be the weather changing quickly. But still it was warm for October.

I heard a small sob below me and bent down to pick her up.

'Oh Mummy, everything's smashed and dirty, I don't like it.'

'Come on dear, it's alright. Come on, you can help me with the dusting and then we'll hoover and then we can have tea. You have to expect a mess after these things, they're not normal you know.'

OK, I thought, let's get this house back to normal. First things first. I must take the cake out of the oven or it will burn. I opened the oven door. It was burnt. In fact it was so burnt the whole of the inside of the oven was black and there was a pile of ash at the bottom that was meant for our supper. Never mind, I'll make another one. I went to get the butter out of the fridge so as to soften it up a bit for when I made another cake. It was already softened. So was everything else in the fridge. I shut the door quickly, not wanting to see. It wasn't right, fridges were cold.

I switched on the light in the kitchen. No light came. Blessed bulb has gone again. But I only changed it two days ago. Oh well I suppose I'd better start cleaning this place. I turned the tap on. No water came out. I turned the other tap on. I screwed it up and down, getting more frantic each time. How am I going to wash without any water? Then I switched on the radio. I don't know what possessed me to, a hidden instinct perhaps. I didn't really want to hear what I heard, in fact I didn't want to hear it at all. A loud crackle, that's all there was. I tried every channel and wavelength, frantically turning the tuner knob, but there was nothing but the most horrible noise.

That's when it hit me. For the past few hours I'd been carrying on as normal, as if nothing drastic had happened, as if we could go back to how we were. A family, happy and together. Now the truth hit me. It would never be the same again, how could it after something so drastic. All the small, so irrelevant necessities were now not there. Water, light, fridge, cooker. My head spun, I wanted to hold on to the dream, I didn't want to face the truth. But I couldn't do anything else. The truth was all around me. I wept. Wept for everything I had lost. Wept for normality and despair. When I could cry no more I stood up and in a daze began to look around me.

Yesterday's newspaper was on the kitchen table, tickets to a quintet playing Schubert at the Phil, a pile of school books on the shelf, an 'Action for Jobs' leaflet on the floor and sticking from under it another leaflet that had been posted through the door, I picked it up. 'The end of the world is nigh' it told me.

I sat down again, weary from crying. I wanted a cup of tea, something to cheer me up. I didn't just want that cup of tea, I needed it. I needed it so much, but I couldn't have it. There was no electricity to boil the water and no water to boil anyway.

Although I had no tears left in my eyes, I wept again in my mind. I wept and wept, but no tears came. I wept for cups

of tea, and newspapers, Schubert and education, 'Action
for Jobs' and the End of the World.
  Which was past nigh.

 EXAMINER COMMENTS

The aim of this assignment was to explore ways of suggesting intense,
desperate emotion without being melodramatic and far-fetched. The key was
to invest an entirely familiar situation with a new significance. This student has
been successful in so far as simple, domestic tasks, such as baking a cake or
making a cup of tea, serve to emphasise the implicit horror. The writing
demonstrates the value of relating *imaginary* circumstances to understandable
experience.

Features worth noting

1   The writer has given the story a clear focus: a mother at home with her
small child. There is no irrelevant information. The **point of view** is the
controlling factor; nowhere do we stray from the consciousness of the
mother.
2   The **beginning** involves us immediately. There is no unnecessary
preamble. It is an opening which combines the directness of a simple, short
sentence with the mystery and awe that comes from being suggestive without
being too specific. Interestingly, the positive effect of the opening is a result of
exercising admirable restraint. The writer resists the temptation to provide an
introduction full of background information which would, in fact, lead us away
from involvement in the story.
3   The beginning has a slightly different tone from the main narration; it has
an almost Biblical ring that chimes in effectively with the **ending** and so the
story is nicely framed.
4   The situation proper is introduced deftly by use of **antithesis**. The simple
dialogue breaks the silence and contrasts with the awesome associations of
the opening. The word 'mummy' also quickly and effectively introduces the
human dimension. There is a danger of sentimentality here, but the writer
doesn't overplay the use of the child to arouse our sympathies.
5   The story is not overlong and is well paced. Information is released
gradually and the little background **detail** that is given, is used positively to
emphasise the sense of isolation. The fate of the husband, for instance, is not
dwelt upon. Rather it is left as a hint of the grim horrors that don't bear
contemplation.
6   The **first person** is used as a positive narrative device. The story is told
from the mother's point of view. Unlike the reader, she can only guess at the
total significance of what has happened. Consequently, a tension is established
between the immediacy of her bewilderment as she tries to return to normal
and the fact that we know it is all hopeless. Remember that using the first
person limits what you can include, but used skilfully that restriction can be
exploited.

7   Although there is quite a variety overall, so that there is no risk of monotony, there are quite a number of short sentences. These are used largely in connection with the mother's actions and so help to convey her feverish desperation as she tries hopelessly to recover normality.

8   The vocabulary maintains an appropriate balance between the conversationally colloquial (OK, I thought, let's get this house back to normal') and the relatively *formal* tones of 'irrelevant necessities'. In fact, the writer grades the comparative formality of expression quite subtly. Instant thoughts and events are conveyed through appropriately direct and immediate language, such as 'That's when it hit me.' Where there is significant reflection, however, the expression is more sophisticated. For instance, the deliberate use of repetition reinforces the moment when the hopelessness of the situation becomes inescapable: 'I wept. Wept for everything I had lost. Wept for normality and despair.'

9   The characters and their environment are well imagined. There are sufficient hints that the woman is well educated and used to a civilised way of life. One of the functions played by the reference to tickets to the concert at the Phil (The Philharmonic Hall in Liverpool) is to suggest something about the family's lifestyle. Notice how that one simple detail helps us to imagine all sorts of other things about the family which are not specifically mentioned. Together with school books and the 'Action for Jobs', all the evidence points to a *Guardian* reader! It is always desirable to select details which lead somewhere.

10   The general selection of detail is well thought out. The writer has kept the overall purpose in mind; throughout, details perform a function. There is no sense that anything is being described for the sake of it. The cake, the oven, the fridge, the light switch, the radio are all things that we take for granted; they are the very image of domestic normality. Other features could have been chosen, of course, but these flow naturally with the course of the narrative. Other details are a focus for another idea, the destruction of the future. The implicit meaning of the introduction of the concert tickets and the jobs leaflet is that the sense of continuity and hope which gives us security is destroyed for ever. But notice how the character does not voice such grand sentiments. How much more effective to cry for newspapers!

11   The ending might seem a little contrived, but how does one end a subject such as this? The introduction of the End of the World leaflet may seem a little obvious, but, as already noted, it ties up well with the beginning, and the final play on words is neatly done. The *deliberate* ignoring of normal sentence structure by making the words 'Which was past nigh' a complete sentence is entirely justified and would not be considered a mistake – sometimes the rules can be bent for special effect.

ADVERTISEMENT

 **INTRODUCTION**

Over the last few years a new kind of advertisement has appeared; one which tells a story in which the advantages of the product or service are highlighted.

You may in some cases not even quite realise at first that you are reading or watching an advertisement. Very often the advertiser's name is deliberately withheld for some time. The example of one such advertisement which follows provided one of the **models** for the piece of student writing which comes after it.

 MODEL

WOULD YOU LEND £3,000 TO SOMEONE YOU'D NEVER MET BEFORE?
MY BANK MANAGER JUST DID

There were only two teeny-weeny obstacles preventing me from going to Australia as far as I could see.

One was persuading my boss to give me 3 weeks off.

The other was persuading my bank manager to give me the cash.

Actually, looking back, it was really all Chris and Kay's fault.

They'd put the idea into my head in the first place.

Ever since they'd both landed plum jobs in Sydney over six months ago, I'd been stricken with a serious mental affliction; out-and-out envy.

The fact that Kay was my oldest friend didn't help. And neither did her letters.

You can imagine. Each one would have lavish descriptions of sun, sea and sand and would tell tales of enormous wages and a positively idyllic lifestyle. Sickening.

Kay always ended with one of those throwaway lines like 'you've got to come over some time'.

Like I said, there were just two flies in the ointment.

Editorial assistants aren't exactly renowned for their astronomical salaries, for a start. And at the place where I work, we're only officially allowed two weeks off at any one time.

So I decided a little emotional black mail wouldn't go amiss.

After a series of particularly hectic afternoons, I complained I was doing more work than anyone else in the department (I was), that it really wasn't fair (it wasn't) and that I really needed a holiday (I did).

And anyway you couldn't travel half way round the world and just take two weeks, could you?

My nagging seemed to work. I got 15 days.

But raising the money, I thought, was going to be far trickier.

For a start, I wouldn't know my bank manager if I bumped into him (or her for that matter) in the street.

And supposing I did, what would I say? 'I'm just popping Down Under for a few weeks to visit some friends, lend us three thousand quid, there's a good chap.'

I could guess the reply.

But I remembered Kay's words of wisdom in her last phone call: beg, steal or borrow.

So the next day, there I was at my local Lloyds Bank.

I'd decided to beg.

My plan was to plead unashamedly. I'd say that it was a once in a lifetime opportunity, that I'd pay them back as soon as I could, honestly.

As it turned out it was a cinch.

They just asked me to fill in one of their application forms and wait.

It must have been all of five minutes later when they came back and said, fine, everything's in order, would I like the money paid into my account?

I thought: get out now while the going's good.

So, calmly I said 'Yes, please' and out I walked £3,000 richer. Without ever even laying eyes on the manager.

Now my bags are packed, I'm ready to go and I don't mind telling you, it feels just brilliant.

I don't even need to pay the loan off in a hurry. They've given me loads of time to do it and at an interest rate that won't budge.

So, Chris, Kay, and Sydney, here I come.

And I raise my glass to you, Mr Bank Manager, whoever you are. I am, if you'll pardon the pun, deeply indebted to you.

(Acknowledgement: Lloyds Bank)

▶ THE STUDENT ASSIGNMENT

IT WAS 7.30: THE MD WAS ARRIVING AT NINE, WHAT COULD I DO?

I could have kicked myself.

Only I could have forgotten about the MD's visit to my house tonight. I remember thinking two days ago about how important it was.

Still, never one to panic (or so I thought) I phoned home in the hope of catching Judith in. Just my luck — no reply.

I rang her mother. Judith was there. There was only one snag — she was ill. However, being a good wife, she said she would be home before the MD arrived.   'What about the dinner?' I asked.

'You'll have to get it yourself.'

Fantastic. My limit is beans on toast. I looked in the fridge. There was nothing I could give the MD. I thought about a take-away, or even taking him and his wife out for a meal. That wouldn't do.

Who did I know who was a superb cook — apart from the wife? The MD's assistant. Quickly, I rang her. She told me what he liked — seafood, steak, good wine, exotic fruit, cheese.

Remembering what was in the fridge — hamburgers, apples and some cheese slices — I wondered what I could do. The assistant had mentioned something about a big superstore nearby.

Taking her advice, I approached the well-lit store, astounded by its size. I drove into the vast car-park and found a convenient space.

Grabbing a trolley I made for the doors, taken aback as they opened before me.

I headed for the meat counter. What a wide variety of meats. All kinds of cuts, cooked meats, steaks, lamb, pork. The list is endless. I bought four T-bone steaks. The man at the meat counter told me how long I should cook them for and what sauces were available.

He also advised me on wines. There was a huge range available.

The same helpful service at the fish counter.

I made off again, looking for fruit and veg.

I came to the end of the aisle. Which way now? I asked an assistant. 'Straight down, past the electrical goods, gardening equipment and it's the first aisle after.'

I felt like an idiot. It was signposted overhead in large letters.

I plumped for peas, tomatoes and mushrooms.

Now for the fruit. Kiwi fruit, pineapple, kumquats and bananas. That should do it. What about apples? Best get two kinds.

I headed for the checkout, down the wide aisles, gazing at the selection of goods.

I stopped.

Were they records? Records in a supermarket? Classical, pop, country and western, R and B. I put a classical music tape in the large trolley.

I came to the checkout. A seemingly endless line of tills, for people with cash, credit cards or less than ten items.

I expected to have to pay for the bags but they were free.

I made for the exit.

When I got home Judith said the MD would be late. That was lucky.

I put the steaks in the oven and followed the meat-seller's instructions.

Judith set the table.

As the MD left he commented on the high quality of the food and drink, especially the steak.

Thanks ASDA.

ASDA — YOU'D BE OFF YOUR TROLLEY TO GO ANYWHERE ELSE!

 EXAMINER COMMENTS

The writer has used the model here to good effect. Many of the features of the model are reflected in the assignment.

Features worth noting

1 The use of short sentences and one-line, one-sentence **paragraphs** is typical of this **colloquial** 'newspaper' style.

2 A lot of *information* about the variety of goods which Asda stocks is included, but only as part of the narrative. Points are also made about the helpful assistants, the space, not having to queue up at a till, free bags, large car-park, etc. without our being conscious of this.

3   The account of the evening divides into *three sections*: the problem and its setting; the process of finding a solution – in which the advertised store is so prominent; and a brief endpiece, capping the 'story'. No attempt is made to write about the actual dinner-party, since this would distract from the central emphasis on the store.

4   The *style* is fairly casual, as if the person involved were recounting this story to you personally. There are asides, little comments such as 'fantastic', 'that was lucky' and 'or so I thought'.

5   The narrator has been given a *personality* and *background*. He's anxious to please his boss, married, can't cook, resourceful, likes classical music and so on.

6   The headline, posing a problem and a puzzle, attracts attention.

7   There is a good sense of **ending**, with the punning slogan and repetition of the name of the store.

MUM

 INTRODUCTION

The task here was to produce a short **biographical** piece about someone you knew well and could go and talk to. The student was asked to focus on a particular incident or a time in this person's life; the intention was not to write the first chapter of a complete biography. The chapter called 'Mother' from Laurie Lee's novel *Cider with Rosie* was read in class, and there was a discussion about ways of combining intimate personal knowledge and the slightly detached, distanced **point of view** expected in biographical writing. The student had to decide who would make a suitable subject, what kind of information she wanted to collect and use, and how to go about collecting that information.

 THE STUDENT ASSIGNMENT

Looking after a one year old child in a hot sticky climate is not the easiest thing to contend with. Being in the middle of Africa away from your parents is another thing. It was an awkward situation to be in but gradually mother learned to cope. She became accustomed to the small lizards that landed on her head as she opened the curtains and fought the fear of the black cockroaches that filled the sink in the dark of the kitchen. Her assertive personality made making friends easy and regularly the house was filled with the hordes of people that mum had collected together. When dad was away she made sure we were safe. The alarm was plugged in by her bed and at the slightest noise she flicked the switch. That home-made device, which dad had produced made more noise than a herd of elephants running through the bush. I can never remember being really scared but there is one incident that is still vivid in her mind. This particular night she lay silently in bed, maybe thinking of home, who knows? Suddenly the bold shadow of a figure appeared at the window. It crept slowly along under the external burglar bars. Generally mother remained calm and collected but on this particular occasion a quick yelp and a kick for my dad appeared to be the only answer. The mysterious figure jumped from the window and it was last seen hurdling the garden fence.

Food was one thing my mother found hard to contend with. It was easy enough to buy but obtaining the food we were used to was not so easy. Having a box of Weetabix in the house was considered sheer luxury! Often, after dinner, Mother would offer such gourmet delights as Black Forest Gateau and strawberries and cream. Our eyes would light up at the very thought and she would chuckle to make us know that we had fallen for her little trick. Soon mum became an expert cook and she still retains that quality to this very day. We were her guinea pigs but we didn't mind one bit; she never failed to delight us with her new dishes and fancy surprises.

Mum soon began to appreciate the large garden, the beautiful flowers and the spacious swimming pool. Her favourite pastime was to lounge around the pool soaking up the blissful, radiant sun. The birds chirped, the sun beamed, the water glistened and the mosquitoes attacked. As long as mum had her pool she could bear the mosquitoes and the insects, and once she discovered insect-repellent her skin was safe from the demons of nature.

Living in Africa is an experience to relish. Mum began to collect small African objects that the salesmen themselves had hand-carved, objects that her friends at home would envy with green eyes. Her tiny collection consisted, and still does consist, mainly of ivory and wooden carvings. She chose only the best models, models with prominent, protruding features and their own special characters. Regularly the models were dusted and polished and each had its own special place on the mantelpiece.

This different lifestyle that mum had grown to like did not prevent her from fulfilling her ambitions as a parent. Most nights she would read to us, relating to the pictures and helping us with the difficult words that our brains could not digest. Often we would dress up as doctors and nurses and she would flop out on the couch pretending to have some drastic incurable disease. We would race to her rescue and quickly she would ask for her blood pressure to be taken and her arms to be checked. As any mother would she made life as pleasant as possible and making her children happy was very important to her.

Like any other place in this world, Zambia had its constant ups and downs. Mum took the good with the bad, the good she made the most of and the bad she fought with determination. Mum had grown to like Africa, she spent many happy times in the country that is now a memory. Those beautiful memories are firmly inscribed on her mind; more than once they have brought a smile to her face.

▶ EXAMINER COMMENTS

Notice first how the work begins. We are immediately transported to the situation of the mother. Our interest is aroused and, as we read on, we find out who is the subject of this piece.

Although the writer does use the more familiar-sounding *Mum* later on, her first reference is to *Mother*, which helps to distance her a little from her subject. Only after she has established her mother as a person does she begin to introduce the personal relationship by references to 'we' and by using the words 'I can never remember'.

The piece does not lose sight of its subject. One of the problems in writing about people whose lives are bound up in your own is that your own memories and responses start to intrude and the focus changes to *you*. Here, the writer's own recollections illustrate her mother's character. Look back at the references to the teasing about unavailable food, or the playing at nurses.

The incident of the burglar, dramatic in itself, is fairly brief (the writer does not get carried away into lengthy narrative), and also shows some of the dangers that her mother had to contend with.

The writer handles information well. We do not feel that we are being told lots of *facts* about her mother, either as a person, or about her life in Africa. But that does not mean to say that the information is not there. We acquire it 'painlessly' as we read. Take the following sentence: 'She became accustomed to the small lizards that landed on her head as she opened the curtains and fought the fear of the black cockroaches that filled the sink in the dark of the kitchen.' and compare it with something like 'My mother had to get used to all the insects and creepy-crawlies. The kitchen was dark and the sink was full of cockroaches. When she opened the curtains lizards would fall on her head.' The original focuses on how her mother reacted to these creatures, rather than their mere existence. It is also concentrated into a single sentence.

Look at the way the **paragraphs** begin; only one starts with 'Mum'. When writing biography, it is very easy to get into the habit of using your subject as the subject of many of your sentences. This piece uses a pleasing variety of paragraph openings, moving us effortlessly from one area of her mother's experience to another. 'Food was one thing . . .' has a sense of directness which 'Mum also had problems with food . . .' is totally lacking. Similarly, 'Living in Africa is an experience to relish . . .' shifts the focus on to her mother's collection and gives the fact that she made this collection a generalised **context** (her reaction to living in Africa), which again helps to distance the writer from her subject. The beginning of the next paragraph very neatly summarises what has gone before and then turns us towards thinking of her mother as a mother.

The writer has also shown skill in the handling of time. She has taken a whole period in her mother's life and suggested the changes that took place by careful use of verbs such as 'accustomed', 'grown to like', 'became', 'began' and 'discovered'. A sense of recurring events is also created by the use of words such as 'regularly', 'often', 'most nights' and 'generally'.

When writing **biography** you can have a double perspective; you can describe the events in the past and also show how they have affected the present. Here, the writer has used this technique very effectively: 'Soon Mum became an expert cook and she still retains that quality to this very day'; 'Her tiny collection consisted, and still does consist . . .'

The writer also produces some pleasingly light touches of **humour**. 'The birds chirped, the sun beamed, the water glistened and the mosquitoes attacked.' Here we are lulled into expecting another rather conventional phrase about the weather, only to get a sudden reversal of direction, shattering the idyll. Notice also the economy of 'a quick yelp and a kick for my dad'.

Finally, the comment 'Mum took the good with the bad' seems a dull cliché, until it is followed by the clever re-statement: 'the good she made the most of and the bad she fought with determination', which transforms it into a crisply contrasted comment on her mother's personality.

GAS (OR A TOOTH EXTRACTION)

 INTRODUCTION

In the following piece of writing, the task was to take a very familiar, even **stereotyped**, situation – a visit to the dentist – and treat it in some new way to rekindle the reader's interest.

THE STUDENT ASSIGNMENT

Here goes.

'OK Clare, sit in the chair, lie back and breathe deeply. You won't feel a thing.'

In, out, in, out. Eyes shutting. Let eyes shut, be a good patient, soon be asleep, everything's fine.

Then the mask was pulled, first to one side of my face and attached behind an ear that wasn't there. Then to the other side, roughly, and attached to the other non-existent ear.

Blackness. Complete blackness.

Then THUD, THUD, THUD, THUD. My whole body was thudding. Rising and falling, rising and falling.

THUD, THUD, THUD.

Then I went in. My body became numb. Starting at the outside it disappeared slowly.

Blackness.

THUD, THUD, THUD.

At every thud I became thinner until I was only a line down my back, my arms and my legs.

THUD, THUD, THUD.

I was a stickman.

Only my head left now. No stickman, only a head. And in that head, blackness. Dazzling blackness that twinkled with black pink and black green. And spun. Round and round, up and down.

THUD, THUD, THUD.

Over and over.

Then it was white. Dazzling white. I wanted to shut my eyes to shut out the dazzle. For ever. But they would not shut. The dazzle went on. From out of the white came a field, and suddenly everyone was there. Julie, Helen, Laura, Dave, Ste.

THUD, THUD, THUD.

Adrian, Angela, Ian, Becky, Jo, Gaynor, Gary and everyone. On the field in a big pile. One on top of the other.

I ran. After Dave. I caught him. We spun.

THUD, THUD, THUD.

Together. Round and round. Above the field. Above the pile. But there wasn't a pile because the pile was spinning too. Spinning all around in pieces. Shattered fragments of pile. Splintered and jagged across the face of the night.

But it wasn't night. It was white. And I was alone. In the white. But I wasn't, because I wasn't there.

Then the thudding. THUD, THUD, THUD. Wasn't big, woolly bangs any more. It was thin, sharp lines. Getting sharper and longer. It wasn't thudding anymore, it was pain. Each jab got longer and longer until it reached from my head to my toes. Which weren't there.

Then one flew from my head right to the core of my body, right down. Too deep. Into me. Deep into me. It struck like a sharpened knife into my depths. Unknown pit. Black.

Split second.

No more, please. And no more came.

I am having my tooth out. I have been given gas. There shouldn't be any pain. There shouldn't.

My god, it hasn't worked. I'm still thinking aren't I? I'm not asleep. Or dead. It will happen soon. Don't worry. Soon.

But too soon I was spinning again. On a ladder. Clinging. Over and over in a huge circle, backwards, up into the sky. There was no sky. But something.

Round and round. Up and down. Over and over. In and out. In and out of the rungs. Slipping.

Hey, I'm bending, I'm slipping through rungs in a ladder. Yes I am. But I wasn't. It was black again.

THUD, THUD, THUD, thud, thud. Gentler now. In the black. Gentle. Rocking. thud, thud, thud, thud, thud, thud.

'Spit, Clare, spit.' Anonymous voice. Not me. Who?

'Spit.'

Then light. A huge weight lifted from my body. I could float. No I couldn't. Not any more.

'Spit.'

I spat.

▶ **EXAMINER COMMENTS**

Perhaps the first thing to notice is the effective lack of a preamble; no long stay in the waiting-room, no butterflies in the stomach, no descriptions of the other patients or the wait, but straight in and on with the account. The writer has tried, with some success, to use language structures to convey the extraordinary experiences of being under an anaesthetic.

Features worth noting

1 The writer uses short sentences, sometimes even single words – 'Starting at the outside it disappeared slowly. Blackness.'; 'No stickman, only a head.'
2 The recurrent sound of her pulse or heart beat combines effectively with the deliberate repetition of words or phrases – 'Blackness, Complete blackness.' 'Then it was white. Dazzling white.' 'Rising and falling, rising and falling'.
3 The shifts in tense from past to present and back again are well handled. 'I'm slipping through rungs on a ladder. Yes I am. But I wasn't. It was black again.'

The writer helps us to share this experience by using a device called *internal monologue* – the thoughts inside her head – 'Let eyes shut, be a good patient, soon be asleep . . .' 'My god, it hasn't worked. I'm still thinking, aren't I?' 'No more please.' In fact, the concentration of the whole piece on the central character, and the writer's refusal to be side-tracked from this into descriptions of anything other than what the narrator sees or feels, is what gives this piece its power.

The visions which the patient experiences have that appropriately dream-like mix of the familiar – the field, friends – and the bizarre – 'shattered fragments of pile', 'only a head', 'black pink and black green'.

The odd sense of detachment which an anaesthetic produces is well conveyed by phrases such as 'an ear that wasn't there', 'I was a stickman' and 'I could float. No, I couldn't.'

The **ending** is handled particularly well. It is always difficult for writing to come out of a dream-like experience. Here we are given a hint by the quietening of the thuds, and the introduction of the dentist's voice – identified by the reader because of what is said, 'Spit, Clare, spit.', but not by the patient. Notice how her gradual coming to consciousness is dramatised by 'Not me. Who?' and the insistent repetition of 'Spit'. The ending is neatly capped (if you'll pardon the pun) by the simple and direct last two words, which indicate the narrator is now fully conscious.

PART 3

EXAMPLES OF COURSEWORK FOLIOS WITH EXAMINER COMMENTS

Part 2 examines *individual* examples of students' work in some detail. This section of the guide considers two examples of *complete* coursework folios.

When assignments are collected together to form a *folio* of coursework, examiners have to consider the *overall balance* of the student's work as well as the individual qualities of each piece. The examples given here represent the work of two successful candidates. Looked at piece by piece, they seem very different. Compare the opening piece in each file, and you might suppose that the first candidate is very much stronger than the second. When you take the folios overall, however, you find that the second candidate displays many positive qualities which go a long way towards compensating for some obvious shortcomings.

The procedures of individual Examination Groups vary, but on the whole examiners try to make an overall assessment of coursework, bearing in mind the candidates' strengths and weaknesses. Naturally you will want to be as consistent as possible in your work, but do not despair if a particular kind of writing is not entirely to your liking. So long as you can demonstrate a *range of skills* and can show that you can write in a *variety of styles*, your coursework can to a large extent be tailor-made to your strengths.

The two examples here are not specific to any particular GCSE English examination, so they should not be viewed as models. Each syllabus lays down particular requirements as to the number and type of assignments which must be included in the coursework. The examples have five pieces each. Make sure that you understand the precise requirements of *your own* examination.

FOLIO: CANDIDATE ONE

▶ PIECE 1: FRIEND OR FOE?

Dear Mum and Dad,

The weather's been beautiful ever since we arrived, and sun has been forecast for the rest of the week. We sailed the inflatable dinghy for the first time yesterday. James reckons it's child's play compared with his exploits at Cambridge.

We both wish you were here. See you next week,
Kathy and James. XX

Heavy breathing told me that James was already asleep. The past two days had seemed to flash by and only now had I the time to stop and realise just how exhausting fun really was.

The heart warming odour of a Traditional English Breakfast brought me to consciousness. Another summer's day awaiting my arrival; a day ready to fly at tremendous speed as soon as I grasped its hand.

The blinding white sand was already scattered with colour and the monotonous screech of gulls with the deafening blare of transistor radios. More colour and music covered the beach as the cool blue carpet rolled back revealing all the more of its shining white floor.

Welcoming waves drew us like buffaloes to a waterhole. The rhythmic thrust of the oars soon became the only music to our ears and the colour and civilisation of the shore became a smudge in the distance; a relic of the past. Here was peace. The sea had become our ally, our escape from the real world, a barrier between our problems and us.

I shivered as if someone had walked over my grave. The sun had gone in and I hadn't noticed. We decided to trace our steps, so James changed direction. Within an instant the dinghy was over turned. Neptune had blocked our path. We had ventured into his kingdom, trespassed on his property, and he had us in his grasp. The welcoming waves turned into mounted armies, the surf as their glittering swords, but our throats weren't to be slit, there was no such easy escape for deserters. We were to be eaten alive, swallowed whole by the rigours of the water. As the pure white incisors of the deep plunged at my neck, a bright hospitable yellow light shone above me like a halo, and I could feel the sensation of my whole aching spirit being lifted from the battle-field.

I became aware gradually of noises around me, which I eventually managed to distinguish as voices.

'You're in safe hands, miss. James has been waiting a long while to speak to you.'

'This could only be the voice of a saint,' I thought to myself. 'Saint Peter, perhaps.' I was glad that James had made it too, he could meet all my ancestors.

'I'm glad you've come round, your mum would never have forgiven me.'

Maybe I hadn't quite made it to heaven. It was a close escape, and I suppose hospital is the second best place.

▶ PIECE 2: THE NIGHT OWLS

Propped for support against the train time-table of Manchester Victoria at 2:30 in the morning is a tramp clad in the faded grey suit of his wedding day, a day only preserved by the worn threads of his garments, a day long since banished from the depths of his heart.

A step nearer and one becomes all the more aware of the putrid aroma of stale liquor mingled with the suffocating stench of many decades of tobacco, a perfume that's even more over-powering as he exhales through his toothless mouth, an opening indicated by an area of tangled grey whiskers, stained yellow with nicotine.

And then his forehead creases, and his eyes squint in what appears to be excruciating pain. He drags one arm from his side, and the other from its previous embrace with a half-empty whisky bottle, and with terrific strain, wraps them about his well developed paunch, as he folds over to utter several bronchial barks, each closely followed by a wheezy air intake.

With this, he straightens up to his usual slouch and

returns to his best friend, and worst enemy, the bottle.

The tramp, however, is not alone at the station. His company is shared between two other citizens, the first being an eccentric college student on his way home from an extremely heavy rock concert. His dirty green cowboy hat, knotted under his chin with a Roland Rat shoelace does its best, but is drastically unsuccessful in hiding the bird's nest like, fraying mat of wild wire sprouting from his skull.

Almost his entire outfit is smothered by embroidered magic mushrooms and mammoths, glued on sew-on badges, pvc patches and cigarette burns, and is veiled by a loud, wide irridescent tie.

The three inch gap between his twenty inch trouser bottoms and split training shoes reveals a 'pair' of horrid orange and glaring green, blinding red and putrid plum Paisley designed socks.

With his grimy hoover tube slung over his right shoulder and sharp metal stud on his left, he waits patiently for his father to arrive in the Mercedes to chauffeur him home at this unearthly hour.

The third person at the station is a smart young woman in her late twenties. Her long blonde hair is coiled and pinned perfectly in place and her wide brimmed candy pink sun hat casts a mysterious shadow over her well-defined cheek bones. Her short, shimmering skirt catches the fluorescent light as she impatiently shifts from one red, four-inch stiletto heel to the other and back again. She glances deliberately at her colour coordinated strapped watch, and fumbles in her clutch bag to touch up her candy pink hat coloured lipstick.

After twenty minutes or so she lets out a short, sharp, indignant sigh, and clacks at top tight-skirted speed to the public telephone. She grabs hold of the receiver, dials the condemned number and then . . .

'WHAT THE . . .' she hesitates, looks self consciously around the station and continues, this time shouting in a whisper, 'Where do you think...'

'Oh no, not at all, that's perfectly alright, I'm sorry to have troubled you.'

'Pardon? . . . no, of course not, I'd be happy to take a taxi!'

She replaces the receiver, stamps her foot, scowls at the telephone box, spins round on one heel, catches the amused eye of the student, annihilates his smirk, straightens her skirt, adjusts the position of her clutch bag, raises her chin and wobbles out of the station.

'Taxi!'

▶ PIECE 3: AN EXPEDITION

Homo Sapiens: thinking man.

How can we consider ourselves civilised when we, mankind, allow the brutal massacre of thousands of week-old, defenceless youngsters to take place every year while their helpless mothers look on? I am referring to the killing of under twelve days old seal pups for no other reason than to provide arctic white fur coats for the upper class. I am speaking from experience. I write about the time I witnessed a mass murder of this kind.

After reading an article about Greenpeace and their attempts to stop the killing of baby seals for their fur, I concluded it was the duty of common people like myself to attend these expeditions to the Arctic with Greenpeace and try to prevent the gruesome activities of the sealers to the best of our abilities.

Thousands of men and women of many nationalities had decided to apply for a position on the 'Rainbow Warrior' and from this number a crew of ten was to be chosen. Greenpeace needs as many nationalities as possible on each mission so that the crew can communicate with the outside world whilst on the expedition to gain as much publicity as possible to prick the consciences of as many countries' peoples as they can.

I was one of the few chosen for this particular expedition. I had never sailed before, few of the crew members had.

Thousands of people were gathered to see us off; friends, family, and those who believed in Greenpeace and the protection of seals. It was as if we were royalty.

Our intention was to spray as many of the pups' coats as we could with a coloured dye before the sealers arrived. If the fur coat isn't pure white then it is of little value to the sealers.

As we entered the Arctic circle our fearless mission became less a fairytale and more of a nightmare. We couldn't stand on deck for more than a few minutes as the bitter cold gales whipped our faces. A few of us were suffering from frostbite and most of us from sea-sickness.

On schedule, with just half a mile to go, in sight of the seals, and suddenly the ship shuddered violently. Cutlery was flung from the shelves and those who were standing fell down. The whole crew hurried on deck to discover the cause of the quake. The 'Rainbow Warrior' had collided with an enormous glacier.

We had a choice of either returning home having accomplished nothing, or mounting the helicopter and landing on the ice, thus breaking the law by the act 'to ensure the safety of seals'; that is: 'No helicopter may land within a mile of any seal'. Not even in an attempt to protect it from death.

Unlike previous Greenpeace breakers of this particular law, there was no one waiting to arrest us. Almost every member of the crew took part in the dyeing of the seal pups. We sprayed every seal we could find, but with time lost going back and forth in the helicopter we couldn't spray every pup.

When the sealers eventually came to carry out their annual slaughter, they left most of the dyed seals untouched since these were invalid. However the pups that we couldn't spray didn't escape quite so easily, despite our attempts to protect them with our own bodies.

I saw one sealer take a pup, drag it to a convenient patch on the ice and taking a pick-axe, he hit the pup's head several times, thrusting the axe through the seal's skull until the pup, if it wasn't dead through blood loss, it was most certainly suffering from a fractured skull. With a knife, he then slit the pup's skin from the head to the tail, and peeled it away from the flesh, leaving a carcass on the ice for the mother to sniff at.

One mother seal followed her pup's body all the way back to the sealer's ship. She might even have mounted it, if another sealer hadn't struck her head because she was in the way.

Thanks to Greenpeace, the sealers left with an almost empty ship. Once we'd shot some gruesome photographs of the bloody carcasses to send to 10, Downing Street and the White House, we also returned home.

Not much was said on our journey home. There was little to say. No conversation had any relevance. It had been an experience that not one of us would forget.

As we were greeted with the idle, meaningless cheers and waves of our supporters on the shore, a faint smile crossed my lips. We were being treated like heroes. Surely that's not correct. If they'd witnessed the sights that we'd seen, they'd know that the real heroes were the seals and their carcasses we'd left back in the Arctic.

Homo Sapiens: Thinking man.

▶ PIECE 4: SHOULD WE HAVE A MONARCHY?

A sea of red, white and blue bodies stretches down The Mall as far as the eye can see. Everyone strains their neck to catch a glimpse of the newlyweds. People are packed into fountains and there are more up trees. The second that the couple appear on the balcony, a deafening roar rises from the masses.

On a day such as a royal wedding with the whole country focussed on Westminster Abbey, all-night street parties in every town and village, and the Royal Couple on the front page of every newspaper, even The Times, it doesn't seem possible that there are people who are opposed to the monarchy.

Arguments against us having a monarchy are that the Royal Family doesn't work for a living, and that their exploits are paid for by the tax-payer. They don't present the realities of the modern world, they are all on private medicine, have private education, and all the monarch's sons are offered a place at Cambridge University, even if their qualifications are inadequate, whereas the average hard-working British citizen is on the NHS, is educated by the state, and even an academic with excellent results stands the chance of being refused at Cambridge University. Should they have these privileges?

It is said that Royalty brings wealth into the country. Why, then, is Britain only eleventh in economic prosperity? Other countries are said to respect our Royal Family, and take a great interest in royal visits. If so, why do they choose not to have a monarchy of their own?

However, if this were the end of the matter, King Charles would never have been permitted to return to England in 1660, after a disastrous eleven years without a monarch.

Maybe the monarchy does consume a lot of money, but think how much money it brings into the country through tourism. Furthermore, if we didn't have a monarch, it is very likely that similar sums would go to support a Head of State. To this, people against the monarchy would say that because a Head of State is elected, they would feel more inclined to subsidise someone that they'd chosen. The disadvantage of having an elected Head of State is that only his supporters would be celebrating events connected with him, and there would be nothing that could unite the whole country.

The Royal Family sets standards that the public tend to follow. For example, 'The Queen's English' is the 'proper' way to speak, and younger members of the family set fashions in clothes and hair styles.

Because the Royal Family is non-political people feel that they can write to the Queen in appeal. Their popularity makes the Royal Family able to open the eyes of the world to the needy. For example, Princess Anne is the head of The Save the Children Fund, and because she is respected world-wide, The Save the Children Fund is able to work all over the world. Being the head of the Anglican

Church, the Monarch is respected particularly by Protestants all over the world.

No matter how much the government changes, the Queen STAYS at the head of the country, and remains a steady influence and support for the people of Britain. The stability of the Royal Family makes them respected by other countries and gives the people of Britain a national heritage to be proud of.

After considering many of the pros and cons of having a Royal Family, I come to the conclusion that we're better off with a monarchy than without one. Furthermore, the vast majority of the British people are proud of the Royal Family, and of being British.

 ## PIECE 5: SEX AND VIOLENCE

Just as statistics show advertising on television to be the most effective method of advertising, many people believe it to be extremely effective at advertising sex and violence. Just as we may catch ourselves whistling the tune for coffee or chocolates, many psychologists and other people believe that most murderers and rapists have been influenced by constant violent scenes on television.

Many people are particularly concerned about these 'video nasties' corrupting the youths of today. Although all films have a rating, it is well-known that children, under-age, go to see films depicting sex and violence because 'it's the thing to do.' Even though an act has been introduced where on BBC no scenes of extreme violence or sex are permitted to be shown before the 9pm news, many children are up after this time, and the use of video-recorders doesn't prevent children from watching obscene sex and violence. While I'm on the subject of children, I can't help stressing that the use of bad language on television almost definitely rubs off on young children. Language not only on soap operas and films, but, in particular, the use of obscene language on children's television programmes. Although children's television programmes tend to stay clear of sex, violence, even if it is the 'goody' punishing the 'baddy', has the effect of making young children violent. For example, a small child hurling his teddy bear across the room, shouting 'He-man', then proceeding to thump his mother in the stomach, and flex his muscles. It's only logical that being violent and swearing every two minutes is the acceptable thing to do, because 'BA' does it all the time.

Not only children are affected by viewing sex and violence on television, although it 'helps' if you can 'catch them when they're young'. Many people think that seeing murder, rape, and other violent activities induces people into thinking that these events are everyday things, and no longer anything to be shocked about. Many people fail to distinguish between fantasy and reality, although reality could have a more influencing effect on prospective criminals. Programmes such as the news, show violence in reality. The riots in Brixton and the war between Iran and Iraq, for example, show a very small part of the world, but because all of the extremely violent activities going on in the world are brought into our living rooms, people come to expect it, and think along the lines of 'Well, everybody's doing it.'

Some dismiss all of these objections with 'It's your own responsibility whether you watch or not.' But can we choose whether we are murdered or raped or not?

EXAMINER COMMENTS: CANDIDATE ONE

This candidate writes fluently throughout the folio of coursework. The most impressive quality is the economy of expression: there are many examples in each piece of expert and attractive phrasing; the writing is never dull.

Just as importantly, there is a *range* of style and subject matter.

Piece 1

The writing is skilfully impressionistic. The candidate attempts the difficult task of describing a personal experience in a detached way, avoiding the most obvious narrative detail. Perhaps the candidate tries too hard for effect, but there is a good attempt at describing the accident by use of *metaphor* and *personification*.

Piece 2

This is the most successful piece. The task was to present a series of characters in a simple situation that would bring them together and describe them purely in terms of their outward appearance. Exaggeration was allowed and humour was encouraged. Although the description of the tramp is possibly somewhat 'over the top', the three portraits are nicely contrasted. Details are well observed with the pleasing quality of humorous exaggeration.

Piece 3

This piece is based on factual information but employs a fictional style. It is quite an effective example of what is sometimes known as 'faction'. The argument is implicit in the narrative and the candidate does well to keep a close eye on the purpose of the task, so that the narrative details contribute to our understanding of the issue in question.

Piece 4

A more traditional exercise in argument. The opening is particularly effective. It avoids the pitfalls of repeating the title by introducing the reader to the subject before explaining its significance. Telling a story first is a technique beloved of preachers and has the advantage of involving the audience and arousing their curiosity. Unfortunately, the main body of the argument is less convincing. The arguments against are well summarised, but the positive points are made up of somewhat disconnected and under-developed assertions. Even so, the expression is crisp and appropriate to this kind of subject.

Piece 5

This is written with some passion but relies rather too heavily on assertion. Equally important is the fact that the piece is just too short and lacking in amplification to do justice to the seriousness of the subject.

Summary

The shortcomings of this candidate are relatively minor, in the face of the writing's clear strengths. There is evidence of positive command of appropriate language in a range of styles. There is a wide-ranging vocabulary. Although the candidate falters somewhat in the last two pieces, there is a firm sense of purpose and a clear ability to plan and structure extended pieces of writing.

On balance, given the assured style and the variety of subject, this selection of coursework would be ranked very highly.

FOLIO: CANDIDATE TWO

PIECE 1: THE ABANDONED STATION

The sunlight streamed through the curtains and dazzled me as I awoke. I clambered out of bed and opened the window. The air was fresh and cool and some skylarks had already started to sing, their tune sailing high in the blue sky. The dew on the grass glistened in the light, whilst the trees stood perfectly still, without being moved by any wind. The appearance of the morning was promising and I decided to walk to the river instead of catching the bus as planned. The farmer had told me that the walk around the river would take me several hours, especially if I had all my fishing tackle with me. It was already half past nine so I thought that the most suitable thing to do would be to walk at a leisurely pace and have an evening fishing.

After a truly appetising meal for breakfast, I asked the farmer's wife if I could miss my evening meal, and take a packed lunch on my walk. She soon got my lunch ready and I set out towards the disused railway which the farmer had shown me the previous day. He said that if I walked down the railway line until I arrived at a tunnel, then the river would just be over a bank on my right. I climbed over the fence and onto the railway line. The sun had now started to heat the air up and there wasn't a cloud in sight. On either side of me there were two steep grassy banks, dotted with splashes of colour in the form of wild flowers and butterflies. The fences at the top of each bank were now old and were covered in moss and lichen. The track settled into a straight line which stretched in front of me as far as I could see. The rails were very rusty and were orange in places. The bolts which held them to the sleepers were also rusty. The sleepers were damp from the dew and looked very rotten.

As I walked I could see varying crops and fields beyond the banks. I passed an occasional tree on the bank but there was no real wooded area anywhere along the route. After about an hour the track turned to an abrupt ending to my right. On my left, however, it continued and to my delight it led me to an old, derelict but quaint railway station. I decided to eat my lunch here and I climbed onto the left-hand platform to take off my rucksack and put it on a bench. The sun was beating down and I stood up to explore the village station. There was a building ahead of me so I walked towards it. The bricks were shaling and the gutters had fallen down in places. The walls were covered in bird droppings, a sure sign of a roosting place. The window frames of the building were still intact although the window panes were very dusty. There was a spider in each one, dominating the glass with their patterned webs.

The door wouldn't open but it did tell me what the building was for; a small sign said 'Waiting room'. I walked to the next building. This turned out to be the toilets. Beyond these there was a small area of the platform which had been taken over by rosebay willow herb. The slight breeze was blowing their seeds all over the surrounding area. Weed-filled plant pots and flower beds were becoming covered in their fluffy seeds and I was also getting my fair share. I walked a few more yards down the platform and started to look at the last building. It was the ticket office. It had a list of the train fares for first, second and third class passengers, all the prices were of pre-decimalisation age and it brought the idea of a working station to life.

There was a white gate and a path which led over the bank behind the platform. This was obviously the way out of the station. An old wooden footbridge led to the other platform. The bridge looked a bit dodgy to me so I simply avoided it and crossed over the rails. There weren't any toilets on this side but the waiting room here was open. The window panes were just as dusty and so when I went in the light was very dim. There were several swallows' nests in the rafters, built with the care and devotion of adult birds. The floor was covered in dust and old leaves, and the walls were quite dirty. A polished wooden bench ran round the perimeter of the room. This was riddled with woodworm. As I stepped out of the dingy room I was once again dazzled by the sunlight. The butterflies were dancing round the flowers and the nettles and the noise of grasshoppers was all that broke the idyllic silence. I crossed back over the line to eat my packed lunch.

I sat on the warm seat and tried to imagine what it would have been like when the station was in use. It couldn't have been too busy but anyone who wanted to go to a town for shopping or the market would probably have travelled this way.

I imagined one or two well-dressed office types, with rolled brollies and bowler hats, a few country women dressed up for a day's shopping and senior schoolboys in uniform with their knee-length shorts going to the nearest secondary school. Most could have been travelling to Shrewsbury in the steam train. I could almost hear the people and the passengers of the past. Images of them coming and going flashed through my mind.

After about half an hour's thought I packed up and started on my trek towards the river. It had been a slightly strange experience but the station was well worth a visit. With the sun still shining I continued down the track towards an enjoyable evening's fishing.

▶ PIECE 2: SHOULD SMOKING BE BANNED IN PUBLIC PLACES?

Every man, woman and child in Britain today smokes two cigarettes per day. In other words, we are all passive smokers; i.e. we breathe in, medically speaking, other people's smoke which is the equivalent of smoking (and inhaling) two cigarettes a day.

This is a disturbing statistic which raises the question 'Should smoking in public places be banned?' The 'public places' would include schools, cafes and restaurants, public transport, cinemas and theatres, public houses, etc.

Many such establishments already recognise the problem of passive smoking and try to reduce its off-putting effects by segregating smokers and non-smokers. However, more often than not, these measures are inadequate and don't take into account the fact that smoke drifts easily.

For example, in cinemas there is often the segregation of smokers and non-smokers into two halves of the room. The dividing line is usually an aisle, which is approximately 4m wide at the most. Smoke easily drifts this far within minutes of the cigarette being lit and often the enjoyment of non-smokers can be ruined by the smell of smoke.

Public transport in the form of trains is usually quite good in separating non-smokers and smokers. The smoke cannot drift because people are in separate carriages.

It is, however, hard to move into a non-smokers' carriage if you are travelling with a smoking friend. People can be forced into embarrassing situations where they may give way and join their friends in a smokers' carriage. If a person does travel in a smokers' carriage, then when he or she comes out of the train they will probably smell of smoke. Apart from the unpleasant smell that person will be less healthy after their journey. A quarter of an hour spent in a smoky room is the equivalent of smoking one cigarette.

Although non-smokers have the right to breathe pure, clean air, don't smokers have the right to breathe in smoke? I'm sure many would argue that smokers should be able to smoke where they want and any ban would be an infringement of their liberty. Surely forcing non-smokers to passively smoke is an infringement on their liberty too.

Smoking is a habit which many people have. Lots probably would find it hard to stop. Statistics show that the number of female smokers in Britain is rising while the number of male smokers is falling.

Smoking advertisements are all around us; we see them at football matches, motor-car racing and other places such as shopwindows, clothes, posters and advertising boards and bags. All these advertisements influence potential smokers, like children, to take up smoking. Children will desire to be accepted by their peers and friends. If they see others smoke, then they will soon start themselves. If the tobacco companies succeed in tempting children to smoke, then there will be a larger amount of smoke in public places. Public houses are very often smoky and for non-smokers it can at times be unbearable. For some it is just the smell; for others the smoke makes their eyes water and hurt.

There is a huge amount of medical evidence to link smoking with different forms of cancer.

Cigarette smoking is usually linked with carcinoma of the lungs. Although pipe and cigar smokers don't inhale as much tar and so aren't as susceptible to lung cancer as cigarette smokers, the risk of contracting lung cancer is thirty times higher for a smoker than a non-smoker. Pipe and cigar smokers tend to contract carcinoma of the lip, tongue, throat and cheek more than cigarette smokers and non-smokers. People may think that passive smokers aren't put at risk by pipe or cigar smokers but as the smoke is just as carcinogenic it is just as dangerous to a non-smoker.

When we come back to the question of a smoking ban in public we must turn to the government. At the moment the government anti-smoking propaganda is hopelessly inadequate. Tobacco is a drug and people do become addicted to it. It should be subjected to the same kind of attack as other drugs. A few photos of tar-filled lungs would soon discourage children and adults from smoking.

At times one wonders how badly our government wants to stop Britain's people smoking. It does of course force smoking adverts to have a health warning on the bottom, but many people feel that the warnings aren't strong enough. Recently, however, the warnings have started to change and become a little stronger.

The government cannot really expect to outlaw cigarettes and ban all forms of tobacco smoking. (I wish they could, but I can see that smokers have got to be allowed to smoke in their own homes.) The government could however, quite easily ban smoking in public places.

The tobacco companies obviously wouldn't like this move because people wouldn't see others smoking and so wouldn't be able to follow their example. This would result in a loss of tobacco sales.

The amount of money given to the government in tax by the

tobacco industry is phenomenal. Apart from this, the government wouldn't want to discourage smoking too much because:

a) less tax would be collected;

b) there would be an outcry from smokers and the tobacco industries;

c) unemployment of cigarette makers in the areas of Bristol and Nottingham would eventually become inevitable.

The government does, on the other hand, do a few things to appease the anti-smoking lobby, such as banning smoking advertisements on television and showing a few anti-smoking adverts themselves. The amount of money the government spends on such adverts is tiny compared with the amount tobacco companies spend on promoting their products. In 1986, the total government spending on anti-smoking propaganda was £3 million. During the same period they paid out £27 million in subsidies to help the Gallagher tobacco giant build a new cigarette factory in Northern Ireland.

I believe that smoking should be banned in certain public places. I have certainly been forced into inhaling other people's smoke in public places, especially in restaurants and theatres. Meals and films can be ruined by smoke and on buses smoke gives me travel sickness. Whenever I am subjected to an excessive amount of smoke, I get a headache. I was very glad to see that a ban on smoking on our local buses was being brought into action several months ago. When I stepped on however, the air was filled with smoke. Whilst I was travelling some people behind me started to smoke and I felt very sickly. It's hardly surprising they were smoking when the driver was chain-smoking.

▶ PIECE 3: RUSTY THE CAT

Rusty had lived down the coal mine since he was a fluffy kitten.

Rusty loved his surroundings and everything around him. He had many friends such as the pit ponies he lived with and the canary birds that sat in the under-manager's office, singing sweet tunes all day.

But there was one thing that Rusty did not like. That was the rats. He hated the naughty rats because they broke the rules of the coal mine. The rules said that each animal must be given their own food. The rats should not have been down the mine and so were not given any food. Instead they stole the food belonging to Rusty's friends, the pit ponies.

When work had stopped at the end of the day, Rusty would run through the tunnels passing other cats, until he reached the under-manager's office. The under-manager was called Albert. He was a jolly, round man with rosy cheeks and waddled from side to side as he walked.

Albert was kind and loving towards Rusty. He always had time to speak to Rusty when they met. As Albert finished work he would ask Rusty to look after and guard his office over night. Rusty was happy to do this for Albert. As he stepped into the cage which would take Albert to the surface, Rusty would leap in beside him, only to be sent back into the tunnels again.

Albert knew how much Rusty would love to visit the surface but rules were rules and none of the cats were allowed out of the mine.

Rusty was devoted to the mine and worked hard every day. All the ponies admired and respected Rusty. In the evenings they would sit with Rusty and talk together for hours at a time. Rusty would purr contentedly as he happily dreamed of the large, open spaces of the surface.

One evening, Rusty noticed that the ponies were excited. They could not settle like they usually do after working all day, so Rusty asked one of the ponies why. Tomorrow all the ponies would be going to the surface for their annual holiday for one week.

Going to the surface! Rusty was so happy for the ponies. He curled up his tail and dreamed once more of his fantasy.

The ponies knew how much Rusty would like to go with them but they knew it was against the rules for them to take him.

The ponies felt sorry for Rusty.

Early next day, Rusty stood at the side of Albert as they both watched all the pit ponies being taken to the surface for their holiday. They were led into the cage one at a time until every last pony was safely in. Then off they went with a hum and a clank of wheels and pullies turning and ropes being wound up.

A man tapped Albert on the shoulder and whispered in his ear.

'The food!' Albert shouted, giving Rusty a shock.
Everyone had forgotten the ponies' food that was kept in the mine. The ponies had to take it on holiday with them, so the food had to go to the surface as well.

But Albert had a problem. The ponies ate oats and the rats had to be kept away from the oats because the rats liked oats too. Albert looked at his feet and saw Rusty twisting himself round his legs. 'If one of the cats were sent up with the oats it could stop the rats eating the oats!'

Everyone's eyes looked at Rusty. Being the hardest working cat in the mine, he was chosen to go up with the oats.

Rusty leaped onto the sacks of oats that were already piled up in the cage in excitement!

Because of the days of hard work, Rusty's dream had finally come true!

 ## PIECE 4: THE HAUNTER

Danny woke up excitedly. This was the big day, the day that he had been told by numerous convincing dreams that he was to meet the 'thing' which would be able to give him everything on earth he had ever hoped for. Danny got up quickly and got dressed. He gulped his breakfast and ran to the corner shop. He pushed the door open and a bell rang. The fat shopkeeper walked briskly to the counter.

'Hi! What can I do for you today then?'

Ernie the shopkeeper looked at his customer. He was about five years old, had fair hair and blue eyes. By just looking at him Ernie imagined that he came from a really caring home. His hair was combed, and his school uniform was spotlessly clean.

'Can you tell me the way to the shore please?'

'Of course, it's right at the end of Conway Street, that's just round the corner by the pub, OK?'

'Thanks. Bye.' Danny said as he ran out of the shop excitedly.

Now all was quiet and the shopkeeper lit a cigarette. As he inhaled, he thought about the boy. It was Wednesday, the 23rd of March, a school day just like any other and yet one lad had asked the way to the shore. Maybe he had to collect shells or something before school; it was very early . . .

Danny ran all the way to the beach. As he ran he tried to remember exactly what had happened in his dreams. He wasn't scared, the dreams had given him confidence. He imagined all the things he had been promised, all the things he had ever wanted, toys and teddy bears, chocolate and money. Greed welled up inside him, the greed was being provoked by the being who almost possessed him at the moment. Danny eventually reached the beach but it was empty. He wandered onto the sand and looked for some special cone-shaped shells. Danny began to wonder if it was all a mistake, maybe nothing would arrive.

As he looked back towards the village a dark figure dodged down behind a wall. Danny started to become scared. He turned away from the wall and looked out to sea. The sun was shining on the clear water. Danny decided to go back to school. His mummy always said not to talk to strangers and never to go anywhere quiet alone. The shore was quiet, too quiet.

Danny turned to run and bumped into the dark figure he had seen behind the wall. Danny looked up at the man's face. The nose was thin and sinister, his lips were small and tight and he was half shaven. The man's eyes seemed to look straight through Danny who slowly began to realise that this was what he had dreamed about. 'Hello, Danny,' the man said with a reassuring kind voice. 'Danny, you know of all the wonderful things I have offered you. If you do as I say, then you will gain a good life with everything you could want, money and riches, and it's your choice, Danny. I'll give you time to decide but you must tell me the next time I see you.' He disappeared and left Danny who ran to school.

Two weeks later, the man appeared in Danny's bedroom. The man stared at Danny and coolly asked him, 'Have you decided yet Danny? What is your answer?' Danny foolishly said yes. The being handed over a crisp pound note. 'Now go and steal a bar of chocolate from Ernie.'

Danny obeyed the man and always got his rewards. Everywhere he went the man seemed to be. Danny started swearing at home and at school. He was told off by his Mummy everyday, but Danny didn't care, he was going to get everything he had ever wanted. His greed, created by the man, overpowered his common sense and all his parental guidance was ignored . . .

The door slammed, the metallic sound echoed around the building. Danny sat with his head cupped in his hands. 'Why did I do it? Why did I of all people kill that poor bloke, why?' He thought back through his crimeful life, his burglaries, drug trafficking, petty shoplifting. Then he remembered the man, the one who he had not seen since he was ten. 'He must have left because Danny Cook had been influenced enough to carry on in an evil life; where was he all those years? Where is he now?'

A familiar voice shouted hello from the top bunk of the prison cell. Danny looked up. His eyes met with those eyes which had pierced him all those years ago.

Danny had now come to his senses and was angry with the man.

'Why do you poison young peoples' minds with your evil temptations? Why aren't you out there now? Why me? Who are you anyway?' All these questions rushed out of Danny's mouth in a garbled torrent but the man answered each one in sequence.

'I find it fun to influence the young and watch their mothers suffer and I am out there now. I am speaking to many children like I spoke to you. I chose you because you were too innocent and your mind was not strong. I don't bother with strong minded people. My servants who are infiltrated into them will deal with all those who are in any way religious and I, my child, I am Lucifer.'

 PIECE 5: MODERN ENTERTAINMENT

Now, more than ever before, sex and violence is a large part of our entertainment industries, chiefly on television, videos and cinema films but also in magazines, children's toys and cartoon books. There are arguments which say that only a very small percentage of our modern films are actually about sex or violence. We do however see many more films that are violent, especially on television. There are numerous films which highlight their main character as being violent. Some use boxing as the violence in the screen, others fighting with guns and modern weapons and some will endeavour to show us scenes of torture in a prison cell or a place where they are being held captive. Rambo, perhaps an overexaggerated example, showed scenes of being beaten, stabbed, etc. One scene showed a man being shot at with an exploding tipped arrow which hit his head and blew out his brains. This is what audiences now like to see. The less violent things like a fist fight have ceased to be exciting or even interesting.

So why is this kind of viewing bad for us and society? Why do people suggest it should more strictly be censored? The US Attorney General released a landmark report linking pornography to violence. An American National Institute of Health says in a recent report that there is now overwhelming evidence to show that viewing excessive violence causes aggressive behaviour.

I think we must see the dangers of this kind of entertainment. If it can cause aggressive behaviour, I'm sure that for an already aggressive person it could cause him/her to do something stupid. The defences put up for violent behaviour are that viewing, or as in children's toys, playing at violence, prevents people from being violent in real life. They have absolutely no proof for this. In the last 10—15 years violence as a form of entertainment has become increasingly popular. The audience became immune to some types of violence so the directors had to start injecting different, worse forms of terror and violence into films. Also in the last 10—15 years the number of rapes, murders, etc. and violent crimes, GBH and so on has risen steeply. Obviously we cannot link this to violence on our screens directly but could it play some kind of part influencing the criminals and provoking them to go out and commit their crime? I doubt it myself but we can't just brush it to one side without actually looking a little closer.

Children's toys, books and stories are now more than ever to do with violence, war, etc. For instance, the cartoons, like Tom and Jerry, which had hardly any violence in, only in the form of a cat chasing a mouse, have been replaced by things like 'Transformers' and 'Masters of the Universe', all of which run purely on the concept of violence. The children can enjoy sitting down and watching He—man kill a few evil robots and then go into battle with some senseless aliens which, of course, the child can buy in the form of plastic model toys, so that he can act out his own adventures. Children have always played with things like toy soldiers, especially the boys.

Pornography too is now a bigger business than it was; films on television often depict sex scenes and some are on quite early. Another point, does putting the worst films on very late make much difference to the amount of viewers and the types of people who watch them? The very bad ones will probably be put on after midnight, so not many people could be bothered to stay up and watch them. Those who do however would probably watch it any time it was put on our screens. It isn't the ones on late we worry about, it tends to be the ones which come unexpectedly during our viewing of a very normal kind of film which suddenly turns violent or sexual.

There is only really one way to stop the general public being able to watch such films. That is by law. If they were banned, lots would object on the grounds of infringement of our liberty, if nothing else. A censorship would therefore be much more appropriate, but here we hit a snag too. Who are we to choose to do the censoring? Who gets that job and how strictly should it be done?

Some would say that even censorship was ridiculous and that sex and violence should be available to viewers who are watching in the privacy of their own homes. There is already a censorship board in Britain but should there be more control?

It is true to say that audiences enjoy a blood-thirsty film, but isn't this somewhat alarming, to see some people crave for such forms of entertainment?
I think violence and pornography can twist our minds into thinking of, debating and, even in some cases, committing, a crime.

Apart from its far-reaching psychological effects, shouldn't we be looking at it from the point of view of morals? Why have our moral standards fallen so low that young people enjoy pornography and will pay for it? It would never have happened a century ago, even 60 or 50 years ago, but now, standards have dropped and we are forced to admit that, to the public of today, lots of morals just don't stand at all.

If violence on screens can lead to aggressiveness, then can pornography have any similar effects? In answer to this question, I would say, perhaps. Maybe it leads to promiscuity or teenage pregnancy. The consequences of teenage sexual experimentation are again far-reaching. They break families up and force marriages. It leads to an increase in venereal disease, abortions, broken relationships, illegitimate babies, and these factors scar people mentally and physically and they leave a sour taste in some people's minds for the rest of their lives.

EXAMINER COMMENTS: CANDIDATE TWO

This candidate writes clearly throughout the folio of coursework but has a somewhat less fluent and varied range of expression than candidate one. On the other hand, in pieces 2 and 5 the candidate shows a greater ability to develop and amplify an argument. On the whole, candidate one shows greater skill and flexibility in **open writing**, while candidate two is more at home at manipulating factual information. Even so, candidate two does display a variety of skills.

Piece 1

This is a sound piece of descriptive writing. It is full of relevant **detail**. The vocabulary is varied and **appropriate** and the expression is clear and fluent. On the other hand, for all its worthy qualities, the writing fails to engage the reader fully. First, the introduction is overlong and is probably unnecessary anyway. Second, there are too many rather matter-of-fact observations – such as 'There was a building ahead of me so I walked towards it' – which are not particularly interesting and do not seem to have much point.

Piece 2

The candidate seems much more at ease, although there is room for shortening and tightening up the argument. Most impressively, the candidate adopts a **vocabulary** appropriate to the task. Words such as 'segregation', 'inadequate', 'passively' and 'infringement' have the right degree of formality and abstraction for this sort of writing.

Furthermore, the candidate is able to distinguish between general principles and specific **examples**. There are weaknesses. At one point the argument drifts away from the subject of smoking in public places and becomes a little bogged down in the reasons young people start smoking. However, the writer does succeed in bringing the discussion back to the topic in hand. The **ending** is a little too personal and is out of keeping with the detached style employed up to that point.

Piece 3

This is the liveliest in the collection, and is a reminder that writing for GCSE does not need to be in the form of the traditional 'essay'. It is also noteworthy that because this piece has a clear **audience**, it is altogether crisper and more engaging than Piece 1, which is rather aimless. This piece succeeds because the language is entirely appropriate to a children's story, there is a sense of proportion and structure, and the writer maintains a nice balance between Rusty's 'human' and animal qualities.

Piece 4

The piece **begins** extremely well, with an excellent sense of mystery and suspense. The first part of the narrative projects the child's psychology skilfully and economically. The clear focus of the opening is lost, however, as the narrative moves on in a more generalised way and the effect of the ending is spoiled by some rather clumsy expression. This was an ambitious piece which would have benefited from further **drafting** and editing.

Piece 5

Here the candidate treats a difficult subject very fully and with some subtlety. The piece manages to put across a clear **point of view** while showing an awareness of the complexity of the issues. Even though the discussion tends to wander from point to point, examiners would recognise that extended argument is a difficult task for GCSE students, and would reward this candidate for the ability to marshal information and ideas into a clear and relevant form.

Summary

In terms of overall achievement there is not a great difference between candidates one and two. Candidate one's folio has many outstanding moments which readily arouse the interest, but the last two pieces tend to tail off rather unconvincingly. Candidate two has less flair with words, is not so interesting to read and so on balance does not rate quite as highly, but the children's story and the two argumentative pieces represent positive achievement of a high order.

Remember that there is *no single route* to success in coursework. Few people are equally gifted in all kinds of writing, and it is not expected that every piece of work should be equally successful. Provided that your writing is fundamentally sound, strengths in one type of task can compensate for relative weakness in another.